24.50

Avoiding War
in the Nuclear Age

100

About the Book and Editor

Given the disappointing history of arms control negotiations and agreements, disconcerting trends in the balance of power, and emerging technologies that challenge conventional assumptions about deterrence, new ways to promote security through negotiations must be identified and utilized if arms control is ever to play an integral role in enhancing deterrence and reducing instabilities. Confidence-building measures (CBMs) may offer one way out of the contemporary arms control morass. Instead of focusing on limiting the number and types of weaponry, CBMs are designed to control how, when, where, and why military activities occur. By clarifying military intentions and regulating the operations of military forces in times of both crisis and calm, CBMs can help diminish the opportunities for war arising from surprise attack or from miscalculation, accident, or failure of communication. This volume assembles leading CBM experts from government and academia to assess the utility of CBMs in a wide variety of areas. It is intended to serve as a basic primer on the subject, as well as to contribute to the ongoing national debate over the role of arms control in strengthening national security by analyzing new and fruitful avenues toward that over-riding objective.

John Borawski is a research associate at the Woodrow Wilson International Center for Scholars, Washington, D.C., with the International Security Studies Program.

For Charlotte E. Thompson,
CBM *extraordinaire*

Avoiding War in the Nuclear Age
Confidence-Building Measures for Crisis Stability

Edited by John Borawski
Foreword by
The Honorable James E. Goodby

Westview Press / Boulder and London

Westview Special Studies in National Security and Defense Policy

This Westview softcover edition was manufactured on our own premises using equipment and methods that allow us to keep even specialized books in stock. It is printed on acid-free paper and bound in softcovers that carry the highest rating of the National Association of State Textbook Administrators, in consultation with the Association of American Publishers and the Book Manufacturers' Institute.

Published in 1986 in the United States of America by Westview Press, Inc.; Frederick A. Praeger, Publisher; 5500 Central Avenue, Boulder, Colorado 80301

Library of Congress Cataloging-in-Publication Data
Avoiding war in the nuclear age.
  (Westview special studies in national security and
defense policy)
  Bibliography: p.
  1. Nuclear warfare—Addresses, essays, lectures.
2. Nuclear disarmament—Addresses, essays, lectures.
I. Borawski, John. II. Series.
U263.A96 1986   355.4'307   85-31505
ISBN 0-8133-7141-4

This book was produced without formal editing by the publisher.

Printed and bound in the United States of America

The paper used in this publication meets the minimum requirements of the American National Standard for Permanence of Paper for Printed Library Materials Z39.48-1984.

6   5   4   3   2   1

Contents

Foreword

In the last quarter of a century, very few arms control efforts have been aimed at eliminating the proximate causes of war, such as crises arising from misperceptions. Arms control negotiations typically have dealt with reducing the perceived threat, whether that be the threat perceived from arsenals of nuclear warheads or from the levels of conventional forces in Central Europe. Little attention has been paid in these negotiations to the problems of preventing miscalculations, of containing crises at their early stages and of reversing military escalations.

This lack of emphasis is surprising, considering that the probability of low-intensity conflict is, relatively, much higher than the probability of conflict at the high end of the conflict spectrum. It is also dangerous, since nuclear conflict is not likely to erupt out of nowhere but would likely be preceded by some kind of conflict at lesser levels of violence.

This book describes the efforts, successful and otherwise, to confront, through international negotiations, the problems of preventing miscalculation, of deterring surprise attack, and of arresting crises or conflict.

The arrangements that have been proposed to deal with these problems are generally, and not very aptly, called "confidence-building measures." "Stabilizing measures" might be a better term, since such measures are most useful precisely where the preconditions for confidence do not exist.

Several factors have combined to make "confidence-building" more topical and the outlook for such negotiations more interesting. One of these is the Stockholm Conference, a 35-nation negotiation dealing specifically with the possibility of instituting an array of confidence-building measures in Europe. Another factor is the sadly unfulfilled promise of "classical" arms control negotiations, and a growing opinion that additional means of contributing to a stable equilibrium must be found. Technological developments also are making "classical" arms control much more complex and the negotiations more prolonged. And, in the meantime, the existence in steadily increasing numbers of rapidly deliverable, highly accurate weapons—both nuclear and conventional—

underscores the urgency of doing everything possible to assure continuing control over these destructive forces by rational human beings.

In reading this book, some common features of confidence-building measures will become apparent. For example, a key difference between "classical" arms control and confidence-building or stabilizing measures is that the former has dealt with the *levels* of forces whereas the latter deals primarily with the *operations* of military forces. "Classical" arms control negotiations typically try to establish *long-term* stability, for example, by providing greater predictability about types and levels of strategic forces over a given span of time. Confidence-building measures, on the other hand, should promote *short-term* stability, especially during periods of intense and possibly turbulent international confrontation.

But such measures also should have a direct, visible, and positive effect on the strengthening of international confidence, stability, and security during normal times. A set of militarily significant confidence-building measures ideally should *oblige* nations to act habitually in a way that would serve to eliminate causes of tension and reduce the dangers of misunderstanding or miscalculation, thus reducing the dangers of armed conflict, including the danger of surprise attack. A set of militarily significant confidence-building measures should install operational barriers against the use of force, particularly by requiring tangible proof of the peaceful intent of military activities that could be perceived by others to be threatening, and imminently so, at that. Such measures should also help, or at least not hinder, efforts to restore equilibrium rapidly in the event of a threat to the stability of the military situation.

Confidence-building measures are not a substitute for efforts to reduce the too-high levels of weapons that exist today, but agreements that serve to eliminate the proximate causes of war would complement those efforts and, perhaps, facilitate their work. In fact, it would be incongruous to work toward the elimination of nuclear weapons, as both the U.S. and Soviet governments have agreed to do, and not work to eliminate the proximate origins of a conventional conflict.

Unfortunately, the case for confidence-building measures has never been fully embraced by the Soviet Union, despite the examples in this book of Soviet agreement to a number of such measures. The obvious reason for this is that confidence-building measures involve varying degrees of openness and even cooperation in military matters, ideas that run against the grain of centuries of Russian tradition. The factors supporting the case for cooperative arrangements to reduce the risk of war that no one wants, however, should also be persuasive to some extent in the Soviet Union. Given persistent and imaginative efforts to negotiate confidence-building measures in a manner that complements arms limitations and arms reduction efforts, the logic of such arrangements may gradually overcome some of the more doctrinaire reasons for resisting them.

With a certain sober optimism, one might even suggest that the potential of confidence-building measures has not yet been fully appreciated anywhere and that the field is ready for serious investigation on a scale far beyond the rather modest efforts devoted to it up to the present. For example, the possibilities of new technologies and their applications to confidence-building have not really been explored, such as in the area of early warning sensors. The methods by which confidence-building measures could work to restore stability during times of crisis have been studied but not to the extent warranted by the nature of the risks. Measures that would impose constraints on certain types of military operations in the interests of promoting stability have also been proposed and these deserve further study, even though differences in military operations make it difficult to produce an equitable military result.

What is needed most of all in this rather neglected area is a concerted effort over time, using all the ingenuity we can muster, to design and build a realistic, workable structure of stabilizing arrangements. This book shows how worthwhile the effort would be, for confidence-building measures can achieve many of the same goals as the better-known areas of arms control—enhanced stability, greater security, and a basis for a more civilized relationship among the major nations of the world.

James E. Goodby
Ambassador
Head of U.S. Delegation, Conference
on Confidence and Security Building Measures
and Disarmament in Europe

Preface

As Commander in Chief of the North American Aerospace Defense Command (NORAD), it is my responsibility to make the assessment as to whether or not North America is under attack. Obviously, a decision of this magnitude must be supported by the maximum quality of data possible and, more importantly, refined by human judgment. Hardware is unquestionably an important part of this assessment process. Our sensors and the secure and redundant communications lines that link them furnish invaluable data that is the bulwark of our strategic defensive posture. However, it is vital to understand that highly trained individuals continuously monitor and evaluate the sensor data to insure its validity. I must consider this data in conjunction with intelligence information and the world situation in arriving at an attack assessment. Human judgment is the cornerstone of the assessment process.

There is no doubt that confidence-building measures can contribute to our assessments. CBMs can help to clarify events depicted in the international political and military scene and events observed by the intelligence community. CBMs in themselves would not drive the assessment process, but could serve as an important data point in determining the significance of a series of ambiguous situations.

The NORAD assessment process is a tried and true one. We observe well over 500 missile and space launches every year, as well as numerous and varied air activities. John Borawski emphasizes early on in this volume the importance of a "credible and survivable deterrent posture that dissuades potential adversaries from contemplating attack." The NORAD assessment is the cornerstone of that credible and survivable deterrent. Our systems are absolutely reliable and accurate, and all potential adversaries need to be aware of that fact. Weakness is a first step in giving incentive to war, and the inability to detect and warn of a potential attack would be a nation's most basic weakness.

The subject of this book, avoiding nuclear war, is one in which all rational individuals share an intense interest. The only way that this may be achieved in today's world is to maintain a strategic defensive posture that makes it unequivocally clear in the minds of potential adversaries that they could not prevail in a nuclear exchange. We must draw on all the assets at our disposal, both military and diplomatic, to ensure that this goal is achieved.

Robert T. Herres
General, USAF
Commander in Chief,
North American Aerospace
Defense Command

Acknowledgments

Too many edited books are memorable for only an unfortunately minute portion of their contents. For making this volume a refreshing exception, I am first and foremost indebted to each and every contributor for the thoughtful chapters contained herein, with special thanks to those who took the time from grueling government schedules for their eloquent and informative contributions. Any flaws in this volume, of course, are unequivocally my own.

This book was produced from start to finish during my stay over 1984-85 as a post-doctoral research fellow with the Project on Avoiding Nuclear War and with the Center for Science and International Affairs, John F. Kennedy School of Government, Harvard University. To Graham Allison, Albert Carnesale, Joseph Nye, William Ury, and all the members of the Avoiding Nuclear War working group, I am sincerely grateful. I am also indebted to all the good people in OASD/ISP, J-5, XOXXI, Op-65, ACDA MA/REG, and the U.S. and Swedish CDE delegations who shared their insights during and after my previous incarnation as a Department of Defense intern, and especially to James Goodby, Jim Hinds, Sally Horn, Arne Kallin, Lars-Erik Lundin, Johan Tunberger, John Matheny, Lynn Hansen, Suzanne Parry, Henny van der Graaf, and Garnett "Charlie" Brown. In addition, I am thankful to my family—my mother Tatiana, Nancy, and Heidi—for their unflagging support.

It is my intention that this compendium serve a twofold purpose: first, to provide a basic primer on the subject of CBMs of interest to arms control specialists, students, and the general public, and, second, to contribute to the ongoing national debate over the role of arms control in strengthening national security by identifying new avenues toward that overriding objective. It represents only a beginning but, one hopes, a useful one worthy of the confidence of our publisher and, most importantly, the reader.

John Borawski
Washington, D.C.

Introduction

John Borawski

For some time it has been apparent that a general state of paralysis has beset arms control. Ambiguous outcomes of past efforts aimed at limiting weapons, current difficulties encountered by competing proposals for arms reductions, bans, and freezes, increasing demands upon verification, and doubts about compliance with existing agreements have all cast, at best, an unsettling shadow on the, future of negotiated force limitations. Concurrently, the pace of force modernization and emerging technologies for earth and outer space application threaten to upset if not nullify altogether the arms control progress that was attainable in the past, while giving rise to operational concepts that defy what many have regarded, rightly or wrongly, as sacrosanct assumptions about deterrence in the nuclear age. One need not concur with the view that arms control is little more than a "virulent superstition"[1] inimical to U.S. security interests to recognize that new approaches to arms control must be found if it is to become a vital, productive, and enduring aspect of maintaining strategic stability.

Questions have also been raised about the kind of arms control that has been pursued. Although the principal East-West arms control negotiations over the past decade and a half—SALT/START, INF, and MBFR—have concentrated on limiting and reducing force levels, several arms control themes of the cold war era have resurfaced in the 1980s in disturbing ways—the remedy for which does not rest solely with quantitative ceilings on arms.

First, war arising by surprise attack has become a greater concern at both the conventional and the strategic nuclear level. By the late 1970s, the Soviets had acquired a "standing-start" conventional offensive option in Central Europe that threatens rapid victory over NATO and, in the context of the demise in the credibility of flexible response, effective denial of NATO's explicit threat of early resort to nuclear weapons to thwart a Pact conventional onslaught. As a May 1985 NATO Military

1

Committee report concluded, the deteriorating European conventional force balance "has permitted the Soviets to develop preemptive attack options for unreinforced attack," while the achievement of "Soviet technological parity in Europe undermines NATO's 'flexible response' strategy."[2] At the central strategic level, the Soviets acquired an ability to pose a significant threat to the land-based elements of the U.S. Triad of ICBMs, SLBMs, and heavy bombers by virtue of an almost 3:1 advantage over the United States in time-urgent, hard-target kill potential[3]—a ratio that could increase to 4:1 by 1993 even if all contemplated U.S. force modernization programs are completed.[4] Although no consensus exists on the exact import and extent of these developments, these trends, coupled with the accelerated effort to develop anti-satellite and ballistic missile defenses and the deployment of potentially undetectable nuclear weapons platforms such as cruise missiles, pose the conceivable risk that in a future superpower crisis, either side may be tempted to launch or threaten to launch a preemptive blow against the other's retaliatory forces in the hopes of attaining some net advantage—however that may be defined in any rational politico-military sense. For example, at some point the Soviets might conclude that they could successfully eliminate a significant portion of the U.S. counterforce capability and still maintain sufficient forces in reserve to deter a U.S. retaliatory strike, with the consequence that, as the Scowcroft Commission suggested in 1983, "they might consider themselves able to raise the risks in a crisis in a manner that could not be matched."[5]

This "crisis instability," in turn, not only enhances opportunities for political coercion and nuclear blackmail, but magnifies the risk of what may be the most likely avenue to war—miscalculation. For instance, one side, because of a perceived need to respond immediately to potentially threatening events, might misinterpret the other's "defensive" activities as preparations for imminent attack, and react disproportionately to the "true" state of affairs—setting off a spiral of uncontrolled escalation leading to unintended catastrophe. These risks are likely to prove especially acute in a crisis, for "The very same action that one side must take to prove that it means business—a nuclear alert or a movement of troops—is indistinguishable from preparation for an attack and may be interpreted as such by the other side."[6] Misunderstanding can also relate to beliefs about the consequences of initiating war, *e.g.*, the widespread belief in 1914 that the first state to mobilize would win and win quickly. Were new technologies, say, to lead to the conclusion that the first to strike would prevail in a nuclear war, any future crisis could run the risk of serving as a potential nuclear Sarajevo.

A second concern that has attracted growing attention involves the problem of catalytic war. Because of the spread of nuclear technology and the worldwide growth of weapons-grade fuel stocks, and the increase over the years in the incidence of international terrorism, the fear has grown that a terrorist group or another third-party actor will detonate a nuclear device in such a way as to induce one of the nuclear powers to believe that the detonation was an attack upon it by another nuclear power—say, a "demonstrative" warning shot in the midst of a conventional war. This scenario is also a type of misunderstanding, but one even further removed from government control and one, as will be argued in these pages, over which neither Moscow nor Washington may possess the means to manage effectively.

The principal means of addressing these and other scenarios that could set the stage for conflagration is, obviously, the maintenance of a credible and survivable deterrent posture that dissuades potential adversaries from contemplating attack, and that allows for time to assess ambiguous situations that could spark precipitate action based on accident, miscalculation, or failure of communication. This objective can be obtained by either unilateral defense efforts or negotiated arms control, or, preferably, a sensible mix of both. However, there are perpetual fiscal and political limits to unilateral efforts, and the history of arms control has proved, to say the least, disappointing. Although the resumption of U.S.-Soviet arms control negotiations in Geneva in March 1985 after over a year's hiatus is a welcome sign, the current stalemate between the sides is unlikely to be broken rapidly. More significantly, the extent to which whatever outcome of these negotiations will seriously address the concerns outlined above remains highly questionable. Continued failure to achieve meaningful progress in "vertical" arms proliferation, in turn, may prompt withdrawals from the 1968 Nuclear Non-Proliferation Treaty, which will expire in 1995, so as to exacerbate further these concerns.

Given the troubling record of prior and contemporary efforts to achieve significant results in arms control, and because of the inadequate attention that has been paid to procedures explicitly directed at preventing and containing the crises that would most likely create the risk of any type of war in the first place, increasing attention has been devoted over the years on a supplementary, or perhaps even alternative, approach to achieving the principal purpose of arms control: reducing the risks of war. This approach has come to be known generically as "confidence-building measures," or CBMs.[7] Although these measures can and have been variously defined, essentially CBMs do not seek to limit forces of whatever kind in terms of restricting their quantity or quality, or in terms of ultimate capability. Instead, CBMs are "management instruments" that seek to control and to communicate about how, when, where, and why military activities are employed—"functional arms control," as it were—in order to multiply the disincentives to the threat or use of force. By regulating the operations of military forces and clarifying the intentions underlying military activities, CBMs should help to inhibit opportunities for conflict arising by surprise attack and miscalculation, and contribute to avoiding and managing the crises that could spark war, whether aggression be premeditated or inadvertent.

This book represents an effort to assemble leading CBM experts from government and academia to assess the utility of CBMs as applied to a wide variety of arms control considerations.

In Part 1, the theoretical underpinnings of CBMs are developed. What exactly can CBMs accomplish? What choices do states have in negotiating CBMs? How do these measures compare with other forms of arms control? What is the historical record, and where can current CBM efforts lead?

In Part 2, the "foundations" of CBMs are developed in depth. Sally K. Horn, Director for Verification Policy in the Office of the Assistant Secretary of Defense for International Security Policy, and a member of the U.S. delegation to the U.S.-Soviet negotiations that resulted in the 1984 Hotline modernization agreement, explains the history of the Hotline, its purpose, and recent Reagan administration proposals to expand direct U.S.-Soviet communication links. Raymond L. Garthoff, Senior Fellow at the Brookings Institution and formerly a member of the U.S. SALT I delegation and U.S. Ambassador to Bulgaria, looks at the 1971 U.S.-Soviet Accidents Measures agreement. Sean Lynn-Jones, Research Fellow with the Project on Avoiding Nuclear War at the Kennedy School of Government, Harvard University, analyzes the 1972 U.S.-Soviet Incidents at Sea agreement. Richard E. Darilek, Senior Analyst with the Rand Corporation and formerly Director of the MBFR Task Force in the Office of the Secretary of Defense, provides an overview of the 35-state Conference on Confidence- and Security-Building Measures and Disarmament in Europe, which convened in Stockholm in January 1984. Charles C. Flowerree, U.S. Ambassador to the Geneva Conference on Disarmament over 1980–81, discusses CBMs in the United Nations setting—a neglected forum of considerable potential in this field. Finally, Bruce Allyn, Research Associate with the Nuclear Negotiation Project, Harvard Law School, and Research Fellow with the Project on Avoiding Nuclear War, surveys Soviet attitudes toward CBMs.

Part 3 specifically focuses on future CBM directions. William L. Ury, Director of the Nuclear Negotiation Project, Harvard Law School, and Richard Smoke, Research Director of the Center for Foreign Policy Development, Brown University, propose an agenda of crisis prevention and management measures. Michael H. Mobbs, Assistant Director of the U.S. Arms Control and Disarmament Agency for Strategic Programs and former Representative of the Secretary of Defense to the U.S. Soviet Negotiations on Nuclear and Space Arms in Geneva, discusses the CBM efforts that have been conducted as part of these bilateral negotiations. Senator Sam Nunn (D-Ga) reflects on his widely acclaimed proposal for "nuclear risk reduction centers." David T. Twining (LTC-USA), Director of Soviet and East European Studies at the U.S. Army War College, Carlisle Barracks, Pennsylvania, sets out a proposal for an East-West Center for Military Cooperation in Europe. Lastly, Jim E. Hinds, Principal Director for Negotiations Policy in the Office of the Assistant Secretary of Defense for International Security Policy, reviews some potential CBM pitfalls.

The conclusion then highlights some of the key themes raised by the contributors and discusses the prospects ahead for CBMs and possible areas for future research. Also offered are a "CBM Handbook" containing selected agreements and proposals, and a selected CBM bibliography for further reading.

Notes

1. George F. Will, "Why Continue the Arms Control Charade?" *Washington Post*, June 6, 1985, p. A27.

2. Quoted in Benjamin F. Schemmer, "Successful Pact Blitzkrieg Possible in 15 Years if NATO Doesn't Produce Better," *Armed Forces Journal International* (July 1985), p. 64.

3. Organization of the Joint Chiefs of Staff, *United States Military Posture FY 1986*, p. 21. As of January 1985, the Soviet force of 308 SS-18 ICBMs alone—out of a total of 2,367 ballistic missiles—possessed greater throw-weight and hard-target kill potential than the entire U.S. force of 1,646 ballistic missiles.

4. Alton Frye, "Strategic Synthesis" *Foreign Policy*, no. 58 (Spring 1985), p. 5.

5. *Report of the President's Commission on Strategic Forces* (Washington, D.C.: U.S. Department of Defense, April 1983), p. 5.

6. Hilliard Roderick, "Crisis Management: Preventing Accidental War," *Technology Review*, vol. 88, no. 6 (August/September 1985), p. 53.

7. For the record, the term "confidence-building measure" first appeared in a December 16, 1955, UN General Assembly resolution. Rolf Berg, *Military Confidence Building in Europe*, mimeo (June 1985).

PART 1

OVERVIEW

The essential feature of arms control is the recognition of the common interest, of the possibility of reciprocation and cooperation even between potential enemies with respect to their military establishments. Whether the most promising areas of arms control involve reductions in certain kinds of military force, increases in certain kinds of military force, qualitative changes in weaponry, different modes of deployment, or arrangements superimposed on existing military establishments, we prefer to treat as an open question.

Thomas C. Schelling and Morton H. Halperin, *Strategy and Arms Control* (New York: Twentieth Century Fund, 1961), p. 2.

1
The World of CBMs

John Borawski

The term "confidence-building measure" is, as Ambassador Goodby observes in the foreword, probably somewhat of an unfortunate choice of appellations in that it implies that CBMs can somehow cause states to have confidence in or to "trust" their potential adversaries. In times of strained relations, hence, or even in the normal course of international relations between states with less than friendly ties, talk of CBMs can appear woefully misplaced. It is important at the very outset, therefore, to clarify what kinds of "confidence" CBMs are supposed to engender.

Actually, CBMs have little direct bearing on what is ultimately the political question of building "trust" among nations. They cannot sweep away deep-rooted suspicions between states of different social systems and perceived ambitions. They cannot dissolve the reasons for current alliance arrangements, or foreclose the possibility of recurrent geopolitical tensions and war. CBMs are not, in other words, a *deus ex machina* whose implementation would automatically allow the West to "trust the Russians" and vice versa. To this extent, therefore, claims that CBMs can directly contribute to "eliminating the causes of tension" among nations, as stated, for example, in the 1975 Helsinki Final Act, are rejected here as unrealistically overreaching.

What CBMs can accomplish, however, is the promotion of stability in both peacetime and crisis by providing tangible and verifiable assurances—"build confidence"—regarding the purpose and character of military activities. The most widely used definition comes from Holst and Melander: "Confidence-building involves the communication of credible evidence of the absence of feared threats."[1] Jonathan Alford defines CBMs as "measures that tend to make military intentions explicit."[2] A recent U.S. Department of State publication defines CBMs as "agreements between countries to increase openness, mutual understanding, and communication . . . designed to reduce the possibility of conflict through accident, miscalculation, or failure of communications and to inhibit opportunities for surprise attack or political intimidation, thereby increasing stability in time of calm as well as crisis."[3] These last few words are important, for CBMs can be designed both to prevent crises and opportunities for sudden attack, and to contain and defuse the crises or armed confrontations that cannot be avoided.

CBMs bear a very broad and fertile relationship to deterrence. CBMs can diminish the possibilities for war arising either intentionally along the lines of World War II, such as by premeditated surprise attack, or unintentionally along the lines of World War I, either in the sense of sheer accident or of deliberate choices based on miscalculation. Of course, how World War III, should it ever occur, will begin cannot be predicted with any certainty. Many observers would concur with the view that "the next global war, if it occurs, will likely be accidental. It would make little sense for either the Soviet Union or the United States to launch a premeditated nuclear strike, or even a conventional assault. . . . It is far more probable that mistakes and misunderstandings during a crisis will lead to tragedy."[4] Others tend to disparage the notion of nations "stumbling into war," viewing the greater danger as that of deliberate aggression. Whichever scenario is more likely, suffice it to concur with Thomas Schelling's observation that "We want to deter an enemy decision to attack us—not only a cool-headed, premeditated decision . . . but also a nervous, hot-headed, frightened, desperate decision that might result from a false alarm or be engineered by somebody's mischief."[5]

To deter both types of decisions, a stable military balance, and arms control efforts directed at securing essential equivalence, are necessary but insufficient objectives. It is also imperative that military factors do not force the pace of crisis, that measures are at hand to avoid, contain, and de-escalate crises and the risks of escalation, that if war begins inadvertently it can be terminated at the earliest possible moment, and that if attack is deliberately intended, then at least an aggressor's task will be complicated and the advantage of strategic and tactical surprise[6] denied. It is in dealing with these concerns, which are not directly related to the nature of the military balance, that, *inter alia*, CBMs can contribute to strengthening deterrence of war, whether conflict begins or threatens to begin by design or by mistake.

CBM Categories

Table 1 sets out three CBM categories and several illustrative applications of each type. These categories are distinct, but any one measure can serve multiple purposes.

Table 1

CBM ILLUSTRATIVE TRIPTYCH

INFORMATION EXCHANGE	OBSERVATION/ INSPECTION	OPERATIONAL CONSTRAINTS
Disclosure of military budgets, major unit and command location and organization, force levels, doctrine	Observers at major maneuvers On-site inspection Sensors at ICBM silos	Ban on simulated attacks Designated troop entry/exit points
Notification of accidental, unauthorized, or unexplained nuclear incidents	Noninterference with national technical means of verification	Ban on forward-basing of "offensive" weapons and support equipment
Notification of maneuvers and missile test launches	Non-concealment undertakings	Ban on multiple missile launches
Dedicated communication links (Hotline)	Enhanced conditions for military liaison mission officers and other accredited military personnel	Maneuver/movement ceilings SSBN sanctuaries/ ASW-free zones
Nuclear Risk Reduction Centers		

Information Exchange

On a basic level, the purpose is simply to enhance mutual knowledge and understanding about military activities so as to "ensure that there is a correspondence between what is said and what is done."[7] While such a measure may sound rather simplistic, it cannot be overstressed that, as the abundant literature on crisis cognition demonstrates, surprise is often achieved not because of lack of warning, but because of its victim's misreading of adversary intentions even when ample warning is available. Thus, Stalin discounted multiple warnings of impending German attack in June 1941 because of his belief that Hitler would not attempt a two-front war. Likewise, Israel in October 1973 did not expect Egyptian attack until at least 1975 on the assumption that considerable upgrading of the Egyptian air force would precede offensive operations. In addition, "surprise relies mainly on the conceptual ability to overcome the enemy's understanding of what is going on,"[8] that is, deception. Hence, in addition to the victims' self-deception noted in the preceding examples, Berlin leaked "intelligence" to the effect that German preparations along the Russian border were actually training exercises related to an invasion of Britain—Operation Sea Lion, whereas Egyptian movements along the Suez led to the plausible conclusion that these troop activities were part of normal annual maneuvers. Hence, the more that is understood about the activities of a potential adversary, the greater the chances of reducing uncertainty in both peacetime and crisis, and, consequently, of diminishing the risks of surprise attack and inadvertent conflict. Furthermore, as Michael Mobbs points out in Chapter 9, the more each side understands about the other's military capability, the lesser the chances of unnecessary competition in arms triggered by "uncertainty or potential misjudgment about the strategic capabilities of the other." Thus, in addition to bolstering crisis stability, CBMs can also promote what has been termed "arms race stability," or the fostering of predictability in the overall military relationship.

Information exchange can assume several forms. It would include military-to-military discussions held on a routine basis for the purpose of exchanging views on strategy, force posture, and other matters of interest to commanders. It would also encompass means of communication such as the U.S.-Soviet Direct Communications Link, or Hotline, which is reserved for the rapid transmission of time-urgent information for the purpose of, *inter alia*, clarifying intentions in periods of tension. Another type of information CBM concerns the advance notification of major military activities—a measure with which the term CBM is probably most commonly associated. The reason for notifying, say, large-scale field or command-post training exercises several weeks in advance along with detailed disclosure on the particulars of such exercises is to enable each side to form a clearer picture of the pattern of routine activities that the other conducts. Given such a framework, anomalies—such as the movement of troops out-of-garrison into areas other than normal maneuver locations—can be detected earlier and better understood, and sudden aggression or the use or threat of force for political intimidation could be inhibited because of this foreknowledge. If a state fails to notify an activity agreed to as notifiable, or if what is notified does not comport with national intelligence information, or if the information disclosed itself causes alarm, a warning of potentially hostile activity is issued, enabling defensive preparations to be undertaken earlier and in a less ambiguous environment. Advance notification also can calm unwarranted fears by avoiding needless misunderstanding. Hence, the first U.S.-Soviet notification CBM, agreed to in 1971, provided for the prior notification of planned ballistic missile launches—misinterpretation of which obviously could lead to catastrophe, particularly when such launches occur in the context of large-scale, worldwide strategic exercises that simulate wartime conditions. As General Herres observes in the prologue: "CBMs in themselves would not drive the assessment process, but could serve as an important linchpin in determining the significance of a series of ambiguous situations."

Observation/Inspection

Observation usually refers to preplanned inspection by invitation, such as observers at notifiable maneuvers. Inspection connotes short-notice surveillance of a more intrusive nature triggered by the demand of the party seeking inspection.

The purpose of both CBM types, nevertheless, is to allow an independent assessment of the character of military activities—notified, suspect, or both—and thereby alleviate or confirm suspicions, and "make it more difficult for a state to prepare for war without detection."[9] Independent observation or inspection by ground and air teams in a situation fraught with the potential for conflict could help defuse a potential crisis by providing reassurance, whereas the physical presence of the other side's personnel could help to inhibit aggression at the outset or, at least, complicate preparations for attack and peel away the layers of attempted deception by virtue of contact with troops in the field. Failure to permit observation or inspection, of course, would provide another indicator of possible aggressive intent. (For opposing views, see Chapter 12).

Operational Constraints

These measures, which are also referred to as "stabilization" or "security-building" measures, restrict military activities by regulating how, when, and where they are conducted. The purpose is to avoid the employment or deployment of military forces in potentially threatening modes and, where possible, to increase warning time by ensuring "that it takes longer for a state to prepare for war."[10] Ideally, constraints, like other CBMs, should capture those activities that provide the leading edge of preparations for war and prove useful by virtue of either compliance or violation. Examples include prohibiting out-of-garrison and mobilization activities above a certain threshold, the forward deployment of "offensive" weapons (*e.g.*, armor-free zones), coded radio traffic or emission-control, the outloading of "live" ammunition at exercises, and multiple ballistic missile and reconnaissance satellite launches.

As illustrations of unilaterally imposed constraints intended to avoid misunderstanding, during the 1962 Cuban missile crisis President Kennedy ordered the suspension of all routine U.S. flights in the direction of the Soviet Union and the removal of the fuses and warheads from U.S. Jupiter IRBMs in Turkey; during the 1968 Soviet invasion of Czechoslovakia, NATO reduced reconnaissance flights over West Germany and even relocated a 30,000 troop exercise 200 miles westward from its planned location near the Czechoslovak border; in 1973 the

Soviets refrained from placing their nuclear forces on elevated alert status despite President Nixon's decision to place U.S. forces on Defense Condition (DEFCON) III; and during the 1981 Polish crisis NATO again abated its intelligence efforts.[11]

Permanently operating constraints, or constraints intended for implementation only in extraordinary situations, of these and other types could prove invaluable in future crises wherein leaders operate under perceived conditions of accentuated uncertainty about objective conditions and adversary intentions. CBMs could help provide an extra measure of reassurance and clarity when it is needed most.

To demonstrate briefly how these three types of CBMs could effectively work to avoid confrontation, assume that NATO begins staging its large-scale, annual Autumn Forge maneuvers in Western Europe. Concurrently, an unanticipated domestic crisis erupts in an Eastern European country that threatens the communist regime and induces the Kremlin to order armed intervention in support of the "Brezhnev doctrine." Just as it would be useful for the Soviets to know, through information exchange and observation/inspection CBMs complementing national technical means, that the NATO exercises would not be employed as a pretext to intervene in Eastern Europe, it would also be useful for NATO to be reassured that Soviet preparations to intervene in Eastern Europe were not intended as a precursor to an attack against NATO. Hence, advance notification of the NATO exercises would help demonstrate the absence of any connection with the unexpected crisis, and notification as an alert of Soviet preparations to intervene in Eastern Europe— coupled with discreet communications perhaps involving even the Hot-line—could help clarify the purpose of the Soviet military activities. Both sides could also go beyond these measures to provide additional reassurance by refraining, say, from conducting military activities that could not possibly be associated only with the routine NATO maneuvers or the Soviet police action—such as the dispersal of nuclear forces. With both sides providing reassuring information and avoiding deployments that could give grounds for assuming the worst, the risks of unintended confrontation would be further reduced.

In addition to their military significance, CBMs can also serve other vital purposes in terms of stabilizing international relations.

First, CBMs reinforce the legal dimensions of inter-state relations. CBMs give effect and expression to the fundamental principle of international law codified in Article 2(4) of the United Nations Charter, which declares that "All members shall refrain in their international relations from the threat or use of force against the territorial integrity or political independence of any state." By promoting consistent adherence to this principle where possible, long-term stability can be forged. Moreover, as a matter of treaty relations, the breach of a CBM—or violation of even a mere politically binding CBM—serves notice to the other parties to the CBM regime of a potential threat and can thus expedite the decision to react in a timely and appropriate manner amidst the often conflicting "noise" generated by warning indicators. A U.S. president and his or her national security council, for example, might draw differing conclusions about adversary intentions in a crisis given the plethora of incoming intelligence and, naturally, because of individual predispositions. The news that the country in question had violated a CBM, however, would presumably register more forcefully with decision-makers, and would, moreover, entitle the other parties to invoke the breach as a ground for terminating the treaty or suspending its operation in whole or in part—thereby enabling rapid defensive preparations with less of a concern for "provocation" of the adversary because the latter had already revealed its hand. Violation of non-legally binding CBMs, of course, can also serve the same purpose, although excessively voluntary measures may prove counterproductive by adding to, rather than diminishing, the ambiguity of intelligence.

Second, CBMs serve a number of political purposes. CBMs prohibiting, for instance, large-scale maneuvers or the stationing of forces near sensitive border areas can reduce opportunities for military intimidation, *i.e.*, "sabre-rattling" or "gunboat diplomacy." Notification well in advance to a large number of states of major military activities can serve to inhibit a state contemplating the display of military prowess at short notice for coercive purposes by raising the political cost of intimidation. Another political CBM dimension is that because these measures can avoid interminable wrangling about the state of the military balance, states otherwise reluctant to engage in arms control may find CBMs more comfortable to adopt. No state has to "give up" anything except for conducting its military activities in threatening ways. CBMs may also prove more likely to command bipartisan support, thereby posing fewer risks for leaders in obtaining domestic support for their arms control initiatives and the agreements that may flow from them. Hence, despite the collapse of the START and INF negotiations at the end of 1983, both superpowers found it possible in January 1984 to participate in the opening of the Stockholm CBM conference, and to agree in July later that year on an upgrade to the Hotline. Finally, CBMs have also been viewed as catalysts toward greater political accommodation and toward achieving more controversial forms of arms control agreements, such as force reductions. For example, Jonathan Alford argues in the case of the Egyptian-Israeli rapprochement that "By first instituting a series of measures to separate forces and reduce military tension in the Sinai, the conditions for a political solution were created."[12] In short, the "confidence" CBMs can generate is invariably manifold, as are the incentives for their negotiation and adoption.

CBMs can also be defined by what they are not. In this sense, their principal difference with other forms of arms control, again, is that they do not affect the size, structure, or ultimate capability of arsenals. No restrictions on the number of ballistic missiles or divisions a state deploys, say, are required. However, when an ICBM is tested or a division moves out-of-garrison, CBMs might require that these activities be conducted only in certain ways so as to avoid misinterpretation. Again, the distinction is that CBMs control the use to which arms may be put, not ultimate military capability. Admittedly, this distinction allows for some grey areas. A comprehensive test ban, for example, could be viewed as a functional constraint in its banning of tests and therefore a CBM. It is not, however, generally regarded as a CBM because the purpose of a test ban is not merely to ban tests for the sake of banning tests, but to affect ultimate military capability by preventing the development of new weapons. Conversely, CBMs for the advance notification of weapons tests do not affect ultimate military capability, but are intended solely for the purpose of clarifying the nature of the test. Therefore, in assessing whether any given measure is or is not a CBM, the intended effect and real purpose must be discerned: does the measure affect ultimate military capability?

CBMs should also be distinguished from political initiatives aimed at the peaceful resolution of disputes that do not directly regulate military activities. CBMs are not synonymous with diplomacy. Although any arms control agreement or, for that matter, an extradition treaty or an agricultural purchase could be said to "build confidence" between the parties, defining CBMs too broadly—or failing to define them at all—would render the term meaningless. Hence, the term CBM as used herein is understood to denote military CBMs, setting aside the question of whether there is any practical purpose to apply the term to other settings.

Finally, although the two are sometimes used interchangeably, CBMs should also be distinguished from verification. This distinction can sometimes prove thorny, for the same procedure can serve both CBM and verification purposes. For example, on-site inspection (OSI) teams at a missile final assembly plant stationed there for the purpose of determining whether a type of weapon is being produced would be part of the verification process associated with a hypothetical treaty regulating the production of that weapon. If, however, inspectors were dispatched to an area to determine whether a suspected threatening activity was occurring, even though no agreement prohibited that activity, then the purpose of the OSI would be to build confidence in terms of threat assessment rather than to verify a particular treaty provision.

Sometimes, both purposes are intended to be served by the same measure. For example, at the Stockholm conference, NATO has proposed a measure under the rubric of "compliance and verification" for on-site inspection on demand of notified or suspect activities. Although inspections would help verify whether the target activity was or was not in conformity with the parameters required for notification, they would also provide threat assessment—the latter being the more important function. In general, however, it may be said that CBMs stand alone as arms control instruments, and will require verification themselves.

CBMs Versus Arms Reductions

Because CBMs focus on politico-military intentions and on the uses to which forces may be put, rather than on directly limiting the wherewithal itself, the temptation exists—for some reason particularly at academic conferences—to regard CBMs as automatically something apart from "arms control" or to otherwise disparage their usefulness. For example, as is pointed out in Chapter 6, certain Third World countries have tended to disparage CBMs as understood in the East-West context as attempts to divert attention from disarmament. It should be clarified here and now, therefore, that CBMs are indeed a type of arms control, and that the distinction between arms control and disarmament should be borne in mind. As Thomas Schelling and Morton Halperin pointed out over two decades ago: "Arms control . . . may involve the straightforward elimination or armaments . . . or may involve communications, traffic rules, or other arrangements superimposed on military establishments."[13] CBMs represent the latter approach.

Too readily dismissing CBMs relative to arms reductions, moreover, overlooks the fact that not only have attempts at securing limits on the testing, production, and deployment of weapons proved extraordinarily difficult to achieve then as now, and are likely to remain so indefinitely, but that such limits may not necessarily prove militarily meaningful or sufficient to bolster deterrence. For instance, deep reductions to balanced levels in nuclear arsenals might not necessarily enhance stability given disparate force postures, the likelihood of technology undermining the significance of numerical limits, and the real possibility that less may be worse, *i.e.*, fewer weapons, even if intended as a step towards the utopian goal of general and complete disarmament, might tempt preemption or make accidental nuclear war more likely under a "use it or lose it" rationale; higher force levels, however, presumably afford a greater confidence margin of assured retaliation and greater flexibility in prosecuting, if necessary, a nuclear conflict. The initial U.S. START proposal, for instance, which called for reducing each side's ballistic missile warheads by one third and ballistic missiles by one half to equal levels, was criticized as increasing the warhead-to-target ratio and thereby making a first strike a more attractive option. Moreover, whether force levels be high or low, surprise attack can neutralize much of the retaliatory capability if serious vulnerabilities are left unaddressed operationally or are finessed by arguments of the type surrounding *Minuteman* vulnerability and follow-on ICBMs. As Richard Betts points out: "The peacetime military balance is an irrelevant indicator of defense capability if surprise radically alters the balance at the outset of war."[14]

Another illustration of the proposition that arms reductions are not enough, or perhaps even disadvantageous, concerns the negotiations on Mutual and Balanced Force Reductions (MBFR) in Vienna. Although the MBFR negotiations are aimed at achieving equal ground and air force manpower ceilings in Central Europe between NATO and the Warsaw Pact, history is replete with examples of superior strategy prevailing over a quantitatively matched or even superior opponent (witness the 1940 German invasion of France, the 1941 German invasion of the Soviet Union, or the Arab-Israeli wars.) Common manpower ceilings, hence, may not necessarily prove stabilizing, particularly in view of geographic disparities between NATO and Warsaw Pact reinforcement capabilities. Moreover, it is not so much the greater levels of troops that the Warsaw Pact enjoys in Central Europe relative to NATO, but the possibility of these forces being employed in a surprise offensive before the full measure of NATO resources could be brought to bear (which would only be possible assuming, of course, early NATO defeat is prevented). Therefore, if warning can be clarified and warning time extended by CBMs, their value could prove greater than the type of force limits currently being negotiated in Vienna, or, for that matter, than the modest NATO conventional defense initiatives presently programmed. As Betts points out: "A Soviet attack could succeed . . . even if the West redresses the conventional imbalance, if the attack were to use unanticipated techniques and catch NATO unready. Strengthening the order of battle offers only additive advantages to NATO; achieving surprise offers multiplicative advantages to Moscow."[15]

Another, and more systematic, way of explicating the potential applications of CBMs in contrast to arms reductions is to review the possible paths to nuclear war and the arms control implications attendant upon their avoidance or containment. Five generic paths, as identified by the Project on Avoiding Nuclear War at Harvard University, are discussed below.[16]

Bolt from the Blue

The first generic path concerns an attack against an opponent's forces executed with complete political and strategic surprise. No preexisting deterioration of relations or actual confrontation forebodes such an attack, but the initiating state nevertheless determines that striking first offers the best of all possible worlds at that time because of, say, its belief that retaliatory damage will be limited to a tolerable level, or even that the defending state will lack the political will to retaliate.

To reduce the remote but conceivable risk of this type of surprise attack—for which no historical precedent exists but upon which strategy for nuclear forces is and must be based—it is obviously essential to maintain relatively invulnerable retaliatory forces and command and control assets such that any adversary would recognize that no plausible outcome of its striking first would represent a success. Arms control approaches that seek to establish essential equivalence, hence, are necessarily germane—although whether they can be realized is quite another question. CBMs too, however, can play a role in deterring surprise attack in a twofold sense. First, processes could be developed to limit misperception and misunderstanding about the objective nuclear balance. In this category would fall information exchange and observation/inspection measures. Second, CBMs could be adopted to help deny the advantage of surprise by ensuring that warning would always be assured in some way. In this category would fall measures ranging from noninterference with national technical means and sensors at ICBM silos to operational constraints on strategic nuclear forces. Such constraints could: (a) increase strategic warning by forcing a state contemplating aggression to signal its hostile intent further in advance, such as prohibitions on SSBN and bomber dispersals beyond prenegotiated thresholds; (b) increase tactical warning, such as by prohibiting the forward basing of SSBNs and thereby increasing SSBN flight time; and (c) help ensure the survivability of some segment of the retaliatory force even after hostilities begin, such as SSBN sanctuaries in which ASW activity would be prohibited.

Preemption in Crisis

The second scenario refers to a situation where one side believes that war is imminent and unavoidable, and that some net advantage will accrue to the side that strikes first (hence, crisis instability). To avoid this course of action, which would most likely also take advantage of surprise, secure retaliatory and command and control assets are, again, vital. Also again, however, CBMs would be useful in developing processes to limit misperception and in constraining opportunities for sudden preemption. In addition, CBMs configured to preventing and containing crises in the first place would prove highly material, drawing upon a wide variety of measures ranging from rapid communications to operational constraints. For example, in 1967 President Johnson resorted to the Hotline to explain the nature of U.S. aircraft carrier operations in the Mediterranean in connection with efforts to rescue the crew of the U.S.S. *Liberty* following the Israeli attack upon that vessel—Soviet misinterpretation of which naturally could have heightened tensions in the midst of an already dangerous situation.

Escalation from Conventional War

A typical scenario for this path would find NATO at the verge of collapse following a surprise Warsaw Pact blitz, with SACEUR requesting authorization to employ nuclear weapons. Perhaps a more plausible scenario would be that of indirect U.S.-Soviet confrontation in a local war that holds out the prospects for direct superpower conflict, such as in the Middle East.

Dealing with such scenarios is somewhat problematic given the fact that in Europe—one but not the only venue of potential superpower conflict—NATO strategy is predicated on the explicit threat to use nuclear weapons first. At least in the NATO context, hence, the more relevant mission for CBMs would be avoiding conventional war and, should it occur, nuclear escalation based on miscalculation. Here, again, the maintenance of a credible military balance constitutes the *sine qua non* of deterrence. However, arms control approaches and unilateral defense initiatives are unlikely to place NATO and the Warsaw Pact on an equal footing even in a limited sense, such as in terms of manpower in Central Europe. Moreover, as already noted, equality in numbers, even if realized in the more relevant combat power indicia such as firepower, cannot *ipso facto* rule out the possibility of war. Hence, while the West cannot expect the East to negotiate away conventional force advantages or to allow NATO defense initiatives to go unchallenged, it is possible to develop procedures to at least help ensure that surprise cannot be achieved and that nuclear war does not begin inadvertently. CBMs for enhancing warning of conventional attack would include the full gamut of CBM types and especially operational constraints. One longstanding CBM for application to Europe concerns a restricted deployment zone along the inner-German border wherein offensive weaponry would be prohibited in such a fashion that "It would then become necessary to resort to highly visible troop movements and/or restructuring in order for a potential aggressor to be able to mount a large-scale surprise attack, thereby increasing the warning time to the other side in case of such an attack."[17] Conceivable measures for avoiding inadvertent nuclear escalation would range from the use of direct communication links to control escalation in wartime to operational constraints on nuclear-capable systems. The withdrawal of tactical nuclear weapons from agreed-upon border zones, for example, has been proposed by various sources in part to reduce the risk of early use of nuclear weapons occasioned by the diminution of positive peacetime controls. SSBN sanctuaries could reduce the risk of unconstrained ASW operations quickly leading to global nuclear exchange. The degree to which constraints can be applied in this context, however, is restricted by virtue of the fact that alerting nuclear forces favors the defending state. Thus, while refraining, for instance, from dispersing nuclear warheads from peacetime storage sites at the outset of a conventional conflict would theoretically serve a confidence-building function, it could also invite preemption. It should also be pointed out that the uncertainty of when nuclear weapons would be employed in a war that began conventionally may bolster deterrence, whereas nuclear-free zones could be argued to call into question NATO's nuclear deterrent and its applicability to all of NATO territory, and thereby increase the risk of conventional probes and, consequently, of nuclear war. It may, nevertheless, be possible to devise an agreed-upon set of standard ceasefire procedures that would serve to defuse conventional conflict if both sides were interested in avoiding further escalation. As William Ury and Richard Smoke note: "such procedures could facilitate a temporary halt to hostilities in order to allow negotiations to begin. Precious hours and days spent settling procedural questions might be saved by some prior thought, and might conceivably make the difference between war and peace in a rapidly moving conflict."[18] Of course, CBMs for wartime application are the hard case, but the stakes involved are such that states cannot afford the folly of neglecting investigation of this area.

Accidental or Unauthorized Use

Despite a complex net of procedural safeguards and redundant warning systems, a highly unlikely but nevertheless not impossible risk exists that nuclear war may arise through sheer error, *e.g.*, radar warning of a first strike of Canadian geese (in 1979 NORAD and other commands reportedly experienced 1,500 false missile warnings)[19] or the unauthorized acts of a local commander (the insane submarine captain scenario). Arms control efforts that seek to shape the military balance are largely irrelevant to this case. Although it should be observed that a credible military balance would allow for time to assess the incident without the need for immediate response, if such events occurred in the midst of a deep crisis, it is not difficult to imagine what different consequences might obtain. Moreover, as Paul Bracken notes, "when forces are placed on alert, the complexity of the warning system may not only cease to provide redundancy; it may also amplify the mistakes."[20] Hence, the more relevant arms control approach would be to make use of CBMs to help clarify promptly the nature of such military incidents and provide assurances that the act was indeed accidental or unauthorized. As Henry Kissinger observed in 1960: "If accidental war is to be avoided, there must be means by which the nuclear powers are able to inform each other rapidly and convincingly that an ambiguous action was not intended to be the prelude to a surprise attack . . . everything may depend on the ability to reassure the opponent clearly and convincingly."[21] Toward this end, Kissinger proposed the establishment of crisis control centers by way of "Joint Western-Soviet offices . . . in Moscow and Washington with their own communications equipment" together with "special surveillance teams" under joint or international control, with both running frequent exercises "designed to guard against the dangers of accidental war and miscalculation."[22] Kissinger's proposal was, of course, a precursor to contemporary proposals for "nuclear risk reduction centers," discussed in Chapters 8 and 10.

Accidents can also relate to non-nuclear events that could spark inadvertent war. For example, during the height of the Cuban missile crisis, a U.S. reconnaissance plane accidentally strayed over Siberia— setting off a Soviet fighter scramble that could have triggered war, as Khrushchev pointed out.[23] What if during a future U.S.-Soviet crisis one side's ASAT weapon undergoing a routine test accidentally blinds the other's satellites? Or, what if one side's cruise missiles undergoing routine tests accidentally stray over the other's territory? Again, in these and, indubitably, more imaginative scenarios that may occur to the reader, although a stable military balance can reduce the risks of precipitate response, it is also important that events are clarified promptly and that appropriate use is made of evaluation time.

Catalytic War

By this term is meant a situation where a third country or non-state actor detonates a nuclear device for the purpose of triggering superpower nuclear exchange. A common scenario involves a deranged Third World leader or a terrorist group setting off a nuclear explosion on the territory of one or both of the superpowers. This event is misinterpreted as an attack by one superpower against the other, with the consequence of general nuclear war. Given the inability to control nuclear proliferation fully, such a scenario is not inconceivable—some observers would say inevitable. By way of historical example, in 1914 the German battleship *Goeben* ran up the Russian flag prior to shelling the Algerian coast, and in World War II the *Luftwaffe* bombed Hungary with Russian-manufactured munitions—inducing Hungary to declare war on the Soviet Union.

Inadvertent escalation can also arise even when a third party nuclear incident or other action is not calculated to trigger superpower conflict. For example, it took more than an hour for the U.S. government to determine that the U.S.S. *Liberty* had been attacked by Israeli, and not Soviet, forces, during which time U.S. ships stood poised to launch attacks against Soviet forces in the area. Again, although a stable military balance can reduce the impulse for immediate response, it is also imperative that measures are at hand to clarify the origins of a nuclear detonation or other events and to manage cooperatively the ensuing confusion such that the superpowers do not find themselves in a war that neither intended. One such CBM, suggested by Thomas Schelling, would involve both sides placing nuclear "signatures" on their weapons, such that analysis, perhaps conducted jointly, performed immediately after the incident would reveal that the weapon could not have originated from the superpowers.[24]

In sum, CBMs may be said to play a complementary as well as an independent role in the arms control process. While it is important to reduce the capabilities for war, it is also imperative to reduce the possibilities for crisis and conflict.

CBMs Past and Present

CBMs constitute a novel arms control approach only in terminology. In 1816, for example, Lord Castlereagh proposed that all the Great Powers, prior to considering arms reductions, explain the nature and extent of their arsenals as a means of dispelling alarm—the equivalent of contemporary proposals for information exchange on military posture and defense allocations. An early "notification" measure concerns the 1930 Greco-Turkish protocol which required each side to provide the other with notice six months in advance of the acquisition of naval vessels, and which because of "mutual statements of intent and frequent consultations served to control an incipient arms race."[25] An early "constraint" CBM involved the 1936 Montreux Convention, which regulates warship deployment in the Black Sea and passage through the Turkish straits. President Eisenhower's 1955 "Open Skies" proposal for mutual aerial inspection provides an early illustration of an observation regime.

The first CBM agreement, however, is generally regarded as the 1963 U.S.-Soviet Direct Communications Link, or Hotline. A child of the Cuban missile crisis and based on U.S. initiative, the Hotline has been upgraded twice, in 1971 and 1984, and has been used in connection with several major global incidents since 1967, *e.g.*, the two Arab-Israeli wars, the 1970 Indo-Pakistani war, the 1979 Chinese intervention in

Vietnam and Soviet invasion of Afghanistan, and in 1982 with regard to events in Lebanon. In 1980 the United States proposed a bilateral direct communications link with China, although this was rejected by Beijing.[26]

In 1971, the Accidents Measures agreement was concluded. It requires each side to maintain adequate safeguards against the accidental or unauthorized use of nuclear weapons; to notify the other immediately in the event of an accidental, unauthorized, or unexplained incident involving the possible detonation of a nuclear weapon; to notify the other immediately in the event of unidentified objects or of interference with missile warning systems; and to notify the other in advance of planned missile launches beyond national territory and in the direction of the other side. Similar "accidents" agreements were concluded by the Soviet Union with France in 1976 and with Britain in 1977.

The 1972 Incidents at Sea agreement requires the parties to observe the International Regulations for Preventing Collisions at Sea, to refrain from provocative acts at sea, and to notify mariners and airmen of actions on the high seas representing a danger to navigation or to aircraft in flight, *e.g.,* missile tests. The agreement is credited with having aided in defusing potential crises and with providing a model for military-to-military consultations.

1972 also witnessed the conclusion of the ABM treaty and the SALT I interim agreement on offensive nuclear arms. The ABM treaty established the Standing Consultative Commission (SCC) to promote the implementation of both the ABM treaty and the SALT I agreement. Although the SCC is primarily a compliance board, it also serves a number of CBM objectives. For instance, Article XIII(1)(d) authorizes the SCC to "consider possible changes in the strategic situation which have a bearing on the provisions of this Treaty"—language presumably broad enough to cover questions falling under the "information exchange" rubric. The SCC is also charged with oversight of the 1971 Accidents Measures agreement.

The 1973 Prevention of Nuclear War agreement requires the two sides to refrain from acts that could exacerbate relations between them, and to enter into urgent consultations should such events arise.

Lastly in the category of bilateral U.S.-Soviet CBM agreements, Article XVI of the SALT II treaty requires notification in advance of all multiple ICBM launches and of single launches planned to extend beyond national territory, regardless of direction. This measure closed a significant loophole in the Accidents Measures agreement in that neither side launches ICBMs in the explicit direction of the other, and it also captured multiple launches not planned to extend beyond national territory (but which, nevertheless, could give rise to misinterpretation—the first warning of missile launches being, after all, infra-red detection of the boosters).

The superpowers are also party to the 1975 Helsinki Final Act of the Conference on Security and Cooperation in Europe (CSCE). The Final Act, which appears to be the first agreement to employ the term CBM, provides for five measures for application in Europe, although excluding Soviet territory save for a 250-km strip of Soviet territory facing or shared with other CSCE participating states. The measures are: politically mandatory notification 21 days in advance of ground troop maneuvers exceeding 25,000 personnel; and, on a voluntary basis, prior notification of troop movements and of smaller-scale maneuvers, exchange of observers at notifiable maneuvers, and exchange of goodwill military delegations.

An ambitious array of CBM initiatives is also currently underway in various fora that build upon the aforementioned agreements. The remainder of this section discusses U.S. and NATO proposals, with discussion of Soviet proposals reserved for the following section "The Soviet CBM Approach."

START and INF

In these two negotiations, now ongoing as part of the bilateral Negotiations on Nuclear and Space Arms in Geneva, the United States proposed in 1982 that all launches of ballistic missiles at or exceeding 1800 km in range—ICBMs, SLBMs, and land-based, longer-range INF (LRINF) ballistic missiles (Pershing II, SS-20, SS-4)—be notified in advance. These initiatives build upon the 1971 Accidents Measures and SALT II accords by including all ICBM launches, whether multiple or single and whether or not confined to national territory, and, for the first time, all SLBM and LRINF ballistic missile launches. Because any launch of a ballistic missile, except for "pop-up" tests, conceivably could generate alarm on the other side—just as the accidental intrusion into Soviet air space by a U.S. reconnaissance plane during the Cuban missile crisis could have sparked inadvertent escalation—a comprehensive missile launch notification regime is long overdue. As William Perry has observed: "Test notification . . . is not an academic issue. A number of years ago, the Soviets launched a whole squadron of operational missiles, thereby making room for a new type of missile in the vacated silos. The Soviets were either displaying an incredible insensitivity or a blind faith in the reliability of our sensor and warning systems—a greater faith than I have. On these occasions, we did recognize the firings for what they were, but this was a dangerous game."[27]

Inclusion of SLBM and INF missile launches has special importance for crisis stability for several reasons. Whereas ICBMs are normally tested from known test ranges, such as Vandenberg AFB in California, SLBMs are normally tested from operational submarine tubes. Coupled with the fact that SLBMs do not have permission action links (PALs), which are devices that preclude the arming or launching of a nuclear weapon until the insertion of a prescribed code, SLBM launches may be more prone to misunderstanding. In addition, the short flight times of INF ballistic missiles and forward-based SLBMs, especially if depressed trajectories are employed, also hold out the potential for generating alarm in the event of an unexplained launch, particularly in times of tension.

Furthermore, in START the United States proposed that each side provide advance notification of all major military exercises involving nuclear forces. Because large-scale exercises simulate wartime conditions, a reciprocal information exchange regime would serve a useful purpose indeed in avoiding misinterpretation (recall the large-scale April 1984 *SpringEx* Soviet SSBN flush into the Norwegian Sea, the size and rapidity of which caught the intelligence community by surprise). In both START and INF, the United States also proposed expanded information exchange on nuclear forces so as to aid in understanding force postures as well as in verifying force ceilings.

As President Reagan stated on June 11 1982: "Taken together, these steps would represent a qualitative improvement in the nuclear environment. They would help reduce the chances of misinterpretation in the case of exercises and test launches. And they would reduce the secrecy and ambiguity which surround military activity "[28]

Mutual and Balanced Force Reductions

In December 1979, NATO proposed a series of "associated measures" at the MBFR negotiations primarily to enhance verification of a treaty providing for common, collective ground and air force active duty manpower ceilings in Central Europe. The associated measures, however, also included two CBMs: notification 30 days in advance and by annual calendar of out-of-garrison activities by one or more division-size formations, and the exchange of observers at these activities. These CBMs, unlike the rest of the associated measures, would apply to the territory of all European MBFR participating states, including the western Soviet Union, and not just to Central Europe.

The Weinberger Report

On April 11, 1983, Secretary of Defense Caspar W. Weinberger issued a report to Congress recommending four new CBMs, which were subsequently endorsed by President Reagan on May 24, 1983.[29] The first measure proposed upgrading the Hotline with the addition of a high-speed facsimile capability that would enable the two sides to transmit more and more complex data, including, for the first time, graphs, maps, and photographs, more rapidly and reliably. Instead of the present rate of 1 page of text per 3 minutes, or roughly 67 words per minute, the facsimile capability would allow for the transmission of 3 pages of text per minute. On July 17, 1984, the Hotline modernization was concluded through an exchange of notes in Washington.

The second measure called for the establishment of a "Joint Military Communications Link," or JMCL, that would supplement the Hotline to facilitate communications below the head-of-state level regarding the military aspects of an emergency (the scenes depicting communication between U.S. and Soviet officers in the motion picture *Failsafe* come to mind). The JMCL could be used for information-sharing in peacetime as well as for communications in crisis.

The third measure called for an improved Embassy-Capital link between the U.S. Embassy in Moscow and the State Department, and between the Soviet Embassy in Washington and the Soviet Foreign Ministry. Together with the Hotline and the JMCL, this communication link would contribute to resolving urgent situations as rapidly as possible.

The fourth measure called for a multilateral agreement open to all states providing for consultation in the event of a nuclear incident involving a terrorist group or some other non-state actor. Presumably, such an accord would supplement existing U.S.-Soviet fora such as the International Atomic Energy Agency Board of Governors and General Conferences.

Despite the July 1984 Hotline modernization agreement, the Soviets have not expressed enthusiasm thus far for the JMCL or the Embassy-Capital link, whereas U.S. European allies have not expressed interest in the multilateral nuclear incidents accord. These initiatives, however, represent possible areas for future negotiation, either on a multilateral or bilateral basis. In this context, it is encouraging to note that on June 14, 1985, the SCC issued a communique announcing that the United States and the Soviet Union had signed a "common understanding" regarding the 1971 Accidents Measures agreement that reaffirmed the commitment to urgent consultations via the Hotline in the event of unexplained nuclear incidents (*e.g.*, terrorist activities).

On May 8, 1985, President Reagan, addressing the European Parliament in Strasbourg, France, proposed the JMCL anew as a "channel for exchanging notifications and other information regarding routine military activities, thereby reducing the chances of misunderstanding and misinterpretation. And over time, it might evolve into a 'risk reduction' mechanism for rapid communication and exchange of data in times of crisis."[30] The President also proposed regular exchanges of U.S. and Soviet military observers at military exercises and locations, and regular, high-level military-to-military contacts "to develop better understanding and to prevent potential tragedies from occurring." Citing the September 1983 Soviet shootdown of a Korean airliner and the March 1985 Soviet shooting of a U.S. military liaison mission officer in East Germany, the President declared "as terrible as past events have been, it would be more tragic if we were to make no attempt to prevent even larger tragedies from occurring through lack of contact and communication."

Space Arms Control

Although prospects for progress in space arms control in Geneva remain highly uncertain—the United States avowing to occasion a transition over time from offensive to nonnuclear defensive systems, the Soviet Union apparently determined to thwart the U.S. Strategic Defense Initiative—CBMs conceivably could play a role in averting destabilization if deployment of anti-satellite (ASAT) and anti-ballistic missile (ABM) weaponry goes forward. For example, with regard to ASAT, President Reagan stated on March 31, 1984, that among the options being studied were the regulation of "certain threatening activities related to space."[31] Conceivable options for both ASAT and ABM CBMs range from modest information exchange measures on planned tests and programs to observation of certain launch and deployment areas to operational constraints, such as bans on simulated attacks, close passes by ASATs near the space platforms of the other side, high-altitude ASAT tests, and on various types of concurrent testing. For example, on June 14, 1985, the United States and the Soviet Union reportedly agreed in the SCC to ban the concurrent testing of air defense and ABM systems. Although this measure is intended to aid in verification of the ABM treaty's ban on the testing of SAMs in an ABM mode (Article VI),[32] it is a precedent that could be extended in the CBM field to capture additional activities for the purpose of avoiding provocative events— such as occurred in 1982 when the Soviets conducted, within a 6-hour period, an ASAT interceptor test and launches of two ICBMs, two ABMs, one SLBM, and one SS-20[33] (on another occasion, the Soviets launched 30 ballistic missiles over a two-day period). Although space CBM considerations ultimately will be determined by the conclusions both sides draw about the character of deterrence and defense in the next century, the desirability of rules of the road in space to manage this competition and to prevent miscalculation of, say, accidents or ambiguous events, is rather self-evident.

The Stockholm CDE Conference

On January 17, 1984, the United States, Canada, and 33 European states convened the "Conference on Confidence- and Security-Building Measures and Disarmament in Europe," or CDE. Although future stages of the CDE may be devoted, as its title connotes, to questions of arms reductions, the first stage, which meets in Stockholm at least until November 1986, will be concerned exclusively with CBMs—or "CSBMs" (plus "security") in CDE parlance to reflect the more substantive thrust of the CDE relative to the modest Final Act CBMs. The objective of the CDE, which is integrally related to the CSCE, is to negotiate a regime of militarily significant, politically binding, and verifiable CSBMs applicable to the whole of Europe as far east as the Urals. The NATO proposal, advanced on January 24, 1984, calls for: (1) information exchange on the organization and location of major ground and air force formations and on regulations governing accredited military personnel; (2) notification by annual forecast of military activities notifiable under measure 3; (3) notification 45 days in advance of out-of-garrison land activities at the divisional level or at 6,000 troops, mobilization activities at 3 divisions or at 25,000 troops, and amphibious activities at 3 battalions or at 3,000 personnel; (4) observers at notifiable activities; (5) noninterference with national technical means of verification, and on-site inspection upon demand of notified or suspect activities; and (6) enhanced communication links among governments. The NATO proposal builds upon the Final Act by lowering the notification threshold from 25,000 to 6,000 troops, extending the notification period from 21 to 45 days, expanding the types of notifiable activity, and introducing new measures such as information exchange, notification by annual calendar, on-site inspection, and European "hotlines." The overall effect is to capture a larger array of military activities and thereby better inhibit potentially threatening events. Similar ideas have been advanced by the neutral and nonaligned countries, whose initiatives are likely to play an important role in arriving at a concluding document.

United Nations

The U.N. Disarmament Commission has been exploring the elaboration of guidelines for appropriate types of CBMs on both a global and regional basis. Although the Commission has thus far failed to accomplish anything of tangible significance, the role of the United Nations in facilitating the establishment of CBM regimes is potentially substantial. In addition, President Reagan has twice employed his annual addresses to the General Assembly to launch new CBM proposals. For example, on September 24, 1984, President Reagan proposed periodic U.S.-Soviet consultations at cabinet level; exchange of outlines of five-year military plans for weapons development and procurement; and exchange of observers "at military exercises and locations," presumably on national territory.

Nuclear Risk Reduction Centers

Congress has also been involved in the CBM business. Indeed, the Weinberger report referred to above was prepared by way of response to a September 1982 amendment to the 1983 Department of Defense Authorization Act by Senators Sam Nunn (D-Ga.), John Warner (R-Va.), and the late Henry Jackson (D-Wash.) for a study of possible measures for improving the containment and control of nuclear weapons use, particularly during crises.

Although the senators praised the Weinberger intiatives, they also concluded that more comprehensive arrangements would be required to manage nuclear crises. To this end, they proposed the establishment of separate national "nuclear risk reduction centers" located in Moscow and Washington that would maintain a continuous watch on any events with the potential to lead to nuclear confrontation. Senate Resolution 329 urging the negotiation of these centers passed by an 82:0 vote on June 15, 1984.

Although the Weinberger report rejected the idea of risk reduction centers for at least the present in favor of the JMCL—which, as President Reagan stated on May 8, 1985, could evolve into some form of risk reduction center—the United States and the Soviet Union agreed on November 21, 1985, to study at the experts level the question of nuclear risk reduction centers. In Chapter 10, Senator Nunn discusses the background of the risk reduction proposal.

The Soviet CBM Approach

The Soviet Union, although having proposed measures similar if not identical to those of the United States, appears to approach CBMs from a different perspective which, very generally speaking, could be characterized by its extremes in terms of ostensibly reciprocal military significance and by an enduring distaste for "transparency"—as recently evidenced by the murder of a U.S. military liaison mission officer, Major Arthur D. Nicholson, in East Germany on March 24, 1984, for alleged "espionage." Indeed, the Soviets reject the term "transparency" (*prozracnost*) in favor of the more ambiguous and subjective term "openness" (*otkrovennost*).[34] However, as evidenced by historical experience, areas of U.S.-Soviet congruence do appear to exist that offer the promise of productive negotiations.

On the one hand, the Soviets have long favored "declaratory" measures that amount to little more than pledges of benign intent—"instant" CBMs, as it were. For example, in the CDE, the centerpiece of the Soviet proposal is a treaty on the non-use of force and on the no-first-use of nuclear weapons. Although neither NATO nor the neutral and nonaligned countries regard these pledges as CSBMs (for they are not militarily significant or verifiable), then Soviet foreign minister Andrei Gromyko declared on January 18, 1984, that adoption of either pledge would constitute "the greatest accomplishment" of the Stockholm conference. Concerning the NATO CSBMs, the Soviets argue that the information exchange and inspection measures are instruments of espionage, the real purpose of which "is to lay bare the structure and activity of the Soviet armed forces and their allies to the detriment of their security."[35] The Soviets do, however, favor improved notification and observation measures, albeit of a more modest scope than the NATO measures, as well as means for crisis consultations.

On the other hand, the Soviets have proposed CBMs of a much more ambitious scope than the U.S. and NATO measures—operational constraints. Soviet proposals on this score including prohibiting maneuvers exceeding 40,000 troops (advanced in both MBFR and the CDE), limits on naval activities (various fora), and constraints affecting strategic and theater/tactical nuclear forces (such as in the CDE and at START). For instance, a Moscow radio broadcast criticized the Weinberger report because it allegedly ignored the "specific and far-reaching" Soviet CBMs advanced in START—citing bans in agreed zones adjoining national territory on flights by heavy bombers, on aircraft carrier patrols, and on ASW activity in SSBN sanctuaries[36] (all measures that the United States has long opposed for several reasons, as discussed in Chapter 9). Although Soviet constraint proposals tend not to disfavor their authors (to wit, aircraft carrier constraints), at least conceptually constraints are of greater military significance than information exchange and observation/inspection CBMs because they actually do something about potentially threatening activities in an operational sense. According to Gromyko: "the Soviet Union stands for preventing dangers and crisis situations, while the United States proposes simply to exchange information."[37]

Another factor to take into account in gauging Soviet CBM attitudes concerns the inadequate record of Soviet compliance with the Final Act CBMs. Until 1981, Eastern compliance had been adequate if less than stellar. For example, Eastern notifications typically were extremely sparse and observers were invited on few occasions and generally from only a select group of countries. U.S. observers, for example, were invited to Warsaw Pact maneuvers only twice and not at all since 1979. Whereas over 1975–84 NATO and the neutral and nonaligned countries invited observers to 31 out of 39 notified maneuvers, the Warsaw Pact invited observers to only 7 out of 22 notified maneuvers.[38] However, in August 1981, the Soviets failed to disclose required information concerning the number and type of forces and designation of a large-scale exercise held in the Belorussian and Baltic military districts. Subsequently, TASS, rather than the required normal diplomatic channels, revealed that the exercise—designed *Zapad*-81—involved roughly 100,000 troops (one of the largest Soviet exercises in post-World War II history and one intended to pressure Poland). With additional compliance issues raised in connection with at least two other known exercises—*Soyuz*-81 and *Shield*-82, Soviet willingness to comply with even more ambitious measures, such as are being discussed in the CDE, cannot but be called into question. Of course, since it is not NATO that will start a war in Europe, and since it is not NATO that has created the problems of surprise attack capability and military secrecy in Europe, it is still not clear what exactly the Soviet Union has to gain from CSBMs in Europe. Be that as it may, the Soviet record of compliance with the Final Act CBMs casts a shadow over the veracity of expressed Soviet interest in pursuing CBMs, at least in the European context.

It should also be observed that, despite conclusion of separate CBM accords in the past, the Soviets tend to view CBMs as integrally linked to agreements that limit force levels. Separation of the two, Soviet commentators charge, is akin to what the Soviets charged during the 1950s-era disarmament negotiations—that the West seeks control but not disarmament. Thus, whereas in START and INF the United States tabled separate CBM agreements, believing that progress should go forward where possible, the Soviet proposals were framed as articles in their START and INF treaty proposals. Likewise, even though the Stockholm Conference is concerned solely with CSBMs in its current stage, the Soviets nevertheless went ahead and introduced a variety of vague disarmament proposals concerning nuclear and chemical weapons. Hence, although both the United States and the Soviet Union view CBMs as complementing arms reductions, this has been expressed in different ways. It should, therefore, not be expected that bilateral CBM negotiations can advance very far in the future without concurrent progress in arms reductions.

Nevertheless, despite these differences, there do exist particular CBM areas that are of mutual superpower interest and where progress can be expected. Soviet statements indicate that addressing the third party nuclear danger, containing regional crises, and improving communications and consultations constitute fruitful areas for exploration. Overall, a fair summation of the Soviet approach is provided by William Ury: "the Soviets will engage in crisis control and prevention, not just passively but actively, when it serves their interest to do so."[39]

Prospects: The Future as Prologue

The salience of CBMs is likely to grow in the forseeable future and beyond in a wide spectrum of possibilities for land, air, naval, and space application encompassing nuclear, exotic, and conventional weaponry. Although explication of conceivable CBM arrangements deserving of greater attention is reserved for the following chapters, at least three points are worth stressing at this juncture by way of review.

First, given the likelihood that potential geopolitical flashpoints and Soviet power projection capability will increase in the years ahead, CBMs can aid in managing some of the risks of war that may arise both among regional actors and, most importantly, between the super-powers. The Stockholm conference, discussed in Chapter 5, could provide a model for regional applications in this regard. The United Nations may also have a practical role to play in facilitating CBM configurations, perhaps based in some instances along the lines of the Sinai monitoring arrangements in addition to other measures (zones of restricted deployment and so forth).

Second, CBMs can provide a valuable complement to nuclear non-proliferation efforts by reducing the dangers inherent in the diffusion of nuclear technology, whether these concerns be addressed by way of U.S.-Soviet nuclear risk reduction centers or other consultative and even cooperative arrangements.

Third, regardless of whether force levels are reduced and stabilized in the future, there will continue to exist a need for CBMs to deal with some of the enduring proximate causes of and paths to war, such as miscalculation and surprise attack. As Ambassador Goodby stresses: CBMs "are not a substitute for efforts to reduce the too-high levels of weapons which exist today, but agreements which serve to eliminate the proximate causes of war would complement these efforts and, perhaps, facilitate their work. In fact, it would be incongruous to work towards the elimination of nuclear weapons . . . and not work to eliminate the proximate origins of a conventional conflict."

In attempting to offer some preliminary thoughts on the future of CBMs, however, a number of qualifying observations must be borne in mind.

First, thresholds will always exist for what sovereign states will prove willing to undertake for the sake of confidence-building in an uncertain world. Intrusive inspection measures will always be suspected as a cover for independent fishing expeditions. A joint superpower risk reduction center poses obvious risks of compromising intelligence sources and methods. Despite the CBM objective of precluding the threat or use of force and of engendering military transparency and predictability, instances necessarily will continue to occur wherein military suasion can serve vital interests, and whereas a degree of uncertainty about military activities and intentions may enhance deterrence—to wit, NATO's doctrine of flexible response. Furthermore, measures that may limit the opportunities for surprise attack may also unacceptably constrain defensive readiness. The Soviet constraint proposal for a 40,000 troop ceiling, for example, would impact disproportionately on NATO: whereas over 1975–83 21 out of the 27 notified NATO major maneuvers were at or exceeded 40,000 troops, only 4 out of 18 notified Warsaw Pact major maneuvers were at or over this threshold.[40] CBMs cannot be allowed to pose the risk of paralyzing necessary action in ambiguous situations, and the trade-offs between offensive and defensive flexibility presented by any given CBM are unclear. Finally, another threshold is the internal, bureaucratic process. Although the rationales for resisting more ambitious CBMs are usually supported by sound strategic reasoning, predictable parochial obstacles can be expected to persist grounded in little more than bromides such as "freedom of the seas." The pros and cons of any proposal must, of course, be examined on an individual basis, and entirely legitimate disagreements on a variety of sub-issues associated with a proposal may arise, *e.g.*, the different perspectives discussed in this volume on the means for enhanced U.S.-Soviet direct communications and risk reduction centers (Chapters 2, 8, 10, and 11) or on the usefulness of observation and inspections in terms of promoting stability (Chapter 12). Nevertheless, the point remains that CBM negotiations occur not only between but within governments, and that sometimes the controversy surrounding a given CBM may prove just as substantial as that attendant upon other arms control proposals.

Second, the risk cannot be erased that CBMs will be deliberately misused for purposes of deception (*maskirovka*). Notification measures are particularly prone to dissimulation, such as by announcing as routine maneuvers or troop rotations what are in reality preparations for aggression—as was the case with the 1939 German invasion of Poland and the 1968 Soviet intervention in Czechoslovakia, and with what could have been the case with respect to Poland in 1980.[41] Advance notification of "maneuvers," in other words, could amount to a clandestine declaration of war. Moreover, despite advanced imagery, electronic, and other intelligence assets—or, more precisely, because of them—it goes without saying that a surprise attack will be accompanied by an ubiquitous deception plan. One side about to attack may wish to create the impression that its actions are purely defensive, and that calm will be restored if only cool heads prevail on the other side. As Douglas Hart observes regarding possible Soviet attack preparations: "it is [vital] that NATO leaders realize what type of crisis they are in. Soviet steps to defuse a 1914-type scenario by maintaining low alert levels for key military forces would be exactly the effect a deception planner would want to create vis-a-vis NATO prior to a sudden attack."[42] And, as Betts cautions: "Justified confidence in the excellence of early warning intelligence . . . means that leaders may be less sensitive to what they do *not* know about enemy capabilities; hence they may be more vulnerable to successful measures of deception and concealment than were earlier leaders who recognized that limited monitoring capabilities had left them with blind spots."[43] Therefore, comprehensiveness and verifiability are two absolute conditions for a militarily significant CBM regime; otherwise, CBMs pose the risk of contributing to the "noise" of intelligence that they are supposed to help clarify. Even then, however, any one type of CBM could be considered a double-edged sword, as it were, upon which full reliance can be placed only at the risk of inviting disaster.

Third, it must be borne in mind that CBMs do not affect ultimate military capability. The solution to *Minuteman* vulnerability, for example, will hardly be found in, say, advance notification of ICBM launches. At the same time, however, arms control by way of quantitative or qualitative limits does not provide a complete solution either. Hence, CBMs, like other forms of arms control, cannot substitute for prudent force planning, and must be seen as only one of many elements in a sound security policy.

Fourth, CBMs do not avoid the thorny problem of verification that has historically hampered arms control. The first problem is whether a measure is verifiable at all. For instance, verification of ICBM launch notifications is clearly attainable by national technical means, whereas out-of-garrison notifications can be verified by a combination of national technical means and cooperative measures. However, a constraint proposal to ban ASW activity (including detection) in SSBN sanctuaries is probably unverifiable and too easily circumventable. For example, passive and active ASW equipment can be placed on non-military vessels and aircraft (*e.g.*, Soviet "fishing trawlers" are said to be equipped to sabotage U.S. ASW installations) and on space-based systems (*e.g.*, satellite-based radiometers, synthetic aperture radar, and blue-green lasers). A second issue is whether measures beyond national technical means are negotiable. The perpetual problem of on-site inspection in Europe is among the issues being addressed at the Stockholm conference. The NATO proposal calls for on-site inspection on demand by annual quota of notified or suspect military activities. The Soviets, conversely, have rejected this measure and have placed primary emphasis on national technical means, although suggesting that unspecified measures beyond national technical means could be considered, such as "requests for clarification" and "consultations." Whether inspection of the type that NATO proposes, or of the type that the Swedes have advanced ("by challenge" or voluntary), will ever prove acceptable to all CDE parties (and it is not just the Soviet Union that resists on-site inspections) remains a very open question. A third issue is whether measures beyond national technical means are advisable. For example, intrusive verification measures that would reveal the location of SSBNs (say, trailing balloons) for the purpose of assuring compliance with bans on forward SSBN basing or with SSBN sanctuaries would also nullify the principal advantage of maintaining the sea-based deterrent—that is, survivability via undetectability.

Fifth, there can rapidly approach a point where CBMs stop making sense when other aspects of security planning diverge from the purpose of the CBM regime. For example, elementary reason dictates that U.S.-Soviet communications should prove survivable such that even if war begins leaders will maintain the means to facilitate war termination. As Kant observed in 1795, in words even truer in the nuclear age: "some sort of confidence [and the means to receive proof thereof] in an enemy's frame of mind must remain even in time of war, for otherwise no peace could be concluded, and the conflict would become a war of extermination."[44] However, if either side's nuclear weapons employment (as distinct from declaratory) policy affords time-urgent emphasis to leadership and command and control targeting, what good are proposals for, say, placing a Hotline link on the President's E-4B National Emergency Airborne Command Post (NEACP), or JMCL links in the National Military Command Center, NORAD headquarters, or on Strategic Air Command airborne command posts ("Looking Glass")? Likewise, how can war termination be occasioned if communication and observation satellites are destroyed at the outset of hostilities? If wartime operational plans work at cross purposes with effective crisis management procedures, then obviously the principles and purposes of confidence-building measures will be undermined.

Lastly, although CBMs can prove critical for preventing and containing crises, crisis avoidance and management, except for truly inadvertent causes such as accidents, are ultimately and primarily political questions not susceptible to technical "solutions" (an extreme example being Chinese refusal in March 1969 to accept Soviet prime minister Kosygin's "hotline" call following Sino-Soviet border clashes).[45] Clarifying military intentions does not equate with forging political consensus on the permissible exercises of power.

So, in the final analysis, CBMs do not offer a panacea for the current plague upon arms control. They cannot replace efforts to restrict the level and type of armaments, avert destabilizing force postures that tempt preemption, and promote, where possible, political accommodation. CBMs do, however, offer the hope of playing far more useful roles in narrowing the possibilities for confrontation and conflict, and opportunities for strengthening existing CBM foundations exist in abundance. With the requisite political will and analytical creativity, CBMs hold out a strong prospect for helping to reinvigorate the arms control process by providing militarily significant and indispensable complements to other means of enhancing security. Although the Herculean task of reducing nuclear and other forces to the lowest levels consistent with stable deterrence must persevere, it is also imperative that effective rules of the road be emplaced in an era of deepening uncertainty about the nature of deterrence in the 21st century.

Notes

1. Johan Jørgen Holst and Karen Alette Melander, "European Security and Confidence-Building Measures," *Survival*, vol. 19, no. 4 (July/August 1977), p. 147.

2. Jonathan Alford, "The Usefulness and the Limitations of CBMs," William Epstein and Bernard T. Feld, eds., *New Directions in Disarmament* (New York: Praeger Publishers, 1981), p. 134.

3. "Arms Control: Confidence-Building Measures," *Gist* (Washington, D.C.: U.S. Department of State, Bureau of Public Affairs, January 1985), p. 1.

4. Hilliard Roderick, "Crisis Management: Preventing Accidental Nuclear War," *Technology Review*, vol. 88, no. 6 (August/September 1985), p. 50.

5. Thomas C. Schelling, *Arms and Influence* (New Haven and London: Yale University Press, 1966), p. 230.

6. Strategic warning refers to indications that an adversary is mobilizing and deploying forces in preparation for an attack; tactical warning refers to indications of the actual launching of the attack.

7. Alford, "The Usefulness and the Limitations of CBMs," p. 135.

8. Lt. General Bar-lev (Israel) quoted in Julian Critchley, *Warning and Response* (New York: Crane, Russak, 1978), p. 75.

9. Alford, "The Usefulness and the Limitations of CBMs," p. 135.

10. *Ibid.*

11. Richard K. Betts, *Surprise Attack* (Washington, D.C.: Brookings Institution, 1982), p. 85; and Paul Bracken, *The Command and Control of Nuclear Forces* (New Haven and London: Yale University Press, 1983), p. 72.

12. Alford, "The Usefulness and the Limitations of CBMs," p. 133.

13. Thomas C. Shelling and Morton H. Halperin, *Strategy and Arms Control* (New York: Twentieth Century Fund, 1961), p. 141.

14. Betts, *Surprise Attack*, p. 4.

15. *Ibid.*, p. 16.

16. Discussion of these paths draws directly from Graham T. Allison, Albert Carnesale, and Joseph S. Nye, Jr., eds., *Hawks, Doves, and Owls: An Agenda for Avoiding Nuclear War* (New York: W. W. Norton, 1985), pp. 10–17.

17. John G. Keliher, *The Negotiations on Mutual and Balanced Force Reductions: The Search for Arms Control in Central Europe* (New York: Pergamon Press, 1980), p. 158.

18. William Langer Ury and Richard Smoke, *Beyond the Hotline: Controlling a Nuclear Crisis* (Cambridge, MA: Harvard Law School Nuclear Negotiation Project, 1984), p. 58.

19. Roderick, "Crisis Management," p. 55.

20. Bracken, *The Command and Control of Nuclear Forces*, p. 53.

21. "Arms Control, Inspection and Surprise Attack," *Foreign Affairs*, vol. 38, no. 4 (July 1960), p. 566. Emphasis added.

22. *Ibid.*, p. 567.

23. As Khrushchev wrote to Kennedy: "Is it not a fact that an intruding American plane could easily be taken for a nuclear bomber, which might push us to a fateful step?" Quoted in William L. Ury, *Beyond the Hotline: How We Can Prevent the Crisis that Might Bring On a Nuclear War* (Boston: Houghton Mifflin, 1985), p. 79.

24. Cited in Ury and Smoke, *Beyond the Hotline*, p. 55.

25. Barry M. Blechman, *The Control of Naval Armaments: Prospects and Possibilities* (Washington, D.C.: Brookings Institution, 1975), p. 983.

26. Raymond L. Garthoff, *Detente and Confrontation: American-Soviet Relations from Nixon to Reagan* (Washington, D.C.: Brookings Institution, 1985).

27. William J. Perry, "Measures To Reduce the Risk Of Nuclear War," *Orbis*, vol. 28, no. 3 (Winter 1984), pp. 1033–1034.

28. Quoted in *Security and Arms Control: The Search for a More Stable Peace* (Washington, D.C.: U.S. Department of State, Bureau of Public Affairs, 1984), p. 52.

29. *Report to the Congress by Secretary of Defense Caspar W. Weinberger on Direct Communication Links and Other Measures to Enhance Stability*, April 11, 1983 (Washington, D.C.: Department of Defense, 1983).

30. "Excerpts from Reagan's Address to the European Parliament," *New York Times*, May 9, 1985, p. A22.

31. *Report to the Congress on U.S. Policy on ASAT Arms Control*, March 31, 1984 (Washington, D.C.: White House, 1984), p. 16.

32. Leslie H. Gelb, "Soviet May East 'Star Wars' Stand," *New York Times*, July 7, 1985, p. A1. The understanding closes a loophole in a 1978 Protocol to the ABM Treaty that defined SAM testing in an ABM mode, which the United States had been seeking to define since 1972. The reported exception to this ban is when one side provides notification that it is facing a situation of unidentified approaching aircraft, at which time air defenses may be activated even during an ABM test.

33. "Soviets Integrating Space In Strategic War Planning," *Aviation Week & Space Technology* (March 14, 1983), p. 110. See also "Soviets Stage Integrated Test of Weapons," *Aviation Week & Space Technology* (June 28, 1982), pp. 20–21.

34. Falk Bomsdorf, "The Confidence-Building Offensive in the United Nations," *Aussenpolitik*, vol. 33, no. 4 (1984), p. 377.

35. Foreign Broadcast Information Service (FBIS), *Soviet Union*, February 5, 1985, p. AA4. This line of reasoning, of course, is hardly novel. For example, the U.S. "open skies" proposal of 1955 was viewed by the Soviets "as a military intelligence measure . . . [to] strengthen the weakest link in U.S. nuclear war-fighting plans," which at that time "lacked only the accurate targeting data" necessary to execute a first strike against the USSR. Allan S. Krass, "The Soviet View of Verification," William C. Potter, ed., *Verification and Arms Control* (Lexington, MA: Lexington Books, 1985), p. 41.

36. FBIS, *Soviet Union*, April 14, 1983, p. AA2.

37. *New York Times*, June 17, 1983, p. A8.

38. James E. Goodby, CDE plenary statement, September 24, 1984, p. 1.

39. Ury, *Beyond the Hotline*, p. 135.

40. "The Helsinki Process and East-West Relations: Progress in Perspective" (Washington, D.C.: Commission on Security and Cooperation in Europe, U.S. Congress, March 1985), pp. 22–30.

41. Zbigniew Brzezinski, *Power and Principle* (New York: Farrar, Straus and Giroux, 1983), pp. 466–468.

42. Douglas Hart, "Soviet Approaches to Crisis Management: The Military Dimension," *Survival*, vol. 26, no. 5 (September/October 1984), p. 218.

43. Betts, *Surprise Attack*, p. 9.

44. Quoted in Trevor N. Dupuy and Gay M. Hammerman, *A Documentary History of Arms Control and Disarmament* (New York: R. R. Bowker, 1973), p. 35.

45. Garthoff, *Detente and Confrontation*, p. 203. The Chinese did, however, agree in 1970 to reinstate the Sino-Soviet telephonic hotline. *Ibid.*, p. 984.

PART 2

FOUNDATIONS

[I]f arms control is to have any meaning, a means of coping with the problem of surprise attack must be devised. . . . If the two sides cannot act constructively on the basis of this manifestly common interest, the danger is real that future arms control negotiations will be reduced to a largely symbolic effort, devoted to ritualistic incantations of general goals and producing agreement on measures that are meaningless.

Henry Kissinger, "Arms Control, Inspection and Surprise Attack," *Foreign Affairs*, Vol. 38, No. 4 (July 1960), p. 567.

2
The Hotline

Sally K. Horn

On July 17, 1984, after eleven months of negotiation, the United States and the Soviet Union formally agreed, in an Exchange of Notes, to upgrade the Direct Communications Link (DCL), or Hotline, by the addition of a secure facsimile transmission capability. This improvement, only the second in the almost twenty years of the Hotline's existence, has the potential to expand significantly both the nature and the amount of direct and rapid communications between the U.S. and the USSR, particularly in crises. Included in this agreement was a commitment by both sides to reviews to improve further the Direct Communications Link. In the long run, this commitment may prove equally as important a facilitator of improved direct communications as the decision to upgrade the Hotline itself.

Modest Beginnings

The desirability of a direct, rapid, and reliable means of communication between the heads of the governments of the United States and the Soviet Union was first recognized in the late 1950s, as experts within and outside of government considered ways to reduce the danger that accident, miscalculation, or surprise attack might trigger a nuclear war. Initially, however, there was no consensus domestically or internationally that a direct communications link would prove beneficial, much less that it could help reduce the risk of direct nuclear confrontation. Indeed, in some quarters in the United States, there was a deep-seated concern that such a link would be used by the Soviet Union for deception and disinformation and therefore would increase, rather than reduce, the tensions in a time of crisis.

The views expressed herein are those of the author, and are not necessarily shared by the Department of Defense or any other department or agency of the U.S. Government.

The fact that a DCL exists today is the result of continued pressure by academicians and journalists who believed that some form of direct communication between U.S. and Soviet leaders was necessary in the nuclear age, continued lobbying by like-minded individuals within the U.S. government, and events, most notably the Eighteen Nation Disarmament Conference (ENDC) and the Cuban Missile Crisis.

The ENDC was established by the United Nations in 1962 to address disarmament, ways to prevent accidental war, and the military use of outer space and the oceanbed. It focused the attention of U.S. and Soviet government leaders on the question of how to reduce the risks of war. It also provided an avenue for private bilateral negotiations on the margins of the larger international setting to negotiate the 1962 Memorandum of Understanding that established the DCL.

In response to the ENDC mandate, on April 18, 1962, the United States submitted a draft treaty outline which proposed, *inter alia*, the "establishment of rapid and reliable communications" among the heads of governments and with the Secretary General of the United Nations. Shortly thereafter, on July 16, the Soviets amended the draft treaty on disarmament which they had submitted earlier to include a proposal for improved communications between heads of governments and with the U.N. Secretary General. While both governments on principle appeared to be in favor of better communication, no action was taken to negotiate these proposals outside of the context of the broader and diametrically different disarmament treaties which the U.S. and USSR had proposed.

The Cuban Missile Crisis of October 1962 underscored dramatically for the entire international community the need for a direct and rapid line of communication between U.S. and Soviet leaders. At the height of that crisis, delays in U.S.-Soviet communication proved to be a major impediment to discourse and crisis resolution. On December 12, the United States submitted a working paper to the ENDC that proposed, *inter alia*, the establishment of communications links between major capitals to ensure rapid and reliable communications in time of crisis— either as part of a broader arrangement or as a separate measure. In the spring of 1963, the Soviet Union agreed to address as a discrete issue the establishment of a DCL between U.S. and Soviet leaders. Technical negotiations began on May 5. They were concluded seven weeks later, when on June 23, 1963, U.S. and Soviet representatives to the ENDC signed the *Memorandum of Understanding between the United States of America and the Union of Soviet Socialist Republics Regarding the Establishment of a Direct Communications Link*. Less than two months later, on August 30, 1963, the DCL was activated.

Contrary to popular belief, the Hotline that was established permitted exchange of printed messages, not telephone calls. This reflected the shared view of the U.S. and Soviet governments that printed messages were far preferable to voice communications. Specifically, both sides believed that printed messages ensure against possible misunderstanding of communications or their mistranslation, and provide a permanent, accurate written record for later use.

The original Hotline consisted of two full-time duplex telegraph circuits connecting teletype-equipped terminals within the Kremlin and Pentagon. The primary circuit was a wire circuit, routed over land (and under ocean) Washington-London-Copenhagen-Stockholm-Helsinki-Moscow. The back-up was a radio circuit, routed Washington-Tangier-Moscow; it was also to be used for service communications and coordination of operations between the two terminals. The system had the capability to transmit 66 words per minute. By agreement, each government pledged to "take the necessary steps to ensure continuous functioning of the link and prompt delivery to its head of government of any communication received by means of the link from the head of government of the other party." The sides also agreed that each government would be responsible for the arrangements for the link on its territory and that additional wire circuits might be established if experience showed the need for them.

The sides further agreed that to facilitate more rapid communications, Hotline messages would be transmitted in the sender's native language. They further agreed that to assure reliability, circuits would be tested hourly using a variety of non-political test messages [editor's note: for example, "When not disturbed, the larvae of one species hang nearly motionless," began one test message on the life cycle of mosquitoes]. To ensure the privacy of communications, all messages including test messages would be encoded upon transmission and decoded upon receipt. Finally, they agreed that each side would maintain a 24-hour capability at its terminal to transmit messages and translate those that were received. These procedures remain in effect to this day.

The precise number of times that the original Hotline was used has not been disclosed. The most notable—and publicly acknowledged—use of the Hotline in this time frame was during the 1967 Arab-Israeli war, when Soviet Premier Kosygin used it to contact President Johnson after the Israeli preemptive strike and subsequently President Johnson used it to prevent possible Soviet misunderstanding of U.S. ship movements in the Mediterranean.

First Upgrade

The initiation of strategic arms talks in 1969 was the catalyst for the first upgrade of the Hotline.

The Hotline generally had worked well. There were occasional, rare interruptions in service, mostly affecting only one of the two original Hotline paths, although on occasion affecting both circuits. These accidental outages were caused by such events as a farmer in Finland cutting a Hotline cable with his plow, a manhole fire near Baltimore resulting in the loss of the primary circuit, telephone workers in the United States inadvertently severing both Hotline cables, and commercial cable service interruptions. However, by and large the Hotline system worked well.

The Soviets first raised the general issue of protecting against the consequences of nuclear accidents, in the preliminary round of SALT talks in Helsinki in November 1969. A particular concern seemed to be the possibility of third-country nuclear activity. In May 1970 the United States proposed also considering the feasibility and desirability of improving the Hotline. In June the United States elaborated on this proposal, suggesting the contribution that advances in satellite communications capability could make to improving the reliability and survivability of the Hotline. In December, it proposed a Joint Technical Group for this purpose. In March and April 1971, two special working groups were established under the direction of the SALT delegations. One addressed arrangements for exchanging information to reduce uncertainties and prevent misunderstandings in the event of certain types of nuclear incidents (see Chapter 3). The second addressed improving the DCL. By the end of the summer, these working groups had completed their work. On September 30, 1971, agreements in both areas were signed by U.S. Secretary of State William Rogers and Soviet Foreign Minister Andrei Gromyko.

The first, the *Agreement on Measures to Reduce the Risk of Outbreak of Nuclear War Between the United States of America and the Union of Soviet Socialist Republics*, requires both parties to:

- Maintain and improve, as necessary, existing organizational and technical arrangements to guard against the accidental or unauthorized use of nuclear weapons under its control;
- Notify the other immediately in the event of certain incidents, if those incidents create a risk of outbreak of nuclear war. These incidents include an accidental, unauthorized, or other unexplained incident involving a possible detonation of a nuclear weapon and detection by missile warning systems of unidentified objects or of signs of interference with these systems or related communication facilities;
- Notify the other in advance of planned missile launches that extend beyond national territory in the direction of the other;

• In other situations involving unexplained nuclear incidents, act in a manner that will reduce the possibility of its actions being misinterpreted.

The agreement further specifies that the Hotline will be the primary means of communication for the transmission of urgent information, notifications and requests for information in situations requiring prompt clarification.

The agreement relating to the Hotline entitled *Agreement Between the United States of America and the Union of Soviet Socialist Republics on Measures to Improve the U.S. and USSR Direct Communications Link* updated and modified the 1963 Understanding by:

• Establishing two satellite communications circuits for the transmission of printed messages between the leaders of the U.S. and USSR, with each side providing a satellite communications system of its own choice. The U.S. side selected INTELSAT; the Soviet side, MOLNIYA;
• Establishing a system of multiple terminals in each country, with the locations and numbers to be determined by each side.

This system maintained the original wire telegraph circuit as a backup; the original radio circuit was terminated in 1978, when the two satellite communications circuits became operational.

This new system, while it retained the 66 words-per-minute transmission capability of the original system, incorporated many significant advantages over the earlier cable systems to better insure reliability and survivability. The system of multiple terminals—as opposed to the single terminal established by the original system—ensures that the leaders of both nations have more than one point through which they can receive and send messages. Transmitting messages by satellite provides for higher quality communications than can be achieved by transmission over land. Further, satellite communications are less susceptible to interruptions due to deliberate or accidental cable breaks or to the atmospheric interference problems common to high frequency radio systems. Additionally, the simultaneous operation of two satellite systems —INTELSAT and MOLNIYA—ensures almost 100 percent technical reliability; if one system fails, the other continues to provide communications.

The six-plus year lag between signature of the agreement (on September 30, 1971) and initiation of operations (January 1978) was necessary to work out technical and procedural arrangements, including the construction of satellite earth stations required to support use of INTELSAT and MOLNIYA. (The same earth station could not be used to receive and transmit to both INTELSAT and MOLNIYA because of technical and operational differences between the systems. In the MOLNIYA system, there are four satellites which operate in highly elliptical, inclined orbits. Each satellite is used for approximately six hours a day as the satellites sequentially come within view of both the U.S. and USSR earth stations. In the INTELSAT system, coverage is provided by a single satellite positioned in a geostationary orbit 22,500 miles over the mid-Atlantic at the equator.)

According to published reports, this upgraded DCL was used during the 1973 Arab-Israeli war, during the 1974 Turkish invasion of Cyprus, and during the 1979–1980 Soviet invasion of Afghanistan.

The Reagan Administration Approach to Nuclear Risk Reduction

President Reagan entered office committed to reducing the risk of war and strengthening security. During his first year in office, he focused the attention of his Administration on developing sound proposals for nuclear arms reductions. Toward the end of that year, he turned his attention as well to the role of confidence-building measures.

In his first major speech on national security and arms control, delivered on November 18, 1981, President Reagan stated that one of the main elements of his program for preserving peace is to engage the Soviet Union ". . . in a dialogue about mutual restraint and arms limitations, hoping to reduce the risk of war and the burden of armaments and to lower the barriers that divide East from West." He specifically expressed his commitment to reducing the risk of surprise attack and the chance of war arising out of uncertainty or miscalculation.

The President returned to this theme in his Berlin speech of June 11, 1982, and at the United Nations on June 17, 1982, in which he outlined several possible confidence-building proposals related to nuclear forces. These included advance notification of major exercises involving nuclear forces; advance notification of all launches of ICBMs, SLBMs, and intermediate-range land-based ballistic missiles (*e.g.*, SS-20s and Pershing IIs); and expanded exchanges of information on strategic and intermediate-range nuclear forces.

The Administration's efforts to identify new CBMs were given added impetus by Senators Nunn, Warner, and Jackson. For some time the Senators had been deeply concerned about the problem of inadvertent or accidental nuclear war and particularly the possibility that a nuclear event in a third country or the acquisition or use of a nuclear device by a terrorist organization could precipitate nuclear war between the superpowers. They sponsored Section 1123(a) of Public Law 97–252 (Department of Defense Authorization Act, dated September 8, 1982), which directed the Secretary of Defense to conduct "a full and complete study and evaluation of possible initiatives for improving the containment and control of the use of nuclear weapons, particularly during crises." The law specifically directed the Department of Defense to consider improvements to the Hotline. Further, it directed that the President subsequently report to the Congress his decisions on the initiatives recommended by the Secretary of Defense.

Shortly after the passage of the Authorization Act, a special interagency working group on Confidence-Building Measures, chaired by the Office of the Secretary of Defense [Editor's note: Ms. Horn], was created to pull together the efforts within individual agencies and the interagency community to identify measures that might reduce the risk that accident, miscalculation, or misinterpretation on the part of one of the superpowers or actions of third parties might trigger nuclear war. This group was also tasked to prepare the Administration's response to the Congressional tasking. For the next seven months, this Working Group brought together the widest possible group of experts within the U.S. Government and drew on the expertise of experts outside of government to explore unilateral, bilateral, and multilateral approaches to reducing those risks. In addition, at more senior levels, the Administration kept in close consultation with key members of the Senate on the progress of the Executive Branch's efforts. As directed by the Congress, the Executive Branch examined and discussed with the Senators a range of possibilities, including: multinational military crisis control centers to monitor and contain nuclear weapons activities of third parties or terrorists; a bilateral forum in which the U.S. and USSR might share information pertaining to nuclear weapons that potentially could be used by third parties or terrorists; improvements to the U.S.-USSR Direct Communications Link; improved verification measures for arms control agreements; measures to reduce the vulnerability of both U.S. and Soviet command, control, and communications systems; and measures to lengthen warning time of potential nuclear attack.

The basic premise underlying the Administration's approach was that the United States should pursue every possible avenue to reduce the risk that war could break out between it and the Soviet Union because of accident, miscalculation, or misinterpretation, even though that risk is very remote. The Administration insisted that alternatives be closely scrutinized, that potential benefits and risks be objectively and clearly spelled out—and that the former outweigh the latter. A key requirement was that the measures proposed promote better understanding; alternatives susceptible to exploitation, or likely to create instabilities or divide the U.S. from its friends and allies, were to be eschewed. Finally, the Administration, cognizant of the conservatism of the Soviet Union and its resistance to change, decided to move cautiously, in an evolutionary manner that would establish a solid foundation upon which to build in the future.

The Secretary of Defense's *Report,* on *Direct Communication Links and Other Measures to Enhance Stability,* was submitted to the Congress on April 11, 1983. It concluded that one of the most effective ways to enhance our ability to prevent unintended nuclear conflict would be to improve the ability of the U.S. and the USSR to communicate about crises and military incidents, and it identified four possible steps as practical and consistent with this objective: (1) the addition of a facsimile capability to the Hotline; (2) the establishment of a government-to-government direct communications link between national crisis centers for the exchange of military and political-military information of a sort which would not normally be done by heads of government (called the Joint Military Communications Link); (3) the improvement in communications between each nation and its embassy in the other's capital; and (4) an understanding providing for consultations in the event of nuclear incidents involving non-governmental or unknown entities. These proposals were endorsed by the President on May 24, 1983.

To ensure that the Soviet Union understood that these were serious proposals to be carefully considered, Secretaries Shultz and Weinberger took the unprecedented step of jointly briefing Soviet Ambassador Dobrynin the week before the proposals were submitted to the Congress. Subsequently, after the President's formal endorsement of the proposals, the United States suggested and the Soviet Union agreed to initiate negotiations on these proposals. Those discussions began on August 9, 1983, and led on July 17, 1984, to the agreement to add a facsimile capability to the Hotline.

The Administration's Proposal to Upgrade the Hotline

The Administration's proposal to upgrade the Hotline was quite simple, yet very powerful—namely, add on to the existing system the capability to transmit with facsimile equipment full pages of text, maps, graphs, or pictures simultaneously with the transmission of shorter, printed messages over the teletype.

Rejected by the United States—as it had been in the past—was the possibility of adding a voice capability to the Hotline. Also rejected was the possibility of video communications. To quote the *Report to the Congress:* "Because voice communication is more difficult than written material to translate, it is far more subject to misunderstanding. In addition, a direct conversation could encourage instant response, thereby denying the head of state the necessary opportunity to consult with advisors and prepare a thoughtful and measured response. For both reasons, emergency voice communications between the two leaders could reduce, rather than heighten, their ability to resolve a crisis. The same considerations apply, in heightened fashion, to the installation of video conferencing capability."

Negotiating with the Soviet Union

The United States and the Soviet Union began negotiations in Moscow on August 9, 1983, and concluded them in Washington July 17, 1984, with a private champagne reception to celebrate their formal agreement to improve the capability for heads of state to communicate on the Hotline. During this time frame, a total of four meetings had been held, alternating between Moscow and Washington. Between meetings, each side examined thoroughly the technical issues involved in the negotiations and prepared materials and questions to move the talks along as rapidly as possible.

The delegations fielded by the two sides were quite different and reflected the different objectives which the two sides had for the talks. The U.S. delegation was headed by the U.S. Deputy Chief of Mission at the U.S. Embassy in Moscow, Warren Zimmerman. The Delegation was weighted toward senior policy-representatives—with representatives from the National Security Council staff and Office of the Secretary of Defense who were competent to speak for the Administration on its proposals to expand U.S.-Soviet crisis prevention communications capabilities. It also included technical communications experts who could discuss implementation of the U.S. proposal to upgrade the Hotline. The Soviet Delegation was headed by A. M. Varbanskiy, a chief of Administration in the USSR ministry of communications. With the exception of one mid-level Foreign Ministry official, the Soviet Delegation was composed entirely of technical communications experts; it clearly had a charter only to discuss the Hotline upgrade.

The discussions between the sides were cordial and non-polemical. From the start, the Soviets accepted the U.S. premise that the technical improvement of the Hotline would be a worthwhile endeavor that would help to reduce the risk of accidental war. They readily endorsed the U.S. proposal to improve the Hotline by adding a facsimile capability that would enable the two sides to send whole pages of text, maps, graphs, and pictures. The sides therefore rapidly were able to enter into discussion of such technical issues as the facsimile equipment to be used, its configuration, satellite transmission paths, etc.

The other U.S. proposals to strengthen communications—the Joint Military Communications Link and improved embassy-to-capital communications—did not fare as well. Despite repeated U.S. efforts and elaboration of these proposals and their rationale, the Soviets expressed no interest in these proposals, terming them unnecessary for crisis management. Whether this disinterest was attributable to the inherent conservatism of Soviet officialdom, skepticism about U.S. objectives, or a political decision to reject any arrangements that might suggest a warming of bilateral relations is open to conjecture. In any case, the Soviets refused to address these proposals.

The agreement reached by the United States and the Soviet Union took the form of an Exchange of Notes between Deputy Secretary of State Kenneth W. Dam and Soviet Charge Viktor F. Sokolov. (Secretary Shultz was in Australia and Ambassador Dobrynin in Moscow on consultations at the time that agreement was reached; hence, their deputies initialed the Exchange of Notes in their stead.)

The agreement commits the United States and the Soviet Union to add a facsimile transmission capability to the existing teletype DCL as quickly as is technically feasible. Like the current DCL, this enhanced system will consist of three transmission links—two satellite circuits plus one wire telegraph circuit to ensure reliability; one earth station in each country for the satellite circuits; and DCL terminals in each country linked to the three circuits and equipped with facsimile as well as teletype capability. Initially, facsimile communications will be transmitted only over INTELSAT and the wire telegraph circuit. The Soviets are in the process of switching satellite systems (from the MOLNIYA to the STATIONAR system) and indicated that, for technical reasons, operations on the Soviet satellite would need to commence after the switch.

The equipment needed for the upgrade includes facsimile terminals, microprocessors with associated disk drives and necessary communications interface equipment. The components of the new system are for the most part off-the-shelf, specially configured for this purpose.

The Exchange of Notes also commits the two sides to conduct reviews as necessary regarding questions concerning improvement of the DCL and its technical maintenance.

Barring unforeseen circumstances, the final technical details should be worked out through technical experts talks (now underway) in time to initiate facsimile transmissions over the Hotline by July 1986, if not sooner.

Prognosis for the Future

The addition of a secure facsimile capability to the Hotline is a modest but positive step to improve bilateral crisis consultations and cooperation. With this upgrade the two sides will be able for the first time to exchange graphic material over the Hotline. The precise, detailed, and often easily interpreted information offered by maps, charts, and drawings could be critical to resolving certain types of military crisis.

Further, both sides will be able to transmit more, and more complex, data more rapidly and reliably. Time will be saved by the increase in transmission speed—a facsimile can transmit a page of text at least three times as fast as a teletype machine. Even more time will be saved by the fact that graphic material, which requires little or no translation, can be sent. This will result in more time for bilateral communication and national deliberation and consultation. Moreover, the addition of facsimile will minimize or eliminate the need for keyboarding, and therefore the possibility of operator error. Finally, the dual teletype-facsimile system will permit different messages to be transmitted simultaneously—a potential advantage in crisis in which a substantial body of information of different types may need to be exchanged.

It is likely that, over time, additional technological changes will occur. These should be facilitated, if not routinized, by the agreement of both sides to reviews of the system.

In terms of usage, in the near term, it is most likely that the facsimile capability will be used sparingly, for communications only in extreme contingencies. In the longer run, as the sides become familiar with the facsimile system and its capabilities—including the greater ease with which communications can be sent over the facsimile system and the system's greater capacity for information exchange—it is possible that the sides may choose to use it more frequently, perhaps to exchange information in other than the most urgent crisis situations. Such an evolution could occur *de facto* or—if the sides chose—be formally agreed to, perhaps in one of the review meetings which the sides have agreed to hold.

It probably will require more time to secure Soviet agreement to go beyond the Hotline, to establish new mechanisms for direct communication—whether they be new communications channels such as the Joint Military Communications Link, which the Reagan Administration proposed to the Soviets, or some form of "risk reduction center" which has been advocated by the Congress and some academic observers. As noted earlier, the Soviets rejected the Reagan Administration proposal for a JMCL as unnecessary. The Soviets may also feel that new communications mechanisms, and particularly risk reduction centers, would dilute their capability to maintain positive, high-level control over the extent and nature of U.S.-Soviet crisis communications and consultations.

Should we be able to secure Soviet agreement to expand the mechanisms for communication, we should take care to avoid jointly-manned mechanisms. As the Secretary of Defense's *Report to the Congress* stated, jointly manned crisis control centers, whether located in a neutral country or in national capitals, most likely would be completely bypassed in national crisis decisionmaking. If not, a center would create a cumbersome extra layer in the national and international decision process, retarding action just when speed was most imperative. Moreover, flexibility in deciding when to communicate would be difficult to achieve in an institutionalized jointly manned U.S.-Soviet crisis control center; the institution would provide a clear and legitimate channel for automatic consideration of any crisis—including those in which Soviet participation would serve to heighten, rather than reduce, tensions.

Further, joint manning of centers in national capitals would entail severe intelligence risks—particularly if colocated with national command centers, as some have advocated, and require such involved bureaucratic procedures that they would be incapable of responding rapidly and efficiently in a crisis.

One feasible approach that could result in greater cooperation to reduce the risk of inadvertent conflict would be to establish the building blocks that would form the foundation for the eventual establishment of separate but linked mechanisms linked in Washington and Moscow. (This, in fact, has been the Reagan Administration's approach.)

A number of the building blocks already exist. For example, the United States—and probably the Soviet Union as well—have in place internal mechanisms (facilities, organizations, and bureaucratic relationships) to respond urgently to crises that might create a risk of nuclear confrontation. For the United States, these include the National Military Command Center—which keeps close watch on all military activities, the State Department Operations Center, and the crisis control mechanisms of the White House. All of these are manned 24 hours a day. Additionally, the United Nations Security Council, on which both the superpowers sit as permanent members, provides a vehicle for multilateral discussions of severe crises.

Further, the United States and the Soviet Union have signed a number of agreements which in principle commit us to cooperate to reduce the risk of conflict. These include the United Nations Charter, the 1971 Accidents Measures agreement, the 1972 Incidents at Sea agreement, the 1973 Prevention of Nuclear War agreement, the 1979 Convention on the Physical Protection of Nuclear Material, and the three U.S.-Soviet agreements—1963, 1971, and 1984—regarding the Hotline.

The building blocks which we must continue to seek include: (1) explicit substantive agreements, for example, to discuss military doctrine and forces and/or to exchange information in the event of unexplained nuclear incidents or in the event of military activities related to nuclear forces that could be misconstrued; and (2) the establishment of an architecture, including technical mechanisms and operational procedures, such as that envisioned for the JMCL, to facilitate dialogue at a level below that of head of government.

These should continue to be pursued as priority matters.

3

The Accidents Measures Agreement

Raymond L. Garthoff

Few people recall that the *first* SALT agreement was not the ABM Treaty or Interim Agreement on offensive arms signed at the Nixon-Brezhnev summit in May 1972, but an "Agreement on Measures to Reduce the Risk of Outbreak of Nuclear War between the United States of America and the Union of Soviet Socialist Republics."[1] This agreement, signed by Secretary of State William P. Rogers and Foreign Minister Andrei A. Gromyko in Washington on September 30, 1971, had been negotiated in the SALT forum as part of a broader effort to build strategic stability through arms control, and stemmed from earlier interest in confidence-building measures to avert nuclear war that had developed in both countries in the 1960s.

Background

In the exchanges between the U.S. and Soviet governments in 1967–1968 leading to the SALT negotiations, the Soviet Union was the first to propose inclusion of confidence-building measures, including a proposal in 1968 "to study the question of taking steps to rule out the accidental appearance of conflict-fraught situations involving the use of strategic armaments."[2]

Signs of a developing Soviet concern over possible accidental or unauthorized use of nuclear weapons were seen during the 1960s.[3] By the late 1960s Soviet writers distinguished among possible *technical, psychological,* and *political* causes of "accidental war."[4] Unofficial exchanges between Soviets and Americans such as at the Pugwash meetings also reflected the growing Soviet interest in the danger of accidental war and war by miscalculation, and in various measures to help alleviate these problems.

Gromyko, in his address to the Supreme Soviet on July 10, 1969, shortly before SALT began, gave equal attention to stopping the buildup in strategic arms as an important aspect of the overall problem that "must not fail to be taken into account in the long range policies of states . . . the fact that systems of command and control are becoming, if one may put it this way, more and more autonomous of the people who create them . . . decisions made by man in the final analysis depend upon conclusions provided to him by computers." He concluded, "Governments must do everything in their power so as to be able to determine the course of events and not become captive to those events."[5] While this concern, and determination to deal with the problem, clearly extended beyond arms control negotiations, it also clearly was regarded as relevant to them. At the next Communist Party Congress, in 1971, General Secretary Leonid Brezhnev's report referred indirectly to the SALT negotiations then underway in Vienna when he stressed that the Soviet leadership "considered it advisable to work out measures reducing the possiblity of the accidental outbreak of war or deliberate engineering of military incidents and their development into international crisis and war."[6]

Preparation for SALT in the United States prior to the negotiations had given little attention to the accidental war problem. A few who had been involved in the earlier exchanges expected Soviet interest in the subject, and on October 30, 1969, just two weeks before the talks began in Helsinki, Ambassador Anatoly Dobrynin told Ambassador Gerard Smith, the chief of the U.S. delegation as well as Director of the U.S. Arms Control and Disarmament Agency (ACDA), that the Soviet Delegation would wish to discuss means of dealing with the problem of "nuclear accidents." Smith indicated agreement, but suggested that this would be appropriate when the talks were well underway. This caution reflected a concern in Washington that the accident problem not delay or distract from the task of limiting strategic arms.[7]

There was, however, a positive interest in some quarters in Washington in developing a dialogue on strategic issues. Secretary of State Rogers, in a speech on the eve of the opening of the SALT talks in November 1969, said that "What counts at this point is that a dialogue is beginning about the management of the strategic relations of the two superpowers," and posed as one specific objective for SALT "To reduce the risk of an outbreak of nuclear war through a dialogue about issues arising from the strategic situation."[8] The official U.S. position adopted for the initial negotiation, however, was *not* to raise the subject, and to be cautiously receptive and request further guidance if the Soviet side raised it.

The Negotiations

In the very first working session of the SALT negotiations, on November 18, 1969, Deputy Foreign Minister Vladimir Semenov, the chief of the Soviet delegation, raised the accidental war problem as one of great importance. After strongly affirming mutual deterrence, and arguing that a continued strategic arms race would not improve but only diminish security, Semenov noted that the differing perspectives and perceptions of the two sides could, nonetheless, lead to "major miscalculations." In addition, "the existing strategic situation by no means excludes the risk of a nuclear conflict either because of unauthorized use of nuclear missile weapons or in consequence of a premeditated provocation on the part of some third power possessing nuclear weapons and means for their delivery."[9] The chiefs of the delegations in their first private meeting two days later agreed that this range of subjects should be discussed in the plenary discussions, and the subject was raised again by the Soviet delegation. A joint "Work Program" for the subsequent negotiations developed at the first session in Helsinki included as one of seven elements "Ways to reduce the danger of the outbreak of a nuclear missile war between the USSR and the USA, including ways to guard against unauthorized or accidental use of nuclear weapons." (It also included a vague reference to the "bearing of third countries on the strategic situation," which could include a provocative attack by a third country, as well as non-transfer of strategic arms to third countries, both of which had been Soviet proposals for the work program not accepted by the U.S. delegation for explicit inclusion.)[10]

The SALT negotiations in the spring of 1970 plunged into proposals for limiting strategic offensive and ABM systems, and initial U.S. concern that the Soviets might sidetrack the talks into the accidental war area abated. Accordingly, negotiation proceeded in parallel on the main track of arms limitations, and on a second track of considering measures to deal with the accident, miscalculation, and provocation problems. Prior to the second session of SALT beginning in April 1970, the U.S. government had included accident measures as one of fifteen analytical areas studied. Clear agreement was reached in Washington on a few areas—mainly improving crisis communications facilities (the Hotline), and exchanging views on nuclear weapons safety and control precautions. There was wariness over possible Soviet efforts not only to constrict U.S. operational military practices, but also to interfere with U.S. alliance arrangements such as shared nuclear support activities. Accordingly, on most aspects of the problem the United States decided to wait and see what the Soviet side had in mind.

The negotiation of the accident measures agreement involved several areas of common and diverging viewpoints. First, the United States tended to emphasize the *technical* aspects of the problem, and of possible solutions, whereas the Soviet side placed greater (although not exclusive) emphasis on the *political* dimension. Minister Semenov stressed that it was a political problem with technical aspects. Second, within the technical and operational sphere, the Soviet side pressed for several measures that the Americans considered would affect adversely U.S. operational flexibility and therefore opposed. (In some instances, however, as discussed below, it was the Soviet Union that preferred not to discuss its own operational procedures.) Third, the United States shied sharply away from the idea of collusive U.S.-USSR measures to deal with the problem of preventing third country provocative attack. Despite differences, nevertheless, the discussions throughout were businesslike and demonstrated mutual recognition of a common problem and mutual interest in reaching agreement.

Negotiation on the accident measures track developed in two phases, from April to August of 1970, and again from April to August of 1971. The 1970 phase involved about half a dozen plenary presentations by the two sides, and a few *ad hoc* experts meetings, interspersed with the continuing discussion of strategic arms limitations approaches. The areas of common interest, and of agreement and disagreement on more specific possible elements of an agreement, were clarified. The subject was then largely set aside during the winter 1970/1971 session because of a U.S. preference to concentrate on the then stalemated strategic arms limitation problem. In March 1971, taking account of the discussion the year before, the Soviet Union introduced a formal proposal. After some delay the U.S. delegation was authorized to proceed.[11] In mid-April 1971, a working group was set up chaired jointly by Ambassador J. Graham Parsons and Minister Roland M. Timerbaev. By the end of May, agreement had been reached on a joint draft document. In mid-July the Soviet delegation then formally advanced a draft agreement based on the working group document (which had not been in the format of a formal agreement). By early August there was full agreement on the text, and on August 20 it was initialled by Ambassador Smith and Minister Semenov.

Meanwhile, one measure to help deal with the problem of avoiding accidental war had been split off for separate negotiations by experts. Whereas the Soviet delegation had taken the initiative in pressing for an accidents measures agreement, the United States took the initiative in proposing an agreement to upgrade the Hotline by use of satellite communications. From March to September 1971, a joint technical group headed by Clifford D. May, Jr., and Vladimir P. Minashin worked out an agreement initialled on September 7, also signed by Rogers and Gromyko on September 30.[12]

Unilateral Organizational and Technical Arrangements

Both sides readily agreed on the need for secure and safe procedures for handling and controlling release of nuclear weapons. The final provision in Article 1 incorporated this agreement: "Each party undertakes to maintain and to improve, as it deems necessary, its existing organizational and technical arrangements to guard against the accidental or unauthorized use of nuclear weapons under its control." As is readily apparent, both the nature of any precise obligation and of any measures to meet it were left entirely to the decision of each party. This provision reflected common recognition of the importance of the subject, but did not prescribe any solutions.

In the discussions, the United States took the lead and went much further in describing its own precautions to guard against accidental or unauthorized launch of nuclear weapons or detonation of nuclear weapons. In a plenary statement in May 1970, Ambassador Smith presented a carefully prepared and cleared statement noting and describing in general terms procedures, command and control arrangements, and weapons design features. He noted positive measures to prevent inadvertent release, arming, launching or firing of weapons; other positive measures to require authentication of any firing release by at least two responsible individuals; weapons design to prevent accidental detonation in an accident from fire or shock; sealing and safety-wiring of critical control switches; and the like. He noted the application of comprehensive human reliability programs for personnel selection, physical guard, frequent inspection, and other precautions against human or technical error or unauthorized access. Finally, he invited more detailed discussion of such safety and other precautionary measures with the Soviet side on a reciprocal basis.[13]

The Soviet delegation did not take up Smith's offer. They offered assurances that the Soviet Union also took thorough and adequate unilateral measures to assure against accidental or unauthorized use, but did not believe it necessary that such matters be further discussed. It is clear that the Soviet military were apprehensive about inadvertent disclosure of any information that might provide an intelligence gain to the United States. Members of the Soviet delegation privately made clear that the Soviet Ministry of Defense had ruled out discussion of operational procedures or doctrine as not necessary for the purpose of negotiating SALT limitations, including measures to prevent accidental war.

This issue had been one of the very few disputed matters on this general subject within the U.S. delegation and the Washington community. Most believed that it was in U.S. interests to inform the Soviet Union about U.S. safety and security procedures and weapons design approaches regardless of whether the Soviets were prepared to reciprocate. Anything that might add to *Soviet* safety and control would benefit both countries. Indeed, a more detailed presentation had been prepared and cleared for unclassified use with the Soviet delegation. The Joint Chiefs of Staff held out, however, for reciprocity on grounds of principle, and the White House was unwilling to overrule their objection, even though it was not shared by any other agency. Accordingly, the discussion on this subject lapsed when the Soviet Union declined to discuss its own procedures.

Constraints on Military Operations

The Soviet Union advanced several proposals for constraining operational movement of aircraft, ships, and missiles [editor's note: similar proposals would be advanced in the START negotiations, as discussed in Chapter 9]. In their initial presentations in 1969, the Soviets raised several longstanding proposals, some dating from the late 1950s. One was the proposal to limit flights of nuclear-armed bombers to the national territorial airspace of each country—a provision that would have greatly curbed U.S. Strategic Air Command (SAC) operations, while little affecting Soviet practice. (An overlapping corollary in the initial Soviet proposal for arms limitations would have eliminated forward-based nuclear armed aircraft—gutting U.S. deployment of tactical and theater nuclear delivery aircraft in Europe and elsewhere.) The other main proposal would have placed restrictions on areas of the oceans in which nuclear-armed aircraft carriers and missile-launching submarines could patrol. The U.S. delegation, in accordance with its contingency instructions, made very clear that the United States would not entertain such proposals.

By the time serious negotiation began in the spring of 1970, the Soviet delegation made one last effort to include geographic constraints on ballistic missile submarine patrols, dropping that line of proposal only when it became clear that the United States was adamant against it. The Soviet delegation then abandoned these broad early proposals constricting operational practices and in late June advanced several propositions for notification and consultation. Two of these concerned operations of the armed forces, but called only for notification: of mass take-offs of aircraft (from airfields or aircraft carriers), and of missile launches extending beyond national borders. (The other two Soviet provisions are discussed later.)

The U.S. delegation discussed the proposal for advance notification of mass take-offs of aircraft, but opposed it. The Soviet delegation remained vague on such questions as the definition of "mass" take-offs and other relevant circumstances. Eventually, the United States made clear that it would not agree to include such a provision, and the Soviet side dropped it.

With respect to notification of planned launches of missiles to ranges extending beyond national territory, the U.S. position was more receptive. The United States argued, and the Soviet side accepted, that from the standpoint both of possible miscalculation and technical accident what was really of potential concern were missile flights in the direction of the national territory of the other side. In due course agreement was reached on Article 4, "Each party undertakes to notify the other party in advance of any planned missile launches if such launches will extend beyond its national territory in the direction of the other party."

A few words are in order on one of the problems that was *not* dealt with in the negotiations. Many of those involved in the Washington preparations and on the delegation feared that the Soviet Union would make an issue about U.S. nuclear support arrangements for allied forces in NATO, claiming risks of accidental war from such third country involvements with tactical nuclear storage and delivery systems. There was suspicion that the Soviets would seek to pry into such matters and hope to cause embarrassment and even division between the United States and its allies by discussion of such sensitive matters. In fact, however, the Soviet delegation carefully avoided this subject. It thus became one of a number of instances in which the Soviet side showed its desire to eschew propaganda or politically disruptive issues and to conduct productive negotiations.

Crisis Communication and Consultation

Both sides had had in mind from the outset the desirability and potential importance of rapid communication and consultation in any case of a nuclear accident, unauthorized use, third party provocative attack, or other event capable of precipitating actions based on misjudgment in responding to an unclear situation. The Soviet delegation in its June 1970 proposals presented two concrete propositions in line with the earlier discussions.

One Soviet proposal was for immediate mutual notification, using all possible means of communication, in the event of an unauthorized missile launch or other act that might lead to the use of nuclear weapons. The United States did not object to that proposition, but considered it too narrow; there was concern over *any* type of nuclear accident. There followed extended negotiation over the next year or so[14] before agreement was reached on Article 2: "The parties undertake to notify each other immediately in the event of an accidental, unauthorized or any other unexplained incident involving a possible detonation of a nuclear weapon which would create a risk of outbreak of nuclear war. In the event of such an incident, the party whose nuclear weapon is involved will immediately make every effort to take necessary measures to render harmless or destroy such weapon without its causing damage."

The second Soviet proposal on notification called for mutual exchange of information in the event of detection of unidentified objects by missile attack warning systems, or signs of interference with these systems and with corresponding communications systems. The United States agreed with the thrust of this proposal, but wished to restrict its application to cases where such events could create a risk of outbreak of war. Accordingly, in due course agreement was reached on Article 3: "The parties undertake to notify each other immediately in the event of detection by missile warning systems of unidentified objects, or in the event of signs of interference with these systems or with related communications facilities, if such occurrences could create a risk of outbreak of nuclear war between the two countries."

Midcourse in the negotiation, the two sides agreed on another provision not initially advanced by either but based on their joint deliberations, Article 5: "Each party, in other situations involving unexplained nuclear incidents, undertakes to act in such a manner as to reduce the possibility of its actions being misinterpreted by the other party. In any such situation, each party may inform the other party or request information when, in its view, this is warranted by the interests of averting the risk of outbreak of nuclear war." In addition, in Article 6, it was agreed that "for transmission of urgent information, notifications and requests for information in situations requiring prompt clarification," the parties would use the Hotline. For less urgent transmissions of information or requests for information each side would, at its discretion, use any appropriate diplomatic or other channels.

Provocative Attack

Far and away the most politically sensitive and far-reaching aspect of the exchanges over possible accidental and unintended war was the subject of provocative (or "catalytic") attack by action of a third country. As noted above, it had entered the dialogue from the very outset of SALT, and from April through June 1970 both delegations referred in their presentations to provocative attack as one possible source of accidental war. In July, the Soviet side then cautiously raised the subject of U.S.-Soviet political cooperation to *prevent* provocative attack by a third party. The reaction in the White House was to drop the subject like a hot potato, seeing it as a possible irritant in relations with our British and French allies, but above all as a spoiler in the secretly planned U.S. effort to improve relations with China. This episode has been discussed elsewhere, and need not be considered here in any detail.[15] It should, however, be noted that decision on such questions was uniquely lodged with Henry Kissinger, and he confused two quite distinct matters: a proposal he received through Ambassador Dobrynin for an early summit meeting to sign a SALT ABM agreement and an accident measures agreement, and the proposal through Minister Semenov in Vienna to consider joint arrangements to prevent provocative attacks. Kissinger believed, erroneously, that the Soviets were trying to use President Nixon's interest in a summit meeting as leverage to get U.S. acquiescence in an anti-China provocative attack agreement. In fact, the Soviet leaders were proposing agreement on accident measures to complement an ABM treaty in an effort to meet the United States' reluctance to agree on an ABM agreement alone.[16] This confusion assured prompt and firm U.S. rejection of any further discussion of the provocative attack issue.[17] The Soviet delegation at SALT was eventually informed that the United States was prepared only to discuss those technical aspects of the provocative attack issue that were covered in the general measures to avoid war by accident or miscalculation.[18]

From the standpoint of the general subject of confidence-building measures and measures to avert accidental war, the Soviet Union had thus taken an initiative in raising the politically sensitive subject of measures to avert possible provocative attack. But once this had been rejected by the United States, it did not press the matter. This strongly suggests that the principal Soviet motivation was in fact a serious security concern over possible third country provocative action increasing the risk of a war by miscalculation, rather than a desire to treat the issue as a political football.

The provocative attack issue also underlined the significance of the relationship of U.S.-Soviet strategic arms limitations, and the risk of war by accident or miscalculation, to third country nuclear proliferation. The Soviet Union sought restraints on transfer of strategic arms to third countries, principally to prevent circumvention of U.S.-Soviet limitations on strategic arms. But there was also an implicit relevance of nonproliferation and nontransfer to prevention of unintended war between the two nuclear superpowers. Finally, there was also a direct relevance, at least in the Soviet view, on agreement on preventing third country nuclear attack and ABM levels. The Soviet side even made this consideration known in connection with possible agreement on a *complete* ban on ABM deployment—a point unfortunately missed in Washington at the time. An opportunity for a total ban on ABM deployment was missed.[19]

No First Use of Nuclear Weapons

Some six months after raising the prevention of provocative attack issue, Semenov also tried out, this time only privately with Ambassador Smith and the present author, the idea of an agreement by both countries not to be the first to use nuclear weapons. This was not a new subject, but it was not irrelevant, and the Soviet leadership evidently thought it worth sounding out the U.S. reaction. Again, the reaction was negative, and the Soviets dropped the matter without even raising it formally in the negotiations.[20]

The Prevention of Nuclear War Agreement

It is also appropriate to note briefly that a subsequent agreement was reached carrying the objective of avoidance of war into the sphere of political behavior. An agreement on the Prevention of Nuclear War (PNW) was signed at the second Nixon-Brezhnev summit meeting in Washington in June 1973, expanding on or complementing the Basic Principles of Mutual Relations signed at the first summit a year before, and on the 1971 Accidents Measures agreement. The parties agreed in the PNW accord that "an objective of their policies is to remove the danger of nuclear war and of the use of nuclear weapons," and accordingly "they will act in such a manner as to prevent the development of situations capable of causing a dangerous exacerbation of their relations, as to avoid military confrontations, and as to exclude the outbreak of nuclear war between them and between either of the Parties and other countries." They also agreed that if the situation would "appear to involve the risk of nuclear war" between themselves or with others, the two powers would "immediately enter into urgent consultations with each other and make every effort to avert this risk."[21]

The PNW agreement thus extended the principles of restraint and consultation from the technical to the political realm, with the continuing objectives of avoiding nuclear war by miscalculation or uncontrolled involvement or escalation, as well as from accident or unauthorized use of nuclear weapons. It stemmed from a persistent Soviet initiative, originally couched in terms of a bilateral commitment not to use nuclear weapons against one another. The United States retained the option of first nuclear use to reinforce deterrence, but was prepared to engage in an effort to avoid nuclear war by broadening the basis for consultation. It should also be noted that the Soviet leaders not only sponsored the

PNW negotiation, but attributed much greater significance to it than did the leaders of the United States.[22]

Allied Consultation

Beginning with the first U.S. approaches to the Soviet Union proposing SALT in early 1967, consultations with the NATO allies kept them well informed. This of course included, although without prominence, the negotiation of the accident measures agreement. One consultation in January 1969 did touch a sensitive nerve in some European allied reaction. It stemmed from a curious last-minute initiative of the outgoing Johnson administration soliciting allied agreement to a proposed U.S. text of "Agreed Principles and Objectives" for the U.S.-Soviet strategic arms limitation talks. The allies were informed that the text had *not* yet been submitted to the Soviet Union, although it took into account various past conversations with them on the subject. While literally true, this was perhaps the least frank and most misleading statement made in all the SALT consultations with our allies. While the text they were shown had not been submitted to the Soviets, much of it was drawn nearly verbatim from *Soviet* proposals to the United States— about which nothing was said. Among the "objectives and principles" given the allies, the one of most immediate relevance to the present discussion—and one of the points which drew the greatest allied concern— was a statement that along with limitations on strategic arms, the two powers would "study the question of taking steps to minimize the possible accidental appearance of conflict-fraught situations involving the use of strategic armaments." Indeed, the very language sounded like a translation from the Russian rather than typical U.S. official language. And it was. While that precise text had not been "submitted to the Soviet Union," the *Soviet* side had earlier proposed to the United States the very same language (with only two small changes: "minimize" had been substituted for "rule out," and "possible" had been inserted). In fact, also not mentioned, the Soviet side had first proposed such "basic principles" for SALT, to be agreed at a planned—until Czecho-slovaki—summit meeting to be held in Leningrad beginning on September 30, 1968, which would have initiated SALT.[23]

Subsequently, there was very little Allied interest in the U.S. reporting on the early Soviet attention to the accident question (in January 1970), advising on the start of negotiations on measures to avert accidental war (in May 1970), the brief U.S. reportage after rejecting the Soviet provocative attack and no nuclear first use proposals (in January 1971), brief updates on continuing negotiation on accident measures, and finally an advance report on the accidents measures (and Hotline) agreements on September 1, 1971. Except for the odd January 1969 episode, the United States kept its allies well-informed, and there were no objections or disagreements over this range of issues.[24]

One aspect of the accident measures negotiation that most directly pertained to at least two allies—Great Britain and France, as nuclear powers—was the question of accession of third parties to the U.S.-Soviet agreement. This subject had not occurred to the United States until the Soviet delegation raised it in May 1971. Washington was wary of involving other parties in any way, in part because it was feared to do so would open up other undesired questions, such as limiting the nuclear forces of Great Britain and France, of U.S. nuclear support arrangements with other allies. Accordingly, the United States turned down the idea. Again in August, after agreement on the bilateral agreement had been reached, the Soviets raised the idea of a joint appeal to other states to endorse the accident measures, and again this idea was turned down. In consultations, the allies were informed after the event of the Soviet proposal on accession and its rejection by the United States.

The United States had, of course, no objection to Great Britain and France also agreeing on similar accident measures agreements with the Soviet Union. Some time later, the Soviet Union proposed such agreements to them, and similar agreements with the Soviet Union were reached by France on July 16, 1976, and Great Britain on October 10 1977.[25]

Implementation

Early in the negotiation, in June 1970, Ambassador Smith had suggested to Minister Semenov that the standing consultative commission (SCC) that was already being discussed as a continuing later forum to deal with SALT implementation and compliance matters also be used to carry forward implementation of an accident measures agreement. Semenov was receptive. At the time the accident measures agreement was concluded in 1971, however, there was yet no SALT agreement of commission. Accordingly, it simply provided for consultations on implementation "as mutually agreed" (Article 7).

The SCC was established in accordance with Article XIII of the ABM Treaty signed on May 26, 1972, and a Memorandum of Understanding signed on December 21, 1972. The Memorandum of Understanding specifically assigned responsibility to the SCC to "promote the objectives and implementation" of the accident measures agreement (as well as of the ABM Treaty and the Interim Agreement on offensive arms).[26]

In 1975 the United States formally proposed that the SCC work out implementing procedures for the accident measures agreement, and the Soviet Union agreed. A confidential Protocol to the accident measures agreement was agreed upon in the SCC in 1976, providing specific guidelines for implementing the provision on notification of missile launches, and establishing a coding system designed to speed transmission of information called for under the accident measures agreement in a crisis situation.[27] The Protocol and, naturally, the prepositioned codes are kept secret.

In 1985 the United States proposed in the SCC, and it was soon agreed, that in case of a nuclear incident instigated by a third party, any unknown or unauthorized group or individuals that had obtained a nuclear weapon, the two powers would use appropriate prepositioned Hotline messages. This agreement was a common understanding embodying a clarification of the 1976 protocol with respect to the accident measures agreement. Incidentally, the U.S. government chose to publicize this understanding through background press briefings in order to take credit for a successful initiative in arms control, and in particular to claim it was doing something about potential nuclear terrorism.[28] The Soviet government maintained silence on the matter, in keeping with the SCC rules of procedure and because it did not wish to draw attention to this relatively minor U.S.-Soviet procedural agreement.

Fortunately, the SCC has only had to deal with routine implementation procedures for the accident measures agreement. Unlike the situation with respect to the SALT agreements, there have been no charges of noncompliance. The SCC is not, of course, a crisis control center, and would not normally even be available (normally holding sessions of several weeks duration twice a year). But it could, under its charter, be used to negotiate additional measures as well as implementing procedures if the two parties decided to use it for that purpose.

Conclusion: Significance
of the 1971 Accident Measures Agreement

The first and obvious question that presents itself when one considers the significance of the accident measures agreement is whether it really helps to avert the outbreak of nuclear war by accident or miscalculation. The main specific provisions have never been tested. Moreover, the clear common interest of the two powers in avoiding a nuclear war—above all one not deliberately launched—may mean that in the event of an incident the two powers would act to prevent the outbreak of war irrespective of whether such an agreement had been concluded. The agreement, in short, might not add all that much to what would happen in any event. On the other hand, that is not certain, and if the agreement *facilitates* the effective exercise of common sense, that may be a not insubstantial contribution. Prompt clarification of even one instance of a nuclear accident under nuclear and possibly very tense circumstances could be a pay-off of colossal importance.

There is also another way of posing the question. The very negotiation and conclusion of the agreement reflected a recognition bv the leaders of both countries that there exists an important common problem and that common efforts were called for to deal with it. They displayed a readiness and ability to work together in reaching the agreement. In short, apart from the effect of the concrete provisions of the agreement, perhaps the greatest significance of the accord was the shared commitment to act together in meeting a challenge to the security of both. The accident measures agreement was, moreover, one of a series of agreements more broadly dedicated to reducing the risk of war. Its contribution is therefore incremental in a confidence-building process that, although subject to sharp vicissitudes of changes in the political climate, has now been developing for more than two decades.

Notes

1. For the full text, see appendix A.

2. Documentation of these exchanges has not been officially released. The comments here are based on the author's direct participation in the exchanges. The verbatim passage cited is from a Soviet proposal in October 1968, stemming from an earlier Soviet proposal.

3. Earlier, Soviet writers had tended to criticize American theorizing about accidental war on the Marxist grounds that wars are caused not by accident, but by basic social (class) conflicts. For example, see V. Berezhkov, "The 'Automobile Accident' Theory of War," *New Times*, no. 16 (April 18, 1962). One important development changing Soviet thinking seems to have been the Cuban missile crisis of 1962, in addition to growing concerns over nuclear proliferation.

4. For example, see G. Gerasimov, "Accidental War," *International Affairs*, no. 12 (December 1966), pp. 33–38.

5. "Session of the Supreme Soviet: Aspects of the International Situation and the Foreign Policy of the Soviet Union, Report by Deputy A. A. Gromyko, USSR Minister of Foreign Affairs," *Pravda*, July 11, 1969.

6. L. Brezhnev, "Report of the Central Committee of the CPSU to the XXIV Congress of the CPSU," *Pravda*, March 31, 1971.

7. This reference, and many to follow concerning developments in the SALT-Accident Measures negotiation, are drawn from the author's knowledge based on his participation in the negotiations rather than on published sources, which are sparse. Ambassador Smith does not mention this particular discussion with Dobrynin in his memoir.

8. "Strategic Arms Limitations Talks: Address by Secretary Rogers," November 13, 1969, *Department of State Bulletin*, vol. 61, no. 1588 (December 1, 1969), p. 467. As one of the drafters, this author would note that Secretary Rogers' remarks on this subject were prepared within the State Department and not on the basis of a cleared government position. ACDA shared this interest, but it was not given similar support in the White House.

9. The proceedings of the negotiation have not been released. Following the first meeting, all presentations of the two sides were classified "Secret." Thus, the availability of the text of the initial presentations without that constraint is an anomaly that permits this direct quotation. Part of the quotation has been cited by Smith in his account. See Gerard Smith, *Doubletalk: The Story of the First Strategic Arms Limitation Talks* (Garden City, N.Y.: Doubleday, 1980), p. 96.

10. Smith provides additional discussion of the Work Program, see Smith, *Doubletalk*, pp. 101–102. However, these quotations are based on information derived from the author's participation, including negotiation of the work program.

11. The bureaucracy in Washington anguished over whether a "separate" accident measures agreement should be negotiated. The White House in November 1970 ruled firmly against a separate agreement (meaning one not tied to progress on SALT more generally or to agreement on a summit meeting). In March 1971, the White House was, however, engaged in its own back-channel negotiations on SALT and did not want to reject abruptly the Soviet initiative in Vienna, so it acquiesced in the U.S. delegation's proposal to proceed with negotiation on the second track and decide later the question of a separate conclusion of the agreement.

12. The Hotline is discussed in Chapter 2. The U.S. proposal was first informally suggested in August 1970 and formally advanced in December 1970.

13. Smith summarizes this presentation in *Doubletalk*, p. 285.

14. Smith describes negotiation on this point in some detail; see *ibid.*, pp. 286, 290–292.

15. The most complete account is in Raymond L. Garthoff, *Detente and Confrontation: American-Soviet Relations from Nixon to Reagan* (Washington, D.C.: Brookings Institution, 1985), pp. 175–181. The subject has also been discussed by both Smith and Kissinger in their memoirs, and had first been publicly disclosed by John Newhouse. See Smith, *Doubletalk*, pp. 96–97, 139–144; Henry Kissinger, *White House Years* (Boston: Little, Brown, 1979), pp. 547–548, 554–555; and John Newhouse, *Cold Dawn: The Story of SALT* (New York: Holt, Rinehart and Winston, 1973), pp. 188–189.

16. Garthoff, *Detente and Confrontation*, pp. 176–180; and Kissinger, *White House Years*, pp. 547–548, 554–555.

17. In fact, Kissinger rejected the Soviet provocative attack proposal even before it was formally presented in Vienna. Semenov had first discussed the subject with the author on July 2, 1970. By arrangement between us, Semenov then raised it informally with Smith on July 7, and formally on July 10. Meanwhile, based on the Semenov-Garthoff and Semenov-Smith discussions, Kissinger (after discussion with President Nixon, but no one else) on July 9

informed Dobrynin that the U.S. categorically rejected consideration of any joint action or political aspect of preventing provocative attack. This was not, however, made known to the rest of the U.S. government, which studied the issue until November. The U.S. delegation was not authorized to respond to the Soviet delegation until December. See Garthoff, *Detente and Confrontation*, pp. 176–180.

18. The Soviets had, in fact, not raised the provocative attack subject again after Moscow had received the firm U.S. rejection from Kissinger in July. The delegation's authorized rejection, as noted, came only in December.

19. A complete ABM ban might even have been reached without any political accord on third-country provocative attacks, but when the Soviet side showed interest in mid-1971, the White House decided not to pursue the possibility. See Garthoff, *Detente and Confrontation*, pp. 143, 151–153, and 181.

20. See Garthoff, *Detente and Confrontation*, p. 182, and Smith, *Doubletalk*, pp. 190–191.

21. *Documents on Disarmament—1972* (Washington, D.C.: GPO, 1975), p. 283.

22. For a detailed account of the PNW agreement and its political impact, see Garthoff, *Detente and Confrontation*, pp. 334–344.

23. This account is based on the author's direct participation in the Washington preparations in 1967–68 and in the NATO consultation in Brussels in January 1969. The NATO consultation began on January 15 and the last discussion was on January 23. The new administration never even alluded to the subject and let it die, both in consultation with the NATO allies and in discussion with the Soviets.

24. This account is based on the author's direct role in the negotiations and the consultations. Incidentally, in contrast to the generally good record of consultation on SALT and the accident measures agreement, the United States failed to consult or even advise in advance most of its allies about the PNW agreement. This fact contributed to substantial European allied dissatisfaction. See Garthoff, *Detente and Confrontation*, pp. 338–341.

25. The French agreement was in the form of an exchange of substantially identical letters between foreign ministers; the British agreement was more formal and was signed by the foreign ministers in Moscow. Both were patterned on the U.S.-Soviet agreement, omitting the provisions on noninterference with ballistic missile early warning systems and notification of missile launches. The texts may be found respectively in the U.S. series *Documents on Disarmament—1976* and *Documents on Disarmament—1977* at pages 466 and 618, respectively.

26. See *Documents on Disarmament—1972*, pp. 201 and 868–869.

27. From interviews with the knowledgeable officials involved. See also Robert W. Buchheim and Dan Caldwell, *The U.S.-USSR Standing Consultative Commission: Description and Appraisal* (Providence, RI: Brown University, 1983), p. 13.

28. See, for example, Flora Lewis, "A Small U.S.-Soviet Step," *New York Times*, July 1, 1985; and "U.S.-Soviet Panel Tackles War Risk: Sides Reaching 'Understanding' on Dealing With Terrorism," *New York Times*, July 6, 1985.

4

Avoiding Incidents at Sea

Sean M. Lynn-Jones

The 1972 Agreement on the Prevention of Incidents at Sea between the United States and the Soviet Union[1] is a virtually forgotten remnant of an era that produced dozens of U.S.-Soviet accords. Although it was almost ignored in both the U.S. and Soviet announcements of the various agreements that emerged from the May 1972 Moscow summit, the agreement has helped to avert potentially dangerous incidents between the superpowers' navies. Most of the achievements of detente have lost their luster with the passage of time, but the agreement's effectiveness appears to have survived the deterioration of U.S.-Soviet relations. The agreement deserves to be considered more closely, not only because it has reduced the oft-overlooked dangers of naval incidents, but also because of its potential utility as a model for other agreements to govern incidents in the air or in space. More generally, the success of the agreement demonstrates that CBMs represent a workable alternative to traditional arms control proposals that impose quantitative or qualitative limits on weapons. The Incidents at Sea Agreement provides a useful example of a CBM that has been in operation for over a decade during a period of increasing superpower rivalry on the oceans.

This chapter reviews the history of the agreement, including the nature, causes, and dangers of the naval incidents that led to its negotiation and signing. The provisions of the agreement are examined to determine their utility, and the implications of recent naval incidents are also considered. After a discussion of some of the factors that may have contributed to the successful negotiation and implementation of the

Reprinted with modifications from *International Security,* vol. 9, no. 4 (Spring 1985), Sean M. Lynn-Jones, "A Quiet Success for Arms Control: Preventing Incidents at Sea," by permission of the MIT press, Cambridge, Massachusetts. Copyright 1985 by the president and Fellows of Harvard College and the Massachusetts Institute of Technology.

agreement, some possible extensions and other applications of the agreement are also offered.

The Nature and Causes of Incidents at Sea

The term "incident at sea" can be applied to a variety of situations resulting from different maritime activities. At the most general level, it means an action on the high seas by a ship or plane that endangers, or is alleged to endanger, another vessel or aircraft. Some actions of U.S. and Soviet naval units that fit into this category include violations of the International Regulations for Preventing Collisions at Sea ("Rules of the Road"[2]), close, high-speed reconnaissance by aircraft ("buzzing"), simulated attacks on ships or planes, accidental firing upon vessels during naval exercises, and other actions that interfere with the safe navigation of ships, such as shining searchlights on the bridge of vessels.

There have been hundreds of incidents involving U.S. and Soviet surface ships and aircraft, although the details of these encounters have not always been made public.[3] Many of these incidents occurred in the late 1960s and early 1970s as the Soviet Union began increasingly to assert itself on the world's oceans. Additional incidents have involved collisions between U.S. and Soviet submarines, some of which were carrying nuclear weapons.[4] The 1972 Incidents at Sea Agreement, however, covers only surface and aerial maneuvering. For reasons discussed below, both the United States and the Soviet Union deliberately excluded submerged submarines from the agreement. This chapter therefore concentrates on the causes and dangers of incidents involving surface ships and aircraft.

The most difficult question to be addressed in considering the causes of such incidents is whether the United States or the Soviet Union has deliberately authorized its naval commanders to harass the other's vessels. Doubtless, some incidents are the result of excessive zeal or incompetence on the part of local naval commanders. Given the intense rivalry between the two countries, it would be surprising if naval personnel did not occasionally play "chicken" with their opponents at sea. The increase of incidents that seems to have occurred in the late 1960s and early 1970s, by this account, was the inevitable result of the larger Soviet presence at sea and more frequent interaction with U.S. forces.

But incidents may also serve some political purpose, possibly justifying their deliberate use as instruments of policy. Seen in this light, naval harassment and dangerous maneuvering are variations on the venerable practice of "gunboat diplomacy." The Soviet Union and the United States may, hence, have purposefully authorized or condoned such incidents.

Although any discussion of Soviet motivations is necessarily speculative, Soviet harassment of U.S. naval vessels appears to have served several purposes. First, and most generally, Soviet harassment of U.S. ships demonstrates to the U.S. Navy that Soviet warships can deny the United States the freedom of action that it has traditionally enjoyed on the high seas. The awareness of the Soviet presence and capabilities may constrain U.S. actions in a crisis, as former U.S. Chief of Naval Operations Elmo Zumwalt has suggested.[5] The Soviets appear to have had this objective in mind. Admiral Sergei Gorshkov, Commander in Chief of the Soviet Navy, has written: "In a series of instances, our ships and naval aviation have demonstrated operational and active actions as a result of which some foreign governments became convinced that they could not consider their aircraft carriers and submarines 'invisible,' 'untouchable,' and in the event of war 'invulnerable' in whatever areas they may be located."[6]

Second, the Soviets have clearly used harassment as a means of conveying their resentment over U.S. naval operations in the Black Sea and the Sea of Japan—areas the Soviet Union apparently regards as home waters. The Soviets have dispatched naval vessels to shadow and harass U.S. ships that venture into the Black Sea, whereas in the Sea of Japan Soviet land-based attack aircraft routinely simulate missile attacks on U.S. carriers.[7] Although these actions could be attributed to the aggressiveness or incompetence of local Soviet commanders, it seems more likely that at least some of them are the result of deliberate policy. Soviet diplomatic protests following incidents in the Sea of Japan claim that "U.S. ships show no regard for existing international norms, grossly violate international norms for the prevention of collisions of ships at sea, and take a number of illegal actions against the Soviet ships in this area, coming dangerously close to them." But the real motivation for Soviet actions seems to be their belief that "the very fact of U.S.-Japanese exercises close to Soviet shores cannot be regarded as anything but a premeditated, organized provocative military demonstration."[8]

Third, the Soviet Union may use harassment for tactical military purposes. Interfering with the flight operations of U.S. carriers and otherwise obstructing U.S. naval activities can prevent the launch of aircraft that might deliver an attack or, more probably, track a Soviet submarine. Soviet vessels may attempt to disrupt U.S. naval operations even when there is no immediate U.S. threat, as such maneuvers would need to be practiced in order to be performed successfully in actual naval combat.

Finally, Soviet harassment, especially simulated attacks, may demonstrate naval capabilities to internal Soviet audiences. Overflights of U.S. aircraft carriers, for example, demonstrate the value of naval aviation and the need to increase spending in this area. Many Soviet naval activities and writings may be intended for domestic consumption by political decisionmakers, as naval expenditures have not always been given priority in the Soviet Union.[9]

U.S. reasons for harassment of Soviet warships probably do not differ significantly from Soviet motivations. Like the Soviets, U.S. units have harassed Soviet vessels to impede their operational effectiveness. U.S. warships may also have harassed Soviet merchant ships or trawlers on the grounds that such vessels were probably engaged in surveillance of U.S. naval forces and operations. Some naval officers have even suggested that harassment be employed deliberately to reduce the ability of Soviet vessels to launch a surprise attack.[10]

There are, however, some differences in the possible U.S. motivations for provoking incidents at sea. The U.S. Navy has long been established as a preeminent force on the world's oceans; it need not engage in deliberate harassment to make its presence felt. In addition, U.S. forces have different missions and capabilities than their Soviet counterparts. Air surveillance of Soviet warships may be considered vital due to the paucity of naval information released by the Soviet Union. The United States also has a much greater capability to engage in aerial reconnaissance, given its monopoly on large aircraft carriers. U.S. naval units are able to track Soviet submarines and force them to the surface. The Soviets lack comparable anti-submarine warfare (ASW) capabilities.

Incidents are also produced by the action-reaction process. In the Sea of Japan, for example, the Commander-in-Chief of the U.S. Seventh Fleet, exasperated by continued Soviet harassment, issued instructions that his ships were to maintain course and speed even if a collision resulted, and he recommended claiming damages from the Soviet Union in the event of a collision.[11] This sort of reaction to incidents at sea can create a vicious cycle in which incidents begin to take on a life of their own and provoke continued reprisals.

The Dangers of Incidents at Sea

Regardless of the potential utility of some forms of harassment, there are clearly inherent dangers in incidents at sea.

First, there is the physical danger to lives and vessels posed by practices that interfere with safe navigation. Although most collisions appear to have involved only the scraping of hulls, there have been incidents that have caused significant damage and even loss of life— such as the apparent crash into the Norwegian Sea in May 1968 of a Soviet Tu-16 bomber that had been buzzing U.S. vessels.[12] Both governments have stressed the threat to human life posed by acts that impede safe navigation,[13] and the importance of avoiding collisions to minimize the risks to ships and personnel should not be underestimated as a factor leading to the 1972 agreement.

A second threat posed by incidents involving U.S. and Soviet warships is the possibility that collisions or other tense naval encounters might increase U.S.-Soviet tensions or even lead to war. Although an incident itself might not directly escalate to major armed conflict, it could create grounds for political demands or reprisals, increase tensions, or needlessly disrupt negotiations or other political discourse—much as the 1960 U-2 incident forced the cancellation of the Khrushchev-Eisenhower summit. The downing of Korean Airlines Flight 007 in September 1983 again demonstrated the sensitivity of superpower relations to military incidents. A naval incident could easily have similar effects.

Historically, naval incidents have often increased tensions and provided the catalyst for the outbreak of war. Incidents at sea precipitated the War of 1812 and brought the United States and Germany into conflict in both World Wars. More recently, the Gulf of Tonkin incident and the seizure of the *Mayaguez* provoked significant U.S. military responses. Although these two incidents did not involve Soviet forces and, strictly speaking, entailed different types of actions than those defined as incidents above, they do indicate that even low-level naval clashes could lead to escalatory military actions.

Finally, the most alarming, although not necessarily the most likely, danger posed by U.S.-Soviet incidents at sea is the possibility that harassment of warships or aircraft will escalate into actual combat as a result of misunderstanding or miscalculation by local commanders, particularly during a period of acute international tension. Some form of harassment might be interpreted as a sign of imminent attack. A U.S. commander might, for example, view Soviet actions such as the training of weapons and fire-control radars on U.S. vessels as the prelude to an attack. Under such circumstances, he might react by launching a preemptive attack against the threatening Soviet combat units. More likely, he might engage in countermeasures to reduce the likelihood of a successful Soviet first strike (*e.g.*, by forcing submarines to surface), which, in turn, could increase Soviet apprehensions over the possibility of imminent hostile actions by U.S. forces.

Several factors contribute to the inescapable instability of contemporary naval interaction. First, current naval technology gives an overwhelming advantage to the side that strikes first.[14] This condition increases the temptation to launch a preemptive attack when threatened. Moreover, most observers believe that Soviet naval doctrine emphasizes the importance of striking first in any naval agreement. The writings of Soviet naval commanders, including Admiral Gorshkov, stress "decisive, offensive actions" and "the struggle for the first salvo."[15] The proximity of U.S. and Soviet forces during a crisis would enable the Soviets to launch an attack from point-blank range without advance warning.[16]

Second, incidents at sea remain unstable because information can easily be misinterpreted in the confusion caused by the proximity of a large number of vessels from various countries, including third parties. The Israeli attack on the U.S.S. *Liberty* in the 1967 Arab-Israeli war could, for example, have been misinterpreted as a Soviet attack.[17] Attempts by national command authorities to control local units might be disrupted or otherwise prove unsuccessful, as occurred in the case of the *Liberty* and the Cuban missile crisis. The "fog of crisis" could also lead to a misinterpretation of a nonhostile act. Harassment meant as a political signal might be misread by local commanders. An attempt by U.S. or Soviet vessels to shake enemy "tattletales" (surveillance ships) might be viewed as a prelude to offensive action, not as a legitimate defensive maneuver. The use of decoys to deceive trailing vessels could be misinterpreted, as such decoys can sound like ASW torpedoes.[18]

Finally, the danger of naval conflict and escalation is heightened by the tendency of naval confrontations to assume a life of their own, prolonging competitive deployments after the crisis has abated. Although the October 1973 Middle East war ended in late October, the U.S. Sixth Fleet continued to operate at DEFCON III readiness until mid-November.[19] The 1971 Indo-Pakistani war ended on December 17, but intense U.S.-Soviet naval interaction did not begin until December 22 and ended on January 8, 1972.[20] These extended confrontations multiply the risks inherent in shorter crises. Moreover, naval units may enjoy greater scope for autonomous action after political authorities are no longer preoccupied with the crisis.

Neither the United States nor the Soviet Union has deliberately and consistently attempted to raise the risks of naval confrontations. Indeed, many U.S. observers argue that Soviet naval activity, like Soviet crisis behavior in general, has been remarkably circumspect.[21] Nevertheless, dangerous incidents have taken place during international crises. In the wake of the seizure of the *Pueblo* by North Korea in January 1968, Soviet vessels engaged in harassment of U.S. warships in the Sea of Japan. U.S. Navy records show a dozen violations of the nautical Rules of the Road by Soviet vessels during this period, as well as a collision between the Soviet merchant ship *Kapitan Vislobokov* and the U.S. destroyer *Rowan*.[22] Following the global alert of U.S. forces during the October 1973 Arab-Israeli war, Soviet units began anti-carrier exercises using U.S. units as targets—the most intense signal they have ever transmitted with naval forces during a crisis.[23] U.S. forces have also engaged in provocative naval acts during a crisis, including following, harassing, and forcing Soviet submarines to surface during the Cuban missile crisis. According to Robert Kennedy, President John F. Kennedy was extremely concerned over the possible dangers of this harassment and sought to control the actions of local naval commanders as much as possible.[24]

The risks of superpower naval confrontation should not be overestimated, or exaggerated. The overall stability of the strategic nuclear balance adds to the incentives for caution and reduces the possibility that either side will see any advantage in initiating war at sea. But even if the probability of war at sea is low, it may be higher than the chance of U.S.-Soviet hostilities in Europe or other regions. It certainly appears greater than the odds of a "bolt from the blue" nuclear strike by either side. Although most scenarios envisage the start of superpower hostilities on land, the risks of naval incidents were apparently great enough to induce both sides to negotiate the 1972 Agreement on the Prevention of Incidents at Sea. In the nuclear age, even a relatively low risk of superpower conflict can justify significant precautions.

Negotiating the Agreement

The increasing frequency and severity of U.S.-Soviet naval incidents led the United States to propose negotiations on the subject in 1967.[25] This overture was ignored for over two years until the Soviets surprised U.S. officials in 1970 by proposing that negotiations be opened in the spring of 1971. The United States did not respond immediately, but initiated an interagency review of the problem to formulate a position. The interagency process was chaired by Ambassador Herbert Okun, a State Department Soviet expert, and involved representatives of the Navy, Department of Defense, and the National Security Council (NSC). National Security Assistant Henry Kissinger and senior NSC staff member Helmut Sonnenfeldt were directly involved. The review team compiled and analyzed information on all previous U.S.-Soviet incidents at sea and the subsequent protests by either party. It sought to develop a negotiating position that would not constrain U.S. or allied naval missions or activities while preventing dangerous Soviet maneuvers. The United States could not, for example, accept the inclusion of limitations on submarine activities, since such a provision, it was felt, might lead the Soviet Union to propose the establishment of submarine operating zones in which ASW would be prohibited. Given the U.S. lead in ASW technology, this step would benefit the Soviet Union. Moreover, the United States was reluctant to discuss submarine incidents, as any negotiated provisions might force the disclosure of submarine locations and compromise strategic and reconnaissance missions.

Navy representatives were also concerned over the possible negotiation of a "distance formula" that would govern how closely U.S. vessels and aircraft would be able to approach their Soviet counterparts. Any form of distance limitation could interfere with naval operations and complicate aerial surveillance. Soviet protests following previous incidents indicated that they were particularly irritated by U.S. close air surveillance. The question of a distance formula thus became a critical issue in the subsequent negotiations with the Soviets.

In contrast to other negotiations, where U.S. negotiators came to listen to the Soviets before offering their own position, the U.S. delegation formulated detailed proposals prior to the start of any talks and considered the likely Soviet responses. The U.S. negotiating position essentially called for clarifying and expanding the Rules of the Road. The United States was particularly interested in preventing Soviet vessels from shouldering U.S. aircraft carriers and thus disrupting their flight operations. Having thus formulated its position, the United States accepted the Soviet offer to negotiate in June 1971, and discussions were scheduled to begin in Moscow in October of that year.

The U.S. delegation to Moscow primarily comprised the participants in the interagency review process. It was headed by then undersecretary of the Navy John Warner, with Okun as vice-chairman. The Soviet delegation consisted of even higher-ranking officials, conveying a clear Soviet interest in the talks. Headed by Admiral Vladimir Kasatonov, deputy commander of the Soviet navy, the Soviet delegation included the second, third, fourth, and fifth highest-ranking officers of the Soviet navy—which may have reduced the constraints that central authorities generally impose on Soviet negotiators.

Although many naval officers and some U.S. Soviet experts had been skeptical about the prospects, the Soviet delegation warmly welcomed their U.S. counterparts. In the negotiations, the Soviets accepted the U.S. agenda and agreed that submarines would not be discussed. The announcement of President Nixon's planned visit to Moscow on October 12 created an even more propitious political atmosphere.

The negotiators discussed the Rules of the Road, signaling, disruption of flight operations, the definition of naval platforms, and the training of weapons and sensor systems on adversary vessels. Among these issues, the most contentious was, as expected, the matter of a distance formula. U.S. negotiators refused to accept Soviet proposals for a distance formula, preferring instead to stress good judgment and general principles.

Despite the lack of agreement on the distance formula, however, the Moscow negotiations made considerable progress. In talks that often lasted up to 16 hours per day, agreement was reached on most issues. The U.S. delegation was not surprised by the Soviet proposals, having anticipated them in its preparation. This advance preparation, as well as Soviet concessions on critical issues such as the dropping of sonobuoys from aircraft, which the Soviets sought to prohibit, enabled the two delegations to initial of memorandum of understanding covering points on which agreement had been reached and listing outstanding issues, including the distance formula, which were to be discussed during the next round in Washington in May 1972.

The negotiations and the memorandum of understanding were subjected to a second, more intensive interagency review before the talks resumed. As the initially skeptical military departments now confronted the possibility that an agreement would actually be reached, they increased their level of representation and vigorously objected to any suggestion that a distance formula be accepted. As the Navy was concerned that the State Department might be overly conciliatory, Lawrence Eagleburger of the Pentagon's Office of International Security Affairs chaired the second interagency review, which ruled out acceptance of a distance formula.

The distance formula was the principal issue in the second round of talks. Although the Soviets initially seemed adamant on the issue, they eventually dropped their objections in return for an agreement to discuss the matter in the future. They apparently continued to feel strongly about the distance formula, however, as indicated by a Soviet captain writing in the September 1972 issue of *Morsky Sbornik*: "It is quite evident that the Agreement would more fully serve its purpose if it contained fixed maximal permissible distances for the approach of ships and aircraft. . . . Therefore the Commission appointed in accordance with Article X will have to develop practical recommendations relative to concrete fixed distances which must be observed when approaching warships and aircraft."[26]

Despite their misgivings, the Soviets were apparently satisfied with the rest of the agreement. Soviet negotiators wanted an agreement and were reconciled to serious concessions to obtain it. The Soviet interest in reaching accord was demonstrated not only by the warm welcome accorded to the U.S. delegation in Moscow, but also by the complacent Soviet naval reaction to the U.S. mining of Haiphong harbor, which occurred in the middle of the Washington negotiations. Admiral Kasatonov actually watched Nixon's speech announcing the mining at Warner's Georgetown home. After a pause, he remarked: "This is a very serious matter. Let us leave it to the politicians to settle this one." This comment implicitly acknowledged that the naval talks were too important to be disrupted even by U.S. actions that endangered Soviet merchant ships. As Okun later remarked of the incident: "We were highball to highball, and they were the first to clink."[27]

The agreement was initialed by Warner and Kasatonov in Washington and formally signed by Warner and Admiral Gorshkov on May 25, 1972, during the Moscow summit. In announcing the results of the summit to Congress, President Nixon contended that the agreement would have a "direct bearing on the search for peace and security in the world" and was "aimed at significantly reducing the chances of dangerous incidents between our ships and aircraft at sea."[28]

The Provisions of the Agreement

The 1972 Agreement on the Prevention of Incidents at Sea serves four basic purposes: (1) regulation of dangerous maneuvers; (2) restriction of other forms of harassment; (3) increased communication at sea; and (4) regular naval consultations and exchanges of information. Its provisions address many of the possible causes of U.S.-Soviet naval incidents, particularly those arising from misunderstanding or misinterpretation.

Regulation of Dangerous Maneuvers. Article II reaffirms the Rules of the Road, and Article III specifically requires ships to remain well clear of one another and to show particular care in approaching ships engaged in launching or landing aircraft or engaged in replenishment underway.

Restriction of Other Harassment. Articles III and IV prohibit simulated attacks, the use of searchlights to illuminate bridges, the performance of "various aerobatics" over ships, and the dropping of various objects that would be hazardous to ships or constitute a hazard to navigation. This last provision apparently reflects Soviet concern over the U.S. practice of dropping sonobuoys from aircraft, but the ambiguous wording probably allows the United States to continue to act as it did before the agreement.

Increased Communication at Sea. Article III requires the use of internationally recognized signals to convey information about operations and intentions and to warn ships of the presence of submarines. Article V requires signals to announce flight operations and also mandates that aircraft flying over the high seas display navigation lights "whenever feasible." Finally, Article VI requires 3–5 days advance notification of actions (naval exercises or missile test launches) on the high seas that represent a danger to navigation or to aircraft in flight, as well as requiring increased use of signals to signify the intentions of vessels maneuvering in close proximity. These provisions reduce the danger of accidental attacks and collisions.

Regular Consultation and Information Exchange. Article VII stipulates that the Soviet and U.S. naval attaches in each other's capitals shall serve as the channel for information concerning incidents at sea. This provision may help to minimize the diplomatic consequences of naval incidents by ensuring that such matters are handled primarily by the two navies. Article IX provides that the United States and the Soviet Union shall conduct annual reviews of the agreement, and Article X specifically establishes a committee to meet within six months to "consider the practical workability of concrete fixed distances to be observed in encounters between ships, aircraft, and ships and aircraft."

U.S. and Soviet negotiators did not reach any agreement on a distance formula, but they did produce a protocol to the original accord on May 22, 1972.[29] This protocol extends some provisions of the 1972 agreement to nonmilitary ships, and prohibits simulated attacks on nonmilitary ships and the dropping of objects near them in a hazardous manner.

Assessing the Agreement

The 1972 Incidents at Sea agreement is generally regarded as a success. Incidents have contined since it was signed, but they have become less frequent and less severe. For instance, whereas the number of serious incidents exceeded 100 per year in the late 1960s, Secretary of the Navy John Lehman, Jr., reported that there were only about 40 potentially dangerous incidents between June 1982 and June 1983.[30] The most dangerous maneuvers and attempts to disrupt formations are no longer commonplace. When incidents do occur, they often are resolved by the two navies without becoming diplomatic controversies. Lehman feels that the annual meetings to review the accord have produced a "stable pattern" of dealing with incidents and that these reviews provide "pretty good resolution" of any disputes in a "rather businesslike" manner.

U.S.-Soviet naval interaction in the October 1973 Arab-Israeli war exemplifies the positive impact of the agreement. The Soviets deployed a peak of 96 vessels during the war, confronting a slightly smaller number of U.S. ships. Despite the heightened political tensions and the proximity of so many hostile vessels, incidents were relatively rare. On the whole, Soviet ships observed the agreement and avoided harassment of their U.S. counterparts.[31] Admiral Worth Bagley, then Commander in Chief of U.S. Naval Forces in Europe, remarked that the "Soviets weren't overly aggressive. It looked as though they were taking some care not to cause an incident."[32]

Nevertheless, more recent naval incidents may suggest that the agreement is not faring so well. Soviet vessels reportedly interfered with salvage operations by U.S. and allied vessels in the Sea of Japan in the wake of the downing of the Korean airliner in 1983. A Soviet frigate apparently attempted to disrupt flight operations of the U.S. carrier *Ranger* in the Arabian Sea before colliding with the U.S. frigate *Fife* in November 1983.[33] In March 1984 a Soviet submarine running without lights collided with the U.S. carrier *Kitty Hawk* in the Sea of Japan. The U.S. Navy began an inquiry to determine whether the Soviet submarine was at fault, although Lehman indicated that the collision appeared to be "inadvertent."[34] Several days later, the Soviet carrier *Minsk* fired 8 flares at the U.S. frigate *Harold E. Holt*. Three hit the U.S. vessel, including one that passed within three feet of the captain. The *Holt* was within 30 yards of the *Minsk*, which had stopped for unexplained reasons. The *Holt* had apparently signaled that it planned to pass the *Minsk* on the starboard side and did so despite several warnings from the Soviet vessel. The U.S. Navy decided to raise the incident at the annual meeting in May 1984.[35]

These incidents do not, however, necessarily signal the demise of the agreement. Soviet vessels in the Sea of Japan may have been reacting to the extraordinary tension that followed the Korean airliner shootdown, or they may have been attempting to prevent the United States from recovering the flight recorder. U.S. Naval officials believe that the harassment was politically motivated, privately acknowledging that incidents tend to become more frequent as U.S.-Soviet political tensions increase. Lehman believes that relations between the two fleets are, nevertheless, still "very professional and workmanlike," and he does not "see anything sinister in the incident with the *Minsk*. . . . The *Minsk* skipper may not have been all on the wrong side."[36] The agreement may still be functioning successfully by reducing the number of incidents and facilitating their diplomatic resolution, even if some incidents continue to take place. Senior U.S. officials have reaffirmed that the incidents of 1983 and 1984 have not changed their interpretation of Soviet behavior, arguing that the "Soviets have made it very clear that they believe in the Incidents at Sea agreement. They want it to continue. They want it to work. They want to live up to it." U.S. officials also point out that "each year we've seen basically a decrease" in the number of incidents.[37]

The May 1984 meetings in Moscow of U.S. and Soviet naval representatives to review the accord provided further evidence of its success. The talks were reportedly conducted in an open, frank, and professional manner. Both sides acknowledged the concerns of the other and avoided political rhetoric and unreasonable demands. U.S. admirals, who said the sessions were the best such meetings in memory, and their Soviet counterparts agreed to renew the agreement for three years. In addition, the Soviet delegation reportedly proposed extending the principles of the agreement to cover additional activities of military aircraft.[38]

The most obvious reason for the success of the agreement is the mutual interest of the superpowers in avoiding dangerous incidents at sea. Neither country has any interest in accidentally triggering a naval conflict that could escalate or disrupt their political relations. Both navies want to prevent accidents that endanger ships and personnel. But more than mutual interest is required for successful negotiations, as the history of U.S.-Soviet arms control negotiations demonstrates. Inept diplomacy and U.S. domestic politics can frustrate even the most promising arms control initiatives.[39]

In this context, the relative ease with which the text of the agreement was negotiated can be attributed to the careful and thorough U.S. preparations, the general political climate, and the absence of any attempt to reduce force levels or to constrain deployments. In addition, the intensive involvement of the U.S. Navy in the preparations and actual negotiations may have helped by ensuring that the U.S. proposals and the memorandum of understanding that emerged in Moscow were acceptable to the operational commanders of the service directly affected by the accord.

The nature of the 1972 agreement may also have reduced any domestic obstacles to its successful adoption. As the agreement does not establish numerical limits on U.S. and Soviet weapons, it is less vulnerable to attacks from congressional and other critics who might allege that it codifies a U.S.-Soviet imbalance. It also does not require the foregoing on any ship building programs. Although it might be argued that avoiding incidents at sea is inherently noncontroversial, it seems more plausible to suggest that the avoidance of quantitative limits reduces the potential for political controversy. Moreover, constraints on dangerous activities, like the Incidents at Sea agreement, may offer greater potential for reducing the likelihood of war than small cuts in existing arsenals.

The actual implementation of the agreement may have been facilitated by the absence of publicity accorded it. The announcement of the agreement was overshadowed by the flurry of agreements that emerged from the 1972 Moscow summit, particularly SALT I and the ABM Treaty. As the agreement is not a treaty, it was not subjected to public debate in the U.S. Senate. The Navy apparently believes that the lack of publicity has contributed to the success of the agreement, and has done, indeed, little to call attention to it.

The success of the agreement can also be attributed to the basic conceptual approach that underlay its negotiation and execution. The Incidents at Sea agreement accepts the reality of U.S.-Soviet competition. Unlike naval arms control measures that would impose geographic limits on deployments, it implicitly assumes that U.S. and Soviet warships and aircraft will continue their rivalry at sea and engage in "gunboat diplomacy" to influence political outcomes in a crisis. Observance of the agreement makes U.S.-Soviet competition safer; it does not alter the basic terms of that competition. By reducing the possibility of misinterpretation of potentially dangerous naval behavior, however, the agreement increases U.S. and Soviet confidence in the nonthreatening nature of each other's naval actions.

Extensions and Applications of the Agreement

The Incidents at Sea agreement could be amended to cover other naval activities or it could serve as a model for similar agreements in other areas. The agreement itself could be improved in several ways. The provisions for notification of dangerous actions, for example, could be broadened to include mandatory notification of all naval exercises. U.S. interests in advance notification have increased as the Soviet Navy has become more capable of actions at great distances from the Soviet Union. Advance notification would reduce U.S. or Soviet suspicions of any sudden, large-scale naval activities that appeared to be of a threatening nature.

The agreement might also be extended to include other countries. Collisions have occurred between Soviet warships and vessels of U.S. allies, including Great Britain. One collision even involved the British aircraft carrier *Ark Royal*.[40] Although a multilateral agreement would be more difficult to negotiate and apply, it would reduce the possibility of harassment by proxy and the dangers of "catalytic" incidents involving third parties. The potential for such incidents has existed in several superpower confrontations in the Middle East and the Indian Ocean, where Indian submarines of Soviet design operate.

The general approach of the Incidents at Sea agreement could be applied to other, analogous areas of potential superpower conflict. A similar agreement might be negotiated to establish procedures for dealing with aerial incidents; agreed-upon procedures might have prevented the tragic destruction of Korean Airlines flight 007.[41]

Outer space is another area in which the principles of the Incidents at Sea agreement seem particularly applicable. If, as seems likely, it is impossible to negotiate the complete demilitarization of space, constraints on threatening activities could work to reduce the danger of unintended superpower conflicts above the atmosphere. Potentially threatening activities, such as the testing of ASAT systems in conjunction with largescale test launches of ballistic missiles, could be prohibited. This type of coordinated operational testing feeds U.S. fears that the Soviet Union is preparing for a first strike, even though most Soviet tests of this kind have not proved successful up to this point.

Application of the principles of the Incidents at Sea agreement could also lead to prohibition of close high-speed passes or passes in geosynchronous orbit by satellites or spacecraft near the satellites of the other superpower. These actions could give rise to fears of imminent destruction of satellites by ASAT weapons as a prelude to a surprise attack. Close passes will appear particularly threatening in the absence of an ASAT ban. Further applications of the agreement's principles may emerge as space technology continues to develop. If U.S.-Soviet military competition in space cannot be prevented entirely through arms control, it must at least be managed.[42]

More generally, additional CBMs relevant to strategic forces could be sought. The agreement is, in many ways, analogous to the Hotline and the 1971 Accidents Measures agreements. These measures could be expanded to require advance notification of all missile tests and limits on multiple missile launches within brief intervals.[43] Like simulated attacks at sea, the latter tend to increase fears of surprise attack. The success of the agreement also suggests the utility of direct military-to-military negotiations between the superpowers. Similar talks could improve mutual understanding and reduce suspicions in other areas.

There are, however, limits to the application of the principles contained in the Incidents at Sea agreement. The agreement does nothing to reduce the instability created by forces that place a premium on striking first. Nor does it resolve any of the political differences that are the basic causes of U.S.-Soviet hostility.[44] Not all issues can be addressed without provoking domestic political controversy in the United States, even though CBMs do not seem to be debated as heatedly as, say, reductions in existing arsenals. Despite these limitations, the Incidents at Sea agreement provides modest yet encouraging evidence of the potential utility of CBMs. Modesty in expectations may be a prerequisite for success in any U.S.-Soviet negotiations. The Incidents at Sea agreement demonstrates that important results can nevertheless emerge from modest expectations.

Notes

1. The full title is: Agreement Between the Government of the United States of America and the Government of the Union of Soviet Socialist Republics on the Prevention of Incidents on and over the High Seas, May 25, 1972.

2. These rules govern nautical lighting, maneuvering, and signaling procedures to ensure safe navigation. For a discussion of recent developments see T. J. Cutler, "More Changes to the Rules of the Road," *U.S. Naval Institute Proceedings,* vol. 109, no. 6 (June 1983), pp. 89–93.

3. Some information on incidents was revealed in U.S. and Soviet diplomatic notes. See Historical Office, U.S. Department of State, *American Foreign Policy: Current Documents 1964* (Washington, D.C.: U.S. GPO, 1967), pp. 562–563, 672.

4. See "Operation Holystone," *Nation,* July 19, 1975, pp. 35–36; and Dan Caldwell, *American-Soviet Relations: From 1947 to the Nixon-Kissinger Grand Design* (Westport, CT: Greenwood Press, 1981), p. 128.

5. Elmo R. Zumwalt, Jr., "Gorshkov and his Navy," *Orbis*, vol. 24, no. 3 (Fall 1980), pp. 491–510.

6. Quoted in David R. Cox, "Sea Power and Soviet Foreign Policy," *U.S. Naval Institute Proceedings*, vol. 95, no. 6 (June 1969), p. 41.

7. Richard T. Ackley, "The Soviet Navy's Role in Foreign Policy," *U.S. Naval Institute Proceedings*, vol. 24, no. 9 (May 1972), p. 55; Abram Shulsky, "Coercive Diplomacy," in Bradford Dismukes and James M. McConnell, eds., *Soviet Naval Diplomacy* (New York: Pergamon Press, 1979), p. 123.

8. Statement issued by the official Soviet News Agency TASS, May 13, 1967, cited in Historical Office, U.S. Department of State, *American Foreign Policy: Current Documents 1967* (Washington, D.C.: U.S. GPO, 1969), pp. 457–458.

9. Steven E. Miller, "Assessing the Soviet Navy," *Naval War College Review*, vol. 32, no. 5 (September/October 1979), p. 65.

10. Frank Andrews, "The Prevention of Preemptive Attack," *U.S. Naval Institute Proceedings*, vol. 106, no. 5 (May 1980), p. 139.

11. D. P. O'Connell, *The Influence of Law on Sea Power* (Annapolis, MD: Naval Institute Press, 1975), p. 178.

12. Thomas W. Wolfe, "Soviet Naval Interaction with the United States and its Influence on Soviet Naval Developments," in Michael McGwire, ed., *Soviet Naval Developments: Capability and Context* (New York: Praeger Publishers, 1973), p. 266.

13. See diplomatic notes in Historical Office, U.S. Department of State, *American Foreign Policy: Current Documents 1964*, pp. 669–673.

14. See George H. Quester, "Naval Armaments: The Past as Prologue," in George Quester, ed., *Navies and Arms Control* (New York: Praeger Publishers, 1980), pp. 1–11.

15. Sergei Gorshkov, quoted in Raymond G. O'Connor and Vladimir P. Prokofieff, "The Soviet Navy in the Mediterranean and Indian Ocean," *Virginia Quarterly Review*, vol. 29, no. 4 (Autumn 1973), pp. 491–492.

16. Stansfield Turner, "The Naval Balance: Not Just a Numbers Game," *Foreign Affairs*, vol. 55, no. 2 (January 1977), p. 350.

17. See Phil G. Goulding, *Confirm or Deny* (New York: Harper and Row Publishers, 1970), pp. 97–98.

18. O'Connell, *The Influence of Law on Sea Power*, p. 180.

19. F. C. Miller, "Those Storm-beaten Ships, Upon which Arab Armies Never Looked," *U.S. Naval Institute Proceedings*, vol. 101, no. 3 (March 1975), p. 24.

20. James McConnell and Anne Kelly Calhoun, "The December 1971 Indo-Pakistani Crisis," in Dismukes and McConnell, eds., *Soviet Naval Diplomacy*, p. 191.

21. See for example Adam Yarmolinsky, "Department of Defense Operations During the Cuban Crisis," *Naval War College Review*, vol. 32, no. 4 (July/August 1979), p. 88; and Dismukes and McConnell, eds., *Soviet Naval Diplomacy*, p. 289.

22. Donald S. Zagoria and Janet D. Zagoria, "Crises on the Korean Peninsula," in Stephen S. Kaplan, ed., *Mailed First, Velvet Glove: Soviet Armed Forces as a Political Instrument* (Washington, D.C.: U.S. Department of Commerce, National Technical Information Service, 1979), p. 9–6.

23. Stephen S. Roberts, "The October 1973 Arab-Israeli War," in Dismukes and McConnell, eds., *Soviet Naval Diplomacy*, p. 210.

24. See Robert F. Kennedy, *Thirteen Days: A Memoir of the Cuban Missile Crisis* (New York: W. W. Norton, 1971).

25. The following chronology is based on a personal interview with Ambassador Herbert Okun, a principal negotiator of the 1972 Agreement, Washington, D.C., November 29, 1983.

26. Captain First Rank V. Serkov, quoted in Anne Kelly Calhoun and Charles Petersen, "Changes in Soviet Naval Policy: Prospects for Arms Limitations in the Mediterranean and Indian Ocean," in Paul J. Murphy, ed., *Naval Power in Soviet Policy* (Washington, D.C.: U.S. GPO, 1978), pp. 244–245.

27. Marvin Kalb and Bernard Kalb, *Kissinger* (Boston: Little, Brown, 1974), p. 306.

28. Richard M. Nixon, "The Moscow Summit: New Opportunities in U.S.-Soviet Relations," *Department of State Bulletin* (June 26, 1972), p. 856.

29. English and Russian texts can be found in U.S. Department of State, *United States Treaties and Other International Agreements*, vol. 24, pt. 1, 1973 (Washington, D.C.: U.S. GPO, 1974), pp. 1063–1066.

30. "Superpowers Maneuvering for Supremacy on High Seas," *Washington Post*, April 4, 1984, p. A18.

31. Roberts, "The October 1973 Arab-Israeli War," in Dismukes and McConnell, eds., *Soviet Naval Diplomacy*, p. 196.

32. Quoted in Caldwell, *American-Soviet Relations*, p. 228.

33. "Soviet Warship, US Navy Vessel Collide in Mideast," *Boston Globe*, November 18, 1983, p. 6.

34. See "Soviet Sub Bumps Into U.S. Carrier," *Washington Post*, March 22, 1984, p. A1; and "Soviet Sub and U.S. Carrier Collide in Sea of Japan," *New York Times*, March 22, 1984, p. A7.

35. "Moscow's Muscle Flexing," *Time*, April 16, 1984, pp. 28–30.

36. *Ibid.*, p. 30.

37. "High Seas Diplomacy Continuing," *Washington Post*, June 8, 1984, p. A15.

38. William Beecher, "Election Clouds Weapons Talks," *Boston Globe*, July 17, 1984, p. 4.

39. See Steven E. Miller, "Politics over Promise: Domestic Impediments to Arms Control," *International Security*, vol. 8, no. 4 (Spring 1984), pp. 67–90.

40. O'Connell, *The Influence of Law on Sea Power*, p. 178.

41. The July 1985 agreement between the United States, Japan, and the Soviet Union to improve communication between their respective air traffic controllers may represent an important first step in this area. See "Monitoring Pact aims to keep jets from straying," *Boston Globe*, July 31, 1985, p. 7.

42. See Daniel Deudney, "Unlocking Space," *Foreign Policy*, no. 53 (Winter 1983–84), pp. 91–113.

43. Johan Jørgen Holst, "Confidence-Building Measures: A Conceptual Framework," *Survival*, vol. 25, no. 1 (January/February 1983), p. 2.

44. Editor's note: For the first time in the 14-year history of the Incidents at Sea agreement, the Soviet Union canceled a regularly scheduled review

meeting that was to be held in Washington over June 11–13, 1984, apparently in retaliation against Secretary of Defense Weinberger's decision to cut short the meeting and eliminate certain customary social engagements by way of response to the Soviet shooting on March 24, 1984, of U.S. military liaison mission officer Major Arthur D. Nicholson, Jr. According to the Department of Defense statement: "The Soviet side informed us on June 7 that they had decided not to come for the talks at this time, apparently not wishing to have the substantive talks without a large social program." However, the statement continued, "both sides agree to seek a mutually convenient date in the future when the talks can be held under appropriate circumstances." Leslie H. Gelb, "U.S.-Soviet Session on '72 Naval Accord Canceled," *New York Times*, June 19, 1985, pp. A1, A9.

5

The Stockholm CDE Negotiations

Richard E. Darilek

By the dawn of the 1980s, it became apparent that arms control efforts were producing far less in the way of reliable results than they seemed to have promised at the beginning of the 1970s. In part, this development stemmed from criticism of such results as had been obtained during the preceding decade—the SALT II Treaty is one well-known case in point. It probably also derived, however, in part from a lack of results elsewhere, for example, in the talks on Mutual and Balanced Force Reductions (MBFR) in Vienna, where NATO and the Warsaw Pact have been negotiating since 1973 without producing an agreement. Moreover, the former promises of arms control, which involved reducing and limiting forces gradually but steadily over time, have waned since the early 1970s as result of the increasing distrust fostered by the USSR's continuing buildup of and obvious willingness to use its military power—whether directly, as in Afghanistan, or indirectly, as in Poland—and by the U.S. force modernization efforts that followed in response.

In the 1980s, therefore, arms control efforts began to change. Their focus began to shift away from gradualism with its incremental agreements, each increment building upon a predecessor, toward greater self-sufficiency for individual agreements, toward agreements justifiable on their own in military terms alone, and toward arms control processes less dependent on an ongoing political process (namely, detente) to sustain them.

Confidence-building measures of the kind represented in the Helsinki Final Act of 1975 were no exception to this general trend. As originally

Reprinted with modifications from the *Washington Quarterly*, vol. 8, no. 1 (Winter 1985), Richard E. Darilek, "Building Confidence and Security in Europe: The Road to and from Stockholm," by permission of the MIT Press, Cambridge, Massachusetts. Copyright 1985 by the Center for Strategic and International Studies, Georgetown University, and the Massachusetts Institute of Technology.

conceived and adopted, these measures promoted notification, in advance
of their starting dates, of military maneuvers and movements in Europe
and encouraged exchanges of observers and other military personnel
among the 35 European (every state except Albania) and American (the
United States and Canada) signatories of the Final Act. Although not
strictly "arms control" measures in the traditional sense, since they
neither reduced forces nor specifically prohibited them from engaging
in any of the notifiable activities, the Helsinki CBMs were nevertheless
intended to inhibit the use of force for intimidation or other hostile
purposes. The Final Act's injunction to notify a major maneuver 21 days
in advance of its commencement, for example, implies that without such
prenotification, the maneuver should not take place. However, the CBMs
were above all an integral part of the Helsinki Final Act, which focused
on human rights and economic as well as military security issues. As
such, the measures were part of a complex political mosaic in which
they represented a politico-military, not simply or exclusively a military,
dimension.

As the politics of arms control shifted at the turn of the 1980s, the
former role of CBMs changed as well. They were roundly criticized at
the Madrid meeting, which from 1980 through 1983 reviewed questions
of compliance with the Final Act, for their military as well as their
political inadequacies; their highly limited application to the European
territory of the USSR; their ill-defined or, in some cases, nonexistent
notification requirements; and their extremely voluntary nature, with its
lack of any sanctions for noncompliance other than political criticism
at such periodic review meetings as Madrid. The Madrid meeting itself
produced, on July 15, 1983, the mandate for new, more geographically
extensive ("the whole of Europe"—including *all* of the European USSR),
militarily significant, politically binding, and verifiable CBMs, as well
as a new conference to convene at Stockholm in January 1984 to negotiate
them. If the Helsinki CBMs were quasi-military measures intended to
build political confidence, the measures to be negotiated at Stockholm
were to be more fully military measures whose objective was to promote
military as well as political confidence. To effect this change in emphasis,
the measures were even renamed confidence and *security* building
measures (CSBMs). Moreover, the Stockholm gathering was itself established as a semi-independent conference; although required to report
its results to the next scheduled review meeting for the Final Act, to
be held in Vienna in November 1986, the Stockholm conference could
put any agreements it reached into effect immediately, without awaiting
subsequent review. While still an appendage of the multi-faceted political
process launched in 1975 at Helsinki, therefore, the Stockholm conference
and any CSBMs it might produce are now somewhat removed from

that process. As such, they have started to resemble other continuing arms control efforts of the 1980s that emphasize immediate military over broader political considerations.

This chapter reviews the various CSBM proposals that have been advanced at the Stockholm conference. The objective is to infer from those proposals what it is that their authors have in mind when they speak of confidence and security building: What are the various images that exist, who holds them, and how do they differ among each other? What hidden agendas have been carried to Stockholm? What might that conference be expected to produce in view of some of the vastly different concepts of confidence and security that clearly exist? To this end, the chapter addresses the NATO, Soviet, Romanian, and Neutral and Non-aligned (NNA)[1] proposals in turn and tries to draw some conclusions both about them and about where the enterprise launched at Stockholm may eventually lead.[2]

The NATO Proposal

NATO has proposed six measures for negotiation and subsequent adoption at Stockholm. Advanced originally on January 24, 1984, and then "amplified" on March 8, 1985, the measures are as follows:

1. Exchange of military information, on a yearly basis, covering: (a) the structure of ground and air forces in all of Europe, giving command organization, unit designations, normal headquarters locations, and the composition of the forces; and (b) the regulations governing the presence and activities of accredited military personnel.
2. Exchange of forecasts of activities notifiable in advance, on a yearly basis; the annual forecasts would include the name and the purpose of notifiable activities, the countries participating, the size and type of forces involved, and the places and times of occurrence.
3. Notification of military activities, 45 days in advance, that involve the field training of ground forces at the division level or 6,000 personnel, mobilization activities at the level of 3 divisions of 25,000 personnel, and amphibious activities at 3 battalions or 3,000 troops. Alerts are to be notified when they commence.
4. Observation of certain military activities, a requirement that states invite observers from all other states to all prenotified activities, including alert activities if they exceed 48 hours in duration.
5. Compliance and verification provisions, by which states would agree: (a) not to interfere with other states' "national technical means" of verification for monitoring compliance with the pro-

visions of an agreement; and (b) to allow each other to send inspectors, on a limited, quota basis, to observe from the ground and/or air activities that seem not to be in compliance with negotiated agreements.

6. Development of means of communication, to enhance capabilities and procedures for urgent communication.[3]

A quick glance at the foregoing list suggests that the quest for information predominates, especially information provided by the other side. Given the expanded CSBM area, which encompasses military forces and activities from the Atlantic to the Urals (in contrast to the CBM area, which extends only 250 km into the western USSR), information that would be required if these measures were to be adopted would be quite substantial. Four of the measures (1, 2, 3, and 6) require that each state provide the other 34 with the necessary information, while the other two (4 and 5) permit these other participants to check for themselves whether the veracity of any information that has been provided is what it should be. Because the information requirement that would be imposed by the NATO proposal is extensive, the Warsaw Pact frequently complains that such "military-technical" measures, as they like to label them for pejorative purposes, are surrogates for an improved Western intelligence-gathering capability. In many cases, however, the information provided would be no different from that already gained by Western "national technical means." What *would* be different is the requirement for the East to provide and help corroborate the information as well—to engage in a constructive dialogue about such information, rather than treat, as now, even the possibility of exchanging it as illegitimate, as a violation of some all-encompassing military secrecy requirement.

A first order assessment of the NATO measures, therefore, might conclude that their emphasis on improving the information flow from the Soviet Union and the Warsaw Pact aims at building confidence and security simply by reducing military secrecy. In other words, the more one is told by a potential adversary in advance about the military activities of that adversary, the better the opportunities provided for corroborating what one is told and for dissipating any unnecessary, suspicion-provoking secrecy surrounding the event. As a result, more confidence is built, and the greater the increase in security all around. From this perspective, the NATO approach to CSBMs may be characterized as a developmental one, derived from NATO's own deep distrust of the Warsaw Pact and reinforced by generally disappointing experiences with CBMs (their inherent weaknesses, noted above, as well as Warsaw Pact failures to implement them fully or properly, discussed in Chapter 1). The objective, therefore, is to change Soviet and Eastern European behavior progressively over time; to this end, NATO wants specific actions, *e.g.*, information exchange and notification, to be the agents of change. In other words, NATO wants deeds, not words or sweeping pledges, to be the basis of confidence and security building efforts in Europe, and it wants more militarily significant deeds now than it might have been satisfied with before, especially in the light of the Helsinki CBM experience.

Further analysis of the NATO CSBMs suggests, however, that something even more far-reaching would be operating in the realm of confidence and security building if the measures were adopted. That something is a belief that the greater openness and predictability of military activities required by the measures would, in the words of the NATO proposal, "reduce the risk of surprise attack, diminish the threat of armed conflict in Europe resulting from misunderstanding and miscalculation, and inhibit the use of force for the purpose of political intimidation." Greater confidence and security, in short, means fewer military surprises—in particular, no surprise attacks. The NATO measures attempt to build such confidence and security by proliferating information, notification, and verification requirements to such an extent that there are few, if any, possibilities left for surprise. In the smooth, flat, wide-open landscape of military activities that the NATO CSBMs seek to create on the European continent, no nooks, crannies, or hideouts sufficient to conceal activities preparatory to launching a surprise attack are supposed to remain.

Such a concept or image of confidence and security building actually goes beyond anything explicitly stated in the NATO proposal, although it is clearly implied. From the Western allies' perspective, after all, what actually creates the risk of surprise attack and the threat of armed conflict in Europe? Whose forces are most likely to be used for purposes of political intimidation? Clearly, for NATO, Warsaw Pact forces fill that bill—in particular, the Soviet Red Army, much of which is forward deployed in central Europe, although it also maintains a menacing presence near NATO borders in northern and southern Europe. At bottom, therefore, building confidence and security for NATO involves changing—in some demonstrable, salutary way—the Soviet Union's conventional military force posture *vis-à-vis* Western Europe. Historically, the Soviets have held an advantage in this regard, and NATO has had difficulty countering that advantage or compensating for it. One of the most difficult counters, in fact, is NATO's historic threat to use nuclear weapons first in a conflict, if necessary, to prevent the USSR from gaining a victory as a result of its advantageous conventional force capabilities. Short of negating those Eastern capabilities through a buildup of conventional forces, which it has always found politically and economically difficult to achieve, NATO must continue to maintain the credibility of its nuclear options, one of which is first-use, and this is becoming increasingly difficult in view of mounting antinuclear sentiment in the West.

NATO has also tried to reduce Warsaw Pact conventional force advantages through negotiation, *e.g.*, the MBFR talks in Vienna which are now in their twelfth year. The Stockholm conference is yet another approach to this same end. Its objective, from a Western perspective, is to limit the politico-military utility of the Soviet Union's and the Warsaw Pact's conventional force superiority in central Europe by means of a negotiated CSBM regime. In contrast to MBFR, the agreement would not reduce and limit conventional forces but, rather, would regulate the activities of those forces so sufficiently as to change what they are able to do and thus vitiate over time their ability to threaten the West. Meanwhile, nuclear weapons would be kept out of the negotiations. As the ultimate guarantor of NATO's own confidence and security for decades, the Western alliance rules them out of bounds at Stockholm and shows no inclination to alter that ruling, even if a new basis for building confidence and security around conventional forces can be initiated at Stockholm.

Whether NATO's objectives are realistic or achievable via the negotiations at Stockholm remains an open question. What is clearer at this stage is the criterion underlying those objectives, *i.e.*, what it takes to build confidence and security among members of the Western alliance. For NATO, some inroads into the conventional force predominance of the Warsaw Pact are prerequisite to any genuine buildup of confidence and security in Europe. Hence, it is not a new but an old problem that is being revisited at the Stockholm conference, even though the problem is being revisited in a different guise (CSBMs) than it has been before.

The Soviet Proposal

Like NATO, the Soviet Union has presented six proposals for consideration at Stockholm. Presumably, these proposals, initially tabled on May 8, 1984, also represent the views of other Warsaw Pact members since, except for Romania, none of these other members has advanced any proposals on its own. Only one of the six proposals corresponds to the kind of CSBMs found in the NATO package— "military technical" measures, as the Soviets tend to categorize them. The one Soviet proposal in this category, however, includes or alludes to the possibility of at least five such measures: (1) a 40,000 troop limit on ground force maneuvers; (2) notification 30 days in advance of major maneuvers exceeding 20,000 troops, 200 aircraft, and/or 30 ships and 100 aircraft;

(3) notification 30 days in advance of force movements exceeding 20,000 troops and/or 100 aircraft; (4) invitation of observers to maneuvers; and (5) some unspecified forms of verification possibly including "requests for information" and "consultations." To justify a limit on the size and scale of maneuvers, the Soviets advance an interesting theory. They argue that "since it is difficult to differentiate between modern large-scale military maneuvers and the preparatory stages of deployment of armed forces for the purpose of commencing hostility in the European theater," the need for such a measure is a matter of some urgency. The irony of this proposal, of course, is that, in the postwar era, the USSR itself has been the prime user of large-scale military maneuvers to mask the commencement of hostilities. Such maneuvers helped cloak preparations for the invasion of Czechoslovakia in 1968; in the early 1980s, they served to put pressure on Poland by threatening it with the possibility of another Czech-style invasion.

The remaining five proposals in the Soviet package represent what the Warsaw Pact considers CSBMs, but what NATO likes to call "declaratory measures," to distinguish them from the more detailed measures it has proposed. Such Soviet measures tend to consist of general pledges not to do something, instead of commitments to positive action (as in the case of a requirement to notify a particular activity). The first Soviet declaratory proposal, for example, calls upon the states participating in the Stockholm conference to undertake an obligation not to be the first to use nuclear weapons. The second proposal promotes a similar obligation not to be the first to use either nuclear or conventional arms, and "hence, not to use military force against each other at all." The third proposal envisages a pledge to freeze and reduce military spending in percentage points or absolute figures. The fourth calls for ridding Europe of chemical weapons. The fifth endorses creation of nuclear-free zones in various parts of Europe, specifically in the Balkans, northern Europe, and parts of central Europe. In the latter area, the proposal calls for the establishment of a zone free from battlefield nuclear weapons on both sides of the borders between NATO and Warsaw Pact states.

A first-order assessment of these Soviet proposals cannot ignore their marked emphasis on making promises to refrain from activities that, for the most part, relate to nuclear weapons—whether those activities involve using the weapons, storing them, or paying for them. This emphasis suggests that confidence and security is built, according to the USSR, by making blanket politico-military commitments, not by exchanging military information as in the NATO proposals. Indeed, the Soviet proposal to cut military expenditures, for example, conspicuously lacks any requirement that such cuts be based on preestablished or agreed data bases for all participants (including the USSR).

Further analysis of the Soviet Union's CSBM proposals also suggests that, unlike NATO's, they are not developmental proposals that tend to promise the building of confidence and security over time; they seem to suggest, instead, that confidence and security can be built instantaneously simply by the adoption of the proposed measures. In contrast to NATO's emphasis on long-term deeds, the Soviets seem to place more emphasis on immediate words—on the instant efficacy of pledges or treaty commitments of the kind the USSR is proposing.

It is curious that the Soviet Union seems to display an emphasis and to be willing to enter into such sweeping commitments with adversaries that it demonstrably fails to trust. Where does it get the initial confidence and security with which to do so? First, it probably gets them from its own residual military power, conventional as well as nuclear. If NATO were actually to forswear nuclear first-use any time soon without providing itself with conventional force alternatives, the Red Army would quickly become the decisive strategic weapon in Europe and redound to the Soviets' further advantage, not least in terms of their own confidence and security. Second, it is possible that the Soviets count on the asymmetries between open versus closed societies to guarantee them a margin of confidence and security as well. In making their proposals at Stockholm, they may believe that Western publics and parliaments, if they ever accept them, will feel more inhibited by such declaratory measures than their authors might and will impose tougher constraints on Western political and military establishments as a result.

In the main, confidence and security building for the USSR implies banning those things that bother the Soviets most in NATO's politico-military strategy and posture—in particular, its stated willingness to use nuclear weapons first, if necessary, to repel a Warsaw Pact attack. Three out of the six Soviet proposals underline this point. One thing that really does stand in the way of complete confidence and security for the USSR in Europe is the existence and potential use of nuclear weapons by NATO, which does not pose an equally credible threat to the Pact in terms of its conventional forces. Confidence and security building from the Soviet perspective, therefore, intimately involves the desire to gain some control over NATO's nuclear stockpiles. Proposals to rid Europe of them are one way to do this, and the Soviet Union makes such proposals in the hope that if the West should ever accept them, it would be more difficult for its officials to return to the *status quo ante* than it will be for officials in Eastern Europe, whose publics and parliaments do not act as watchdogs over military strategy. Moreover, the USSR can draw some support for such a view from the status of nuclear strategy in the West, which is not only highly contested at present but also likely to spark considerable debate in the future. Any proposals in this area from the USSR only fan the flames of a fire already smoldering over intermediate-range nuclear force deployments and other nuclear issues. The USSR is only too happy to make such proposals, at Stockholm and elsewhere, in pursuit of its own distinctive confidence and security building measures.

The Romanian Proposal

Two other sets of proposals have been presented at Stockholm. One set, tabled on January 25, 1984, comes from Romania, a member of the Warsaw Pact long noted for its relative independence from the Soviet Union in matters of foreign policy.

The Romanian proposal bows in the general direction of the NATO CSBMs by calling for prior notification of major military maneuvers, movements, and, to the extent possible, alerts. It also nods in the Soviet Union's direction by calling for an all-European treaty on the non-use or threat of force, for a freeze on military expenditures, and for a maximum limitation on the size of military maneuvers. Interestingly, the Romanians do not ask for agreemeent on no-first-use of nuclear weapons, a key element in the Soviet list of proposals, although they do support the Soviet call for nuclear-free zones in the Balkans, in the north of Europe, and elsewhere on the continent (without specifying precisely where such other regions might be).

Beyond echoing proposals from other quarters, Romania recommends measures that seem uniquely its own. In particular, it calls for creating special security zones along the borders between states. In these security corridors, there would be limits on the armed forces, armaments, and military activities that would be permitted, *e.g.*, there would be no maneuvers, movements, or concentrations of armed forces and armaments, nor could important force components be placed on alert there. The corridors would be free of nuclear weapons and might become, over time, completely demilitarized, except for internal and border security forces. The Romanian proposal also calls for a system of information, communication, and consultation among states on problems relating to the prevention and management of crises, as well as for adoption of measures to prevent nuclear conflict by error or accident.

Such proposals tend to suggest that Romania's concept of confidence and security building centers around longstanding European concerns with the sanctity and inviolability of frontiers, as well as the more recent postwar interest in preventing nuclear war by miscalculation or accident. At a deeper level, of course, what the Romanians appear to be saying is that confidence and security building for them consists of guaranteeing a certain territorial integrity and freedom from attack which, given their geographic location, is most likely to come from their Warsaw Pact allies. Like NATO, Romania would find curbs on the Warsaw Pact and, especially, the Soviet Union's conventional military predominance in central Europe to be fundamentally productive of confidence and security building. But as a member of the Warsaw Pact, Romania also has to worry about the possibility of an East-West conflict that could find Romanians caught in the middle—extremely vulnerable as a member of the Pact to the possiblity of nuclear retaliation by the West in an all-out conflict. Hence, the emphasis on crisis management and measures to prevent nuclear conflict by error or accident. Romania, like other smaller European states in the Warsaw Pact and elsewhere, can only be confident and secure if the major adversaries, who ultimately control its fate, take concrete steps toward reducing the possibilities for mistrust and insecurity, *i.e.*, the possibilities for war, that exist between them.

The Neutral and Nonaligned Proposal

That same or a similar judgment could apply to the NNA states as well (Austria, Cyprus, Finland, Lichtenstein, Malta, San Marino, Sweden, Switzerland, and Yugoslavia), who presented on March 9, 1984, their own set of proposals at Stockholm. These proposals run the gamut from prior notification of various military activities through specific constraints on certain types of military activities, to positive references (for the benefit of the USSR) to the possiblity of reaffirming pledges to refrain from the threat or use of force, to similarly encouraging statements (for NATO) about the need for verification and standardized reporting for military expenditures. Like the Romanian proposal, the NNA document makes no reference to no-first-use of nuclear weapons as advocated by the Soviet Union, nor does it support NATO positions in every particular—for example, it calls for ceilings on the size of maneuvers and for verification provisions in language that is more reminiscent of the Soviet than of the NATO proposal. Above all, however, the NNA proposals for CSBMs seem most directly akin to the language and the spirit of the CBMs that preceded them. More than any other set of proposals, those of the NNA states seem to build consciously and incrementally on the base that already exists in the Helsinki Final Act.

On the one hand, this suggests that confidence and security building for the NNAs consists largely of a developmental approach, begun in the 1970s, that should not be abandoned entirely despite the disappointments of that decade. The NNAs seem to want to build on what is already there (CBMs), incorporating what is new (CSBMs) gradually without abandoning what has gone before. Hence, the similarity of many of the NNA proposals to terms, conditions, and language already existing in the Final Act. Confidence and security building for them means conscientiously preserving what has already been accomplished and trying to inch, not leap, beyond.

On the other hand, the NNA approach goes further and in so doing adds another level of meaning to what it takes to build confidence and security among them. For the NNAs, as for the Romanians, the prospect of an East-West conflict could prove devastating. Although presently remote, the prospect cannot be ignored, especially in view of recent increases in East-West tensions. For the NNAs, the possibilities for reducing those tensions are still paramount in importance. Their interest, therefore, revolves as much around the need to promote political rapprochement, or detente, between the principal East-West adversaries as they do around the need for particular military arrangements. Compared to the Romanians, who want mechanisms to control any crisis that might arise, the NNAs seem to want means to prevent any crisis from arising.

Confidence and security building for the NNAs, therefore, is a political as well as a military endeavor in which specific CSBMs can help with improvements but can never serve as substitutes for good political relationships. Without such relationships between the main East-West adversaries, NNA confidence and security simply cannot be built independently. Hence, the NNAs are ready to assume and play the role of potential compromisers between the two major blocs at Stockholm— in the interest of their own, as well as their conceptions of Europe's, confidence and security building requirements. They have played this role before at Helsinki and Madrid and they expect to play it again at Stockholm (witness the Swedish and Finnish efforts in arranging a compromise formula for working groups, arrived at on December 3, 1984). That role is prefigured in the compromising nature of the document they have submitted for consideration.

Prognosis

What is the likely outcome of the Stockholm conference? What are its chances of building confidence and security along any of the various lines discussed above?

The first answer to this question is that neither of the major East-West adversaries seems likely to have its proposals adopted in full at Stockholm. The USSR, for example, will not get NATO to forswear the possibility of using nuclear weapons first in a conflict, nor will NATO be willing to sign up for the various nuclear-free zones the Soviets are proposing. At this point, NATO does not even consider the subject of nuclear weapons appropriate to Stockholm's agenda, in part because of Western allies' insistence at Madrid that it should be oriented exclusively toward conventional forces in Europe—although the CDE mandate does not explicitly exclude "nuclear" CSBMs from the agenda.

Similarly, NATO seems unlikely to gain complete Soviet acceptance of the extensive information-sharing regime that it has proposed for Europe from the Atlantic to the Urals. The Soviets balk not only at the verification measures envisaged in NATO's proposals, but also at the wide-ranging prenotification and information exchange measures that, together with verification, constitute the main pillars of NATO's approach. The paradox seems to be that both sides require adoption of their respective positions if they are to achieve greater confidence and security for themselves; however, each side also requires that the other's position cannot be fully adopted as well. Compromise solutions, therefore, do not offer a convenient way out of such an impasse, particularly if the overriding objective is to build confidence and security on both sides.

Nevertheless, one potential outcome of the Stockholm meeting is, in fact, a compromise. Such a possibility is suggested in and by the NNA proposal, which already contains a menu of diverse proposals that other participants can pick and choose from if, in the end, they feel compelled to leave Stockholm with at least some concrete results. In fact, the possibility for just such a compromise was suggested in President Reagan's speech of June 4, 1984, in Dublin. In that address, the president stated: "If discussions on reaffirming the principle not to use force, a principle in which we believe so deeply, will bring the Soviet Union to negotiate agreements which will give concrete new meaning to that principle, we will gladly enter into such discussions."[4] This statement could ultimately lead to Western acceptance, in some fashion, of the Soviet Union's non-use of force proposal at Stockholm in exchange for comparable movement on the Soviet side (*e.g.*, in the area of notification and verification). Such a compromise may become more likely as the Stockholm meeting draws to a close and pressure mounts for it to report some results to the next Final Act review meeting in Vienna in 1986.

The NNAs, the Romanians, and others might be happy with such a compromise outcome; it is, after all, the essence of the NNA and, to a lesser extent, the Romanian positions. NATO and the Warsaw Pact, however, will still be at loggerheads with each other despite such compromises and both will remain unsatisfied in terms of their key confidence and security building criteria. Reaffirmation of the non-use of force by the United States and NATO will not satisfy the Soviet Union's hopes for a renunciation of the first-use of nuclear weapons, while agreement to minimal information or verification measures will not sufficiently improve NATO's sense of security or confidence *vis-à-*

vis the conventional forces of the Warsaw Pact. What will likely emerge under the circumstances is some marginally improved set of measures that look more like evolutionary improvements on the Helsinki Final Act CBMs than the quantum leap forward toward more militarily significant CSBMs that was supposed to justify holding the special meeting at Stockholm. Like the Helsinki CBMs, the best that can probably be hoped for any compromise agreements emerging from Stockholm is not that they build confidence and security but simply that they lessen mutual feelings of mistrust and insecurity, while holding open the possibility of greater progress at a later date.

In any event, the future seems clearly to imply that the quest for confidence and security in Europe will continue, whether at Stockholm or at successor conferences. The fundamental incompatibility of NATO and Soviet conceptions of what it takes to build such confidence and security will undoubtedly persist, and their sharply differing views will almost certainly continue to clash at these gatherings. The opportunity for direct interchanges between the main adversaries on such central issues may itself be sufficient to warrant the enterprise. After all, in early 1984, Stockholm was for a time the only East-West negotiation taking place. For the others—the NNAs, the Romanians, and even allies from one side or the other—Stockholm-like meetings will continue to be essential in their never-ending quest to influence the United States and the USSR, to blunt the edges of controversies that arise as a result of those adversaries' differing conceptions of confidence and security, and to search for any available compromises. In the process, a common conception of confidence and security building in Europe is not likely to emerge soon. The continuing need to focus on differing conceptions of what it takes to build confidence and security in Europe, however, which meetings like Stockholm can hardly avoid, may in the long run prove salutary if it forces all parties concerned to recognize and come to grips with their differences, rather than simply paper them over for the sake of agreement.

Notes

1. Editor's note: Malta, an original sponsor of the NNA proposal, advanced its own CSBM package on November 8, 1984, after the writing of this article. The Maltese proposal, which is contained in appendix A, deals entirely with the Mediterranean and includes notification, constraint, and declaratory measures.

2. Texts of and quotations from the four proposals discussed in this chapter may be found in the *Arms Control Reporter 1984* (Brookline, MA: Institute for Defense and Disarmament Studies, 1984).

3. This description of the NATO measures is excerpted from James Goodby, "Security for Europe," *NATO Review*, vol. 32, no. 3 (June/July 1984), p. 12.

4. *New York Times*, June 5, 1984.

6

CBMs in the U.N. Setting

Charles C. Flowerree

Awareness of efforts in the United Nations to promote the concept of confidence-building measures on a worldwide basis is miniscule, even in circles familiar with the effort in Europe. Be that as it may, the General Assembly has devoted a good deal of attention to this question in recent years and the issue has stirred up controversy. The U.N.'s experience with CBMs has reflected the deep philosophical and political differences that divide the major groupings of nations on all issues pertaining to international security.

The West, which is acutely conscious of the role that mutual suspicions and misinterpretations of actions by other nations played in precipitating the First World War and is still playing in exacerbating today's tensions, regards confidence-building as a vital factor in the security equation. In the U.N. this view is translated into support by the Western group (NATO and like-minded countries) for extending the concept of CBMs to the world beyond the European continent.

The Eastern group (the USSR and its allies) has seen the CBM exercise largely as another way of promoting the Soviet Union's longstanding prescriptions for peace and security—nonaggression pacts (eerily reminiscent of the 1939 pact between Hitler and Stalin), no-first-use of nuclear weapons, and so on. They have opposed certain specific aspects of the Western approach such as the concept of openness with regard to military activities and concrete measures rather than declarations of intent.

Most of the nations outside Europe, except those having close ties with the West or the Soviet Union, have varying degrees of difficulty with the European model for CBMs. Many wish to shift the focus away from military measures and to give a very broad interpretation to the meaning of confidence-building. Some seem to suspect that the whole exercise is a calculated diversion from the priority task of eliminating the nuclear threat once and for all.

These conflicting views have recently been given expression in the U.N. Disarmament Commission (UNDC), a deliberative body open to all U.N. member nations that meets for a month each spring to consider specific questions in the disarmament area. One of the tasks assigned for the 1983 session, as stated in UNGA Resolution 37/D/100 of December 13, 1982, was "to consider the elaboration of guidelines for appropriate types of confidence-building measures and for the implementation of such measures on a global or regional basis." Discussion of this item was continued during the 1984 session but there was little progress toward agreement on the content, or in some instances even the form of the draft guidelines. Further consideration is being postponed until 1986 in the hope that intervening developments will make that a more propitious time for a renewed effort.

How the U.N. effort was initiated, how it developed, and the reasons for the resistance to globalizing CBMs is examined in the succeeding sections.

Historical Background

The proposal that the U.N. take up the question of global CBMs was first raised formally at the Tenth Special Session of the UNGA devoted to disarmament (SSOD) in 1978 in a speech by then Chancellor Helmut Schmidt of the Federal Republic of Germany. The SSOD was the occasion for many chiefs of state or heads of government to air their views on arms control and disarmament before a world audience. Several sought to make new proposals or variations on old ones, with which they hoped their countries would henceforth be identified. So it was with the FRG which, since the Conference on Security and Cooperation in Europe, had seized on CBMs as an area of its special concern. At the Vienna MBFR negotiations, the West Germans had also been stressing the importance of CBMs as an element of an eventual agreement. It was therefore not surprising that CBMs would be the centerpiece of Chancellor Schmidt's proposals to the SSOD.

The Final Document produced by the SSOD gave due recognition to the concept of global and regional CBMs, but in a fairly subdued manner. Paragraph 93 was entirely devoted to this question. It stated that in order to facilitate the process of disarmament, it would be necessary to take measures and to pursue policies to strengthen international peace and security and to build confidence among states. The paragraph incorporated certain illustrative measures: improvement of communications between governments (hotlines, for example); an assessment by states of their military research and development activities for possible impact on existing agreements or on future efforts in the field of disarmament; and periodic reports by the Secretary General to the UNGA on the economic and social consequences of the arms race.[1]

These proposals were not intended to limit in any way the U.N.'s consideration of CBMs, but neither did the paragraph as a whole give a clear direction or strong impetus to future work in this area. The proposals concerning research and development and the economic and social consequences of the arms race were indeed followed up by studies that were eventually published, but they were not undertaken in the context of confidence-building as it is generally understood.

To maintain some momentum on the issue, the UNGA, in a resolution sponsored by a group of Western and like-minded countries,[2] commissioned a comprehensive study to be prepared by a group of governmental experts appointed by the Secretary General. This study was completed in August 1981 and was published in 1982, in time for the Second SSOD in May of that year where it was duly noted.[3] The study did a commendable job of reflecting all points of view but the emphasis was on the military aspects of confidence-building. The FRG Chairman of the experts group made a determined effort to achieve a consensus document and managed to limit the reflections of disagreement largely to a single chapter, the one that presented an illustrative list of possible CBMs. The study was straightforward in presenting both agreed measures and those on which there was no agreement, together with an explanation of the reasons why different experts could not subscribe to certain measures.

The "Comprehensive Study on Confidence-Building Measures" did not, of course, constitute a recommendation to U.N. member states by the UNGA. Consequently, the UNGA handed the question to the UNDC, charging it with the task of producing guidelines which could be commended to all countries.

Deliberations of the Disarmament Commission

Once seized with the problem, the UNDC encountered the same divergencies of views that had been reflected in the CBM study. In the UNDC, however, the problems were magnified. The desired end product was a consensus report, or as close to one as possible, containing recommendations which the UNGA would endorse. While the experts group working on the study had been able to find formulations acceptable to all on most issues, except those impinging on the most fundamental areas of disagreement, in the UNDC differences were harder to bridge. One reason was that there were a much larger number of participants, most of whom were operating within the narrow bounds of instructions from their governments.

At the May 1983 session the UNDC established a working group to begin considering the question of CBMs (which was only one of several agenda items). Since a final report to the UNGA was not due until 1984, the UNDC did not attempt to go beyond an airing of views of identification of areas of agreement and disagreement on this occasion.

In addition to the CBM study, the UNDC had before it replies from Member States to the Secretary General pursuant to UNGA Resolution 33/91B of December 16, 1978, which had invited them to give their views on CBMs. Furthermore, at the 1983 UNDC session several delegations circulated working papers the contents of which illustrated graphically the wide divergencies that stood in the way of a consensus report.

The FRG, whose delegation provided the chairman of the working group, submitted a paper outlining specific guidelines and principles recommended for inclusion in the eventual report from the UNDC to the General Assembly.[4] Among the points it stressed were:

- The need for more extensive information exchange about opposing military forces, thereby enhancing "openness, transparency and mutual calculability in security matters;"
- The role of CBMs in facilitating genuine progress in arms control agreements;
- Placing mutually agreed and verifiable constraints on military activities;
- Strict observance of the principles of the U.N. Charter as a prerequisite to and a fundamental source of confidence-building;
- The necessity for concrete actions that can be examined, assessed, and refined, not declarations of intent, as a foundation for effective confidence-building;
- Progressive agreements on measures moving from less to more restraining measures until a comprehensive network of CBMs is established; and
- Recognition that a regional approach is both desirable and feasible, although the global approach should not be neglected.

The FRG paper went on to propose a series of concrete and politically binding measures such as: exchange of observers at maneuvers, the establishment of "hotlines" and crisis management centers, the introduction of peacekeeping forces into a region, and other measures that are familiar elements in the Western position on the CBM issue.

The FRG paper also addressed the role of the U.N. in promoting CBMs. It suggested that the Security Council and General Assembly could further the process of expanding the CBM network by adopting recommendations directed either to all states or to certain states in a particular region. The Security Council would have primary cognizance over security measures such as the introduction of forces and international mediators into an area of tension, actions for which there is a well-established precedent. The General Assembly would concern itself primarily with measures that might be applied in the political, legal, economic, and social fields, but it could, of course, recommend any sort of CBM falling within the scope of the U.N. Charter. Both the Security Council and the General Assembly could call for an evaluation of existing CBMs and, on the basis of this evaluation, recommend their continuation, modification, or extension. The Secretary General, acting in accordance with Article 99 of the U.N. Charter, might bring to the attention of the Security Council such CBMs as might seem appropriate for easing tensions that threaten international peace and security.

Another recommendation of the FRG paper was that the Committee on Disarmament (now the Conference on Disarmament) should identify and negotiate such CBMs as are related to or included in agreements on disarmament and arms control being negotiated in the Committee.

Finally, the FRG suggested that the specialized agencies of the U.N. could contribute, within their respective fields of activity, to the process of confidence-building. For example, they might help through aid programs to alleviate political, economic, and social inequalities, thereby reducing existing tensions and distrust in the broader sense of "confidence-building."

In stark contrast to the West German approach was that of the Indian delegation. Their working paper, submitted at the 1983 session of the UNDC, took a dim view of CBMs in both the general and particular sense. At the very outset the Indian paper declared that ending the nuclear arms race commanded the highest priority and that now was hardly the time to shift attention to CBMs "of marginal significance." Later the assertion was made that there is no direct link between CBMs and security.

Having put CBMs in this perspective, the Indian paper went on to give views on what confidence-building ought to be or ought not to be. Among the points made were:

- Confidence-building is not a narrow, restrictive and regulatory concept; regulatory measures are provided for in the U.N. Charter. It would be a distortion of priority and a waste of resource if the Security Council, the General Assembly, or the Conference on Disarmament started dealing specifically with CBMs;
- Any approach to confidence-building in the wider sense of the term must be a comprehensive one involving measures in the political,

economic, and social fields, such as a restructuring of the world economic system and elimination of racial discrimination and foreign occupation;

- The major powers have a special responsibility for improving the climate of trust and confidence among states; they should dissolve military alliances, dismantle foreign military bases, and remove their military presence from various regions. A regional approach to CBMs cannot be pursued in isolation from the global approach. One cannot really speak of a regional threat to security; today, the greatest threat, *i.e.*, the nuclear threat, emanates from beyond the oceans;
- Confidence-building in disarmament includes such measures as a freeze on the production, stockpiling, and deployment of nuclear weapons, a comprehensive ban on nuclear testing, and renunciation of doctrines of winnable nuclear wars. CBMs should not be used to facilitate verification of arms limitation and disarmament measures;
- Confidence-building can assume the form of a declaration of intent which need not be followed by a concrete and specific commitment. Politically binding or legally enforceable CBMs are a contradiction in terms. If a measure is politically binding or "reinforceable" (sic), it can never inspire confidence.

While the Indians are probably at the extreme end of the spectrum in their negative approach to CBMs, many of their points have been echoed by other non-aligned countries outside Europe.

A more moderate view from the Third World has been articulated by Mr. Hugo Palma, currently Director of Political and Diplomatic Affairs in the Ministry of Foreign Relations of Peru and a participant in the drafting of the U.N. study on CBMs. Writing in the U.N. periodical *Disarmament*, Mr. Palma acknowledged that in the ten years since the CSCE Final Act, "confidence-building has assumed a dimension that would have been difficult to predict at that time."[5] He recognized legitimate European concern about massive arms build-ups and the possibility of the "unexpected outbreak of hostilities" (*i.e.*, surprise attack). In the global context, however, Palma asserted that lack of confidence arises from broader concerns than those on which the European countries have focused. These concerns stem from the "generic behavior of nations," rather than from specific decisions in the military field. Therefore, military and "paramilitary" measures cannot be of great significance. Developing a global prescription for CBMs requires appropriate measures in the political and economic spheres. Summing up, Palma observed: "Of course confidence can and must be built gradually, but I do not see how it can be promoted in a compartmentalized fashion.

We could all agree that confidence-building can, as some have argued, be a specific category of state conduct, but attempts to apply it to only one kind of 'lack of confidence' may already have met with insuperable difficulties."[6]

The Soviet Union and the countries in what in U.N. parlance is called the "Eastern group" did not table a working paper at the 1983 UNDC session, but in their interventions they put forward familiar arguments. At the 1984 session, the Eastern European countries circulated a paper that incorporated the standard Soviet prescriptions for peace, disarmament, and security. Included were a variety of sweeping proposals ranging from a world treaty on the non-use of force in international relations (to be preceded by a similar pact between NATO and the Warsaw Pact) to a prohibition on chemical weapons and non-deployment where none now exist.

The Eastern paper appears to have been a *pro forma* ploy to get the Soviet position on the record yet again in a U.N. forum and to curry favor with the nonaligned. It is doubtful that the Soviets intended to make a serious effort to incorporate all these points in the UNDC's final report except where certain of them might coincide with the proposals of other groups of countries. In the discussions the Soviet representative said he found value in the continuation of the debate on CBMs and observed that the FRG paper had some useful aspects, notwithstanding Soviet objections to certain parts of it. On the question of openness in military matters the Soviets made the familiar objection that openness in the abstract, *e.g.*, information on nuclear weapons not given in connection with specific arms control measures, would only inflame the arms race and complicate arms control negotiations.

Outcome of the UNDC Deliberations

And so the arguments went at the 1983 and 1984 UNDC sessions. Several delegations, including the Dutch and the Finns,[7] made proposals to try to reconcile the differences or to accommodate as many points of view as might be possible in a cohesive set of recommendations, but to little avail. At the end, other than agreement on some very general points, there was insufficient convergence to permit even a start on drafting a report.

In these circumstances the chairman of the working group attempted to capture the thrust of two years of effort in a document labelled "Chairman's Composite Draft," which was circulated after the group's final session on May 25, 1984.[8] The chairman made it clear that this was not a negotiated text and that he was solely responsible for its content. The format followed that of the FRG working paper and was similar in tone, although other viewpoints were reflected to the extent possible.

Under the first main heading, "General Considerations," the draft treated the philosophy of CBMs and their relationship to such things as disarmament and the general political context. The section headed "Guidelines for appropriate types of confidence-building measures and for their implementation" dealt with, inter alia, the objectives of confidence-building, the characteristics of CBMs (*e.g.*, the necessity for tailoring CBMs to specific situations and the importance of the free flow of information concerning military activities), the where, when, and how of implementing CBMs, and prospects and opportunities for their development.

A third and final main heading was called "Illustrative catalogue of types of measures." There was no elaboration under this heading, however, and a footnote explained that it had been included in the agreed structure of the guidelines on a tentative basis but had not been considered during the drafting process. Some delegations had expressed doubts that this section should be elaborated at the present time. Nevertheless, the footnote pointed out that four proposals for an illustrative list of measures had been submitted during the course of the debates by the FRG, a group of socialist states, the Soviet Union, and jointly by Brazil and Mexico. The latter two were appended to the chairman's draft. Also appended were many proposals for amendments and additions to specific paragraphs in the first two major sections of the draft, the most numerous being those proposed by the Soviet Union and other members of the Eastern group. India, Mexico, and Brazil also offered amendments.

The UNDC's final report to the General Assembly clearly laid out the divergencies that had become apparent in the course of the debate. It called for continued work on the CBM question, nevertheless, and recommended that the General Assembly at its 39th session (fall 1984) decide on an appropriate format for concluding work on the guidelines as early as possible. Many delegations had come to the conclusion, nevertheless, that it would be wise to suspend further consideration of the guidelines in the UNDC until 1986 in the hope that progress in the Stockholm CDE would help resolve some of the problems that had hampered achievement of a greater degree of consensus on the guidelines. Accordingly, the General Assembly adopted a resolution, referred to at the beginning of this chapter, noting what the UNDC had accomplished in 1983 and 1984, and requesting that it resume its work on CBMs in 1986.

Attempting to Bridge the Gap
Between the West and the Rest

Much effort was expended by Western delegations in the UNDC in trying to find formulas that would meet the expressed concerns of the Third World while maintaining the core of the Western notion of what constitutes confidence-building. The problem of dealing with the Soviets was secondary. The issues between East and West were either similar to those between the West and the Third World, or were the kind that could not be resolved until there was some agreement at Stockholm.

There is a touch of irony in the fact that the 1975 Helsinki CSCE Final Act accepted the Western concept that security embodies political, social, and economic concerns as well as strictly military concerns. That position appears on the surface to be close to what many of the Third World countries have been arguing. The difference, of course, lies in the fact that the West has looked at confidence-building as a discrete element in the overall effort to promote security. Both sides in the debate, with the possible exception of the Indians, have acknowledged that there is some merit in the other's position, but the basic philosophy underlying each is very different. These conflicting philosophies stem from different ways at looking at the world and from different objectives in U.N. diplomacy.

An admirable effort to bridge the gap by demonstrating points of convergence between the Western position and that of the developing states has been made by a West German academician who served as a consultant to the CBM study group. Writing in *Aussenpolitik*, Dr. Falk Bomsdorf acknowledged that the Third World concept raises some difficult and "tricky" problems, noting that "interests clash forcibly in Third World areas."[9] Nevertheless, he argued that the Third World view should be accommodated by the West. He pointed out that in contrast to the situation in Europe where two advanced military machines (NATO and the Warsaw Pact) face each other, in the Third World national security is jeopardized by a different set of dangers. He cites the well known litany of problems faced by nations recently freed from the bonds of colonialism. There may be intervention by powers from outside the region, either directly by national forces or by proxies. Regional disputes between two or more states often arise from old, unsettled disputes or from post-colonial conflicts of interest. Moreover, there may be domestic strife arising from social or ethnic tensions.

Bomsdorf noted that, at least in conceptual terms, the most feasible measures for limiting threats to the security of Third World countries are those that impact on the ability of outside powers to intervene. But it has to be borne in mind that many of the extra-regional powers, especially the superpowers, regard their ability to project military force into Third World regions as an indispensable element of their foreign policies. In the absence of agreements among the major powers that remove their incentive for intervening in the Third World, there are, nevertheless, some CBMs that could benefit any country in any region. Bomsdorf offered a few examples: publication of military budget and force strength figures, establishment of regional arms import registers, establishment of nuclear weapon-free zones, prohibiting the stationing of offensive weapons near borders, agreements on arbitration procedures, regular meetings of political and military leaders, and exchange of TV and radio programs and other measures of that nature.

As Bomsdorf noted, a substantial number of actions along these lines have already been initiated in the Third World. Latin America has a particularly large number of examples. They include the Inter-American System with its consultation and arbitration mechanisms, the 1974 Ayucucho Declaration on cooperation among eight Andean states, and the 1967 Treaty of Tlatelolco declaring Latin America a nuclear-free zone. Moreover, several Latin American countries have adopted CBMs on the European model through the conduct of joint military maneuvers, visits by warships, exchanges of military missions, training of foreign officers, and annual conferences of chiefs of staff rotating among different capitals.

In Africa the Charter of the Organization for African Unity (OAU) contains provisions that can well be interpreted as pertaining to confidence-building. Article II, para. 2e, states that member countries are to coordinate and harmonize their policies with special reference to cooperation in defense and security. Article III, para. 5, of the Charter bans subversive activities and several African nations have bilateral agreements under this provision—Angola and Zaire, Sudan and Ethiopia, and Malawi and Mozambique.

In Asia confidence-building has not been a prominent feature of inter-state relations, with the exception of the rapprochement between Egypt and Israel which features a wide range of CBMs. The current tensions in the rest of the Middle East, however, appear to be beyond the capacity of CBMs to alleviate. In South Asia, the Indo-Pakistani confrontation would seem to be made to order for some of the classical European-type CBMs, but the political climate at the moment does not give much hope for progress along this line. Farther to the east, the establishment of the Association of Southeast Asian Nations (ASEAN) provides the framework for actions in the political and economic realms that could be subsumed under the mantle of "confidence-building."

As these examples show, there is indeed scope for CBMs in other parts of the world outside the European continent where, in fact, some countries are engaged even now in confidence-building activities, though they may not recognize them as such. And therein lies the rub. Logic may say there is a basis for accommodation between the contending concepts of confidence-building, but politics—both international and internal to the U.N.—stands in the way.

In an attempt to meet the non-European nonaligned nations half way, Western delegations sought during the UNDC discussions to incorporate references to non-military CBMs in the guidelines while maintaining the major thrust in the military sphere. The U.N. study provided a precedent for this kind of approach, but half a loaf has not proved to be enough.

One of the problems for those who view CBMs through Western eyes is that as soon as recommendations begin to wander from the military realm, they become highly general or even abstract. The language takes on a hortatory tone and tends to repeat all the well known prescriptions for world peace and security that were incorporated in the Final Document of the 1978 U.N. SSOD.

A variety of considerations affect the positions of the developing countries, including, in the extreme, a suspicion that CBMs are simply another effort to shift the spotlight away from the heavily armed Western powers and on to the activist nonaligned countries who have been calling so loudly for nuclear disarmament. Other countries, largely in Latin America and Africa, can justifiably point to the absence of any immediate military threat from their neighbors. They are therefore not interested in promulgating guidelines that are tailored to the European situation or similar cases where heavily armed adversaries face each other across common borders. So it can be seen that there are factors on both sides that work to limit flexibility.

Future Prospects

The foregoing discussion suggests some conclusions about the future of CBMs in the U.N. context. The first and most obvious is that, barring diplomatic breakthroughs in arms control negotiations or a substantial improvement in the climate of international relations in general, there is little or no chance that the General Assembly will be able to adopt guidelines for CBMs that will prove satisfactory to all groups of countries. Moreover, the wide variety of problems facing different nations around the globe makes it difficult to devise a universally applicable prescription of any great utility. Success at Stockholm, if it is achieved, would solve only one set of problems—the East-West differences—that have bedeviled the U.N. effort.

To draw such a bleak conclusion about the immediate future of CBMs in the global context, however, is not to say that the question should be put in the deep freeze. There are many ways it can be kept alive without staking all on the achievement of an agreement on measures to which every state can subscribe.

For those who wish to see the concept of confidence-building spread more widely around the world, a low key approach would seem to be the most appropriate. Through interventions in the UNGA or other multilateral fora recognition can be given to efforts that may be taken or contemplated on a regional level or between pairs of nations to enhance confidence. UNGA resolutions designed to recommend or encourage CBMs in specific situations should be introduced only when it is clear that they will be widely supported. Perhaps the Secretary General is in the best position to take initiatives in this area. The U.N. CBM study contained a suggestion that the Secretary General maintain a "voluntary register of types of confidence-building measures applied throughout the world." By doing so he would be giving recognition and encouragement to the entire process and possibly increase public awareness of the vast—and in many cases unexplored—potential for CBMs to make a contribution to strengthening peace and security.

When the UNDC resumes its deliberations in 1986, there may be an opportunity to narrow the differences, especially if there has been progress at Stockholm. In any case, however, efforts should be made to moderate confrontation. If full agreement on guidelines for global CBMs is not possible, that will not be a disaster. Much has been accomplished already to increase awareness of the potential that lies in CBMs. Protecting and nurturing that achievement in the future should take precedence over striving for consensus.

Notes

1. UN Document A/RES/S-10/2, July 13, 1978.

2. UNGA Res. 34/87B, December 11, 1979.

3. UN Document A/36/474, October 6, 1981.

4. *Report of the Disarmament Commission, General Assembly Official Records: Thirty-Eighth Session Supplement No. 42*, A/38/42 (New York: United Nations, 1983).

5. Hugo Palma, "Confidence-Building: Present Situation and Future Prospects," *Disarmament*, vol. 7, no. 3 (Autumn 1984), p. 120.

6. *Ibid.*, p. 123.

7. *Report of the Disarmament Commission, General Assembly Official Records: Thirty-Ninth Session Supplement No. 42,* A/39/42 (New York: United Nations, 1984).

8. Report of the Disarmament Commission, A/38/42.

9. Falk Bomsdorf, "The Confidence-Building Offensive in the United Nations," *Aussenpolitik,* vol. 33, no. 4 (1984), p. 383.

7
Soviet Views of CBMs

Bruce Allyn

When the Stockholm CDE began in January 1984, the discussions immediately and predictably became impaled on the horns of a long-standing policy dilemma: the two different, and apparently opposing, U.S. and Soviet approaches to building confidence in their relationship. When discussing CBMs, the Eastern countries have historically stressed the priority of arms limitation and improving the overall U.S.-Soviet relationship through broad, declaratory principles such as non-use of force. At the onset of the CDE, for example, then Soviet foreign minister Andrei A. Gromyko stated that the "greatest achievement" that could possibly result from the CDE would be the adoption of a pledge of non-use of force, including a no-first-use of nuclear weapons obligation. The United States and its NATO allies, however, aside from their concern over the latter policy's ramifications for flexible response, have tended to reject the utility of such unverifiable declarations promising certain future behavior, and have generally dismissed such Soviet proposals as redundant atmospherics. Moreover, U.S. approaches to CBMs increasingly assume that progress in enhancing crisis stability should not await progress in political relations—or even in negotiated arms reductions.

This chapter analyzes recent official Soviet statements on CBMs, as well as the views expressed in the writings of Soviet specialists in the Foreign Ministry and Academy of Sciences institutes devoted to the study of international relations. Although "CBM" is a term that has come to signify practically any measure designed to reduce the risk of nuclear war without reducing arms, this chapter focuses on CBMs that are particularly useful in crisis situations—including both the Helsinki Final Act-type measures designed to reduce the risk of surprise attack and miscalculation, as well as crisis management procedures which come into play during acute, escalatory situations. This study does not deal in detail with the military dimension of Soviet approaches to crisis management, which has been treated elsewhere.[1]

The Soviet Approach to CBMs

Although in the Soviet literature the term "CBMs" (*mery po ukrepleniu doveriia*) normally refers to the type of measures in the Helsinki Final Act, the notion of measures to strengthen "confidence" (*doverie*) is understood broadly, with the fact of strategic parity considered the fundamental ground for international confidence. For example, in the words of one Soviet specialist, "The approach to defining CBMs should not be narrowly technical, but widely political."[2] In Soviet statements, there is a standard distinction between CBMs of a "political-legal" and "military-technical" type, the former (*e.g.*, non-use of force declarations) claimed to have "the most direct relation to strengthening confidence among states."[3]

As already noted, the general Western approach to CBMs has been to consider CBMs in a somewhat narrow context and independent of arms control in the sense of, say, force reductions. In recent years, along with the general deterioration of East-West relations, the failure of arms control to meet public expectations has heightened Western interest in CBMs. If both sides, this approach suggests, do not take concrete—albeit small—steps to avoid accident, miscalculation, or unintended escalation in times of high tension and crisis, a major opportunity may be missed to ensure that nuclear weapons are never used. To take this point of view to its extreme, the *worse* the U.S.-Soviet political relationship, the *more* essential it is that mechanisms are at hand for bilateral communications and the like regarding military activities and incidents involving the risk of nuclear war. That the U.S.-Soviet agreement of July 1984 to upgrade the Hotline was signed at a low-point in superpower relations allegedly proves this point.

The official Soviet approach, however, is that there is a danger that agreement on "military-technical" measures will create the illusion of improved political relations and divert attention from the "real issues" of arms reduction and general strategic stability. In a recent publication on CBMs, a Soviet specialist observed: ". . . CBMs cannot substitute for measures immediately directed toward limitation and reduction of military potentials. An inaccurate understanding of CBMs as a replacement for measures in the area of disarmament not only would lead to an overevaluation of their positive potential, but it would create the danger of their application as a pretext for refusal to achieve genuine progress in the area of arms control and disarmament."[4]

This view has historically characterized the Soviet approach to CBMs. The Soviet approach to the 1955 U.S. "open skies" proposal, for example, was that aerial surveillance and exchange of military establishment blueprints should be permitted only when the last stages of general and complete disarmament were underway. Soviet stress on the priority of nuclear arms reduction, as well as the persistent claim that the West was primarily interested in espionage, hindered agreement on CBMs at the Geneva Surprise Attack Conference in 1958.[5]

Thus, while the Soviet approach consistently stresses the intrinsic value of CBMs, it has historically linked them to disarmament and to broader political goals. In recent years, the Soviet CBM approach has been linked tightly to Soviet foreign policy aims at the START and INF talks. The cool Soviet response to the U.S. statement in November 1982 directing its negotiators at START and INF to discuss three proposals to reduce the risk of miscalculation[6]—even though the Soviets praised the ideas in terms of their own merits—was allegedly because of "the way the White House put this question and the specific context."[7] The Soviet side clearly was according CBMs a subordinate role to their "peace offensive" against Pershing II and cruise missile deployment, as well as against appropriations for the MX ICBM. Furthermore, the Soviets were not wont to give the U.S. president a victory by agreeing to any measures before the U.S. election. The Soviet side delayed a year, until just a few weeks before the START talks ended, to agree to form a CBM working group.

The one recent example where the Soviet side delinked agreement on a CBM from other foreign policy goals appears to be the Hotline facsimile upgrade agreement. Yet rather than serving as proof that CBMs can be negotiated even in the worst political climate, the Hotline accord was, in the Soviet view, a purely symbolic action: the Soviets wanted the direct communications link to utilize state-of-the-art technology. The Soviets made every effort to downplay the political significance of the technical upgrading of the Hotline, stressing that it did not constitute a significant step toward more peaceful relations.[8] Although both Soviet civilian and military specialists have over time consistently stressed the intrinsic value of the Hotline,[9] Soviet specialists have, however, recently questioned the Hotline's actual effectiveness if political relations are characterized by suspicion and distrust.

In addition to the political linkages discussed above, the Soviet CBM approach is characterized by measures calling for operational constraints. The Soviet proposals for CBMs at START and at the CDE, for example, include such measures as aircraft carrier-free zones and safe havens for SSBNs.[10] These and other measures have called forth objections from the U.S. side about their utility and fairness.[11] Even though the Soviets would probably also have trouble with actual implementation of these constraints (apart from those that are clearly in their interest), they have taken the political offensive. "In brief," Gromyko noted in mid-1984 about the Soviet constraint proposals, "the Soviet Union favors the prevention of dangers and crisis situations, while the U.S., for its part, proposes merely exchanging information about them."[12] The standard Soviet explanation for Western resistance to Soviet proposals at the CDE to constrain the scale of military maneuvers is that continued intensification in the scale of NATO exercises is part of the strategy of "a clearly expressed rehearsal for unleashing and waging an aggressive war," with an additional danger lying in "the fact that the troops are deployed in such a way that it is hard to determine whether ordinary combat training is under way or whether preparations for real large-scale combat operations are being implemented."[13] Apart from the political element, however, Soviet constraint proposals may also suggest that the Soviets view crisis stability less as a function of particular weapon systems which are in themselves considered destabilizing, such as silo-based ICBMs, but more as a result of *how* and *where* weapons such as SSBNs and long-range cruise missiles are deployed in a crisis situation.[14]

A third area of difference concerns verification and the broader issue of transparency as a fundamental CBM objective. At the CDE, for example, the Soviets continue to express the characteristically Russian concern about "legalized espionage." Soviet objections to the NATO CSBM proposal are threefold. The first objection again rests on a linkage between CBMs calling for information exchange and the state of the overall political relationship. In a state of poor relations, Soviet CDE delegates assert, the Western policy goal of "transparency" (*prozrachnost'*) or "openness" (*otkrytost'*) "will provide the possibility of observing contemplatively and helplessly the intensive arms race" and enable "military staffs to choose targets with greater accuracy"[15] (equating information exchange with facilitating target acquisition). The second general Soviet objection is based on the principle of "equal security": because of enduring geographic facts and current geopolitics, the NATO approach (or, more precisely, the language of the CDE mandate) would put the Soviet Union at a disadvantage *vis-a-vis* the United States, whose territory would remain immune from "transparency." The third objection arises in the context of the tiresome polemics which have historically accompanied arms control negotiations, and which, on the Soviet side, takes the form of an objection that the West "tries to make acceptance of demands about verification [*proverka*] into preliminary conditions to work on any CBMs, independent of the concrete context. This introduces into the area of confidence-building the defective idea of the absolute priority of monitoring [*kontrol'*], verification and inspection [*inspektsiia*], which for decades have blocked forward movement to numerous agreements on limiting the arms race. Experience long ago refuted the Western concept 'first monitoring, then disarmament.' "[16]

From the Western side, however, the stumbling block appears as the persistent desire of the Soviet side to preserve military secrecy, despite CDE mandate language requiring the measures negotiated at the Stockholm Conference to be provided with adequate forms of verification. Given the openness of Western political systems, the Soviets have less to gain in information exchange than Western states, despite evidencing a greater degree of openness recently by their willingness to accept some form of on-site inspection in MBFR, a chemical weapons ban regime, and with regard to International Atomic Energy Agency inspection of civilian nuclear power plants. As already discussed in Chapter 1, the Soviet record of compliance with the Final Act CBMs indicates a continuing aversion to "transparency."

The Overall Political Relationship and CBMs

As noted above, the Soviet side has historically pursued a policy tightly linking CBMs to the larger state of U.S.-Soviet relations. Since the demise of detente, Soviet writings have been replete with metaphors to convey the notion that the superpowers cannot reach specific agreement on CBMs until agreement on a basic approach to the problem of strategic stability is "reestablished." To agree on concrete CBMs outside the framework of a broader political approach, Soviet CDE delegate Igor Andropov stated, would be "to erect a roof when the house still has no foundation on which to build."[17] One Soviet specialist suggested a similar analogy for the U.S.-Soviet negotiations on enhancing the Hotline and other steps (discussed in Chapter 2). U.S. overtures to consider measures beyond enhancement of the existing Hotline (for a joint military communications and embassy-capital link) met with no Soviet response because such efforts were like a real estate buyer trying to get agreement on the specific price of real estate which the owner had not yet agreed to sell. In short, the Soviet position is that Western CBM proposals are like efforts to provide answers without addressing a fundamental prior problem.

This fundamental problem, Soviets officially maintain, is how to reestablish agreement on the basic *principles* governing U.S.-Soviet relations, primarily the central strategic aspect. In the 1980s, Soviet writings have placed great stress on the assertion that the principles of the relationship of the early 1970s have now been rejected. Much has been written on Soviet perceptions of detente and the extreme importance they attached to the acknowledgment of strategic parity (which the Soviets are fond of referring to as a "material nonaggression pact")[18] and the framework of "equality" in U.S.-Soviet relations. This framework was embodied in statements of shared intentions in a system of declaratory agreements to which the Soviets repeatedly hearken back, and which contained pledges to prevent the emergence of situations threatening nuclear war and to consult if dangerous crises did arise: the 1972 Basic Principles Agreement pledging both sides to "attach major importance to preventing the development of situations capable of causing a dangerous exacerbation of their relations," and the 1973 Agreement on the Prevention of Nuclear War, which repeats this pledge and obliges both parties to engage in "consultations" if "at any time relations between the parties or other countries appear to involve the risk of nuclear conflict."[19] In addition, the framework of U.S.-Soviet relations included increased trade, cultural exchange, and public statements of mutual respect. It was in this context that Soviet officials and specialists began to mention with increasing frequency the problem of crisis prevention.[20] In 1973, before the Yom Kippur war damaged optimism about the Basic Principles and Prevention of Nuclear War agreements, Georgi Arbatov wrote that the further development of U.S.-Soviet relations required the prevention of new conflicts and crises and also "the creation of a mechanism that would make it possible to solve emerging problems through negotiations."[21] (If Arbatov's comments can be taken as reflecting serious official interest in a crisis prevention and management "mechanism," what did the Soviets have in mind?)

However, the current Soviet reticence to discuss measures beyond the Hotline, the Soviets maintain, is precisely because the "good relations" of the early 1970s have ceased to exist. What was feasible in 1973 is not yet ready for the agenda in the mid-1980s, even though Soviet analyses affirm, along with many Western accounts, that the risks of inadvertent war have increased with the deterioration of superpower relations. For example, Andropov's statement in December 1982 referring to the importance of CBMs would seem to imply Soviet support for CBMs to enhance crisis stability. In that statement, Andropov declared that "Given the swift action and power of contemporary arms, an atmosphere of mutual suspicion is especially dangerous. Even an absurd accident, an error, a technical fault, may have tragic consequences. It is important, therefore, to take fingers off the launching buttons, to put arms on a reliable safeguard."[22] However, agreement on the magnitude of the danger does not necessarily translate into agreement on policy recommendations.

Most recent Soviet writings, which again must be evaluated against the background of short term Soviet foreign policy aims, focus on the increasing danger of inadvertent war arising from advertent [U.S.] actions to deploy weapon systems regarded as destabilizing in the Soviet view. The 1984 Report of the Soviet Institute for Space Research, for example, concluded that a large, space-based BMD system would increase the danger of a preemptive strike and "the probability of making a wrong decision in a crisis situation."[23] Concerning the Pershing II, Marshal Kulikov charged that it "would make it practically impossible to prevent a conflict resulting from an error or technical fault."[24] Given Soviet concerns and foreign policy objectives regarding these systems, U.S. proposals for nuclear CBMs were not seriously entertained—the primary Soviet objective was to stop deployment, not to reduce the risk of a mistake once the weapons were in place.

Apart from the short-term objective of preventing U.S. weapons deployment, however, the Soviet reticence toward crisis management proposals also has deep ideological roots. Soviet ideology has historically stressed the negative aspect of the paradox of crisis control, *i.e.*, the fact that every safety measure reducing the risk of a catastrophic accident can be seen as a license to engage in reckless behavior. Numerous Soviet writings have been devoted to denouncing the "crisis diplomacy" of Western "imperialist" states, defining crisis management (*krizisnoe upravlenie*) as a means by which imperialist states provoke a crisis and manipulate the risk of war in order to attain unilateral foreign policy goals.[25] For this reason, Soviet commentators have suggested that the U.S. Senate proposal for "nuclear risk reduction centers" may be disingenuous. Such a center, some Soviets have suggested, could be used by the U.S. as a "safety valve" to enable it to apply force more flexibly on a global scale while lessening the nuclear risks involved.[26] In recent years, however, Soviet writings have begun to condone the use of the term "crisis management," defining it in the more positive, deescalatory sense of the term.[27] With the achievement of strategic parity in the 1970s, Soviets claim that the U.S. has been less ready to use nuclear alerts to impose its policy goals in a crisis.[28]

Despite the demise of the detente relationship, and the self-righteous Soviet denunciation of U.S. actions, there is an enduring Soviet elite perception that managing an increasingly dangerous and chaotic world can only be achieved by some sort of superpower collaboration. The Soviets perceive this as less likely now than in the early 1970s, but, nonetheless, it is still seen as desirable and natural.[29] This perception explains in part the current Soviet stress on the importance of reestablishing the overall U.S.-Soviet political relationship prior to considering concrete CBMs to enhance crisis stability.

The Role of Declaratory Principles

According to Soviet statements, a primary path to reestablish an overall framework for U.S.-Soviet relations, and thereby open the way for further consideration of concrete CBMs, is through the mutual adoption of declaratory principles. To understand the Soviet emphasis on statements of benign intent, it is useful to examine elements of Soviet domestic political culture. Many analysts have noted that Soviet Marxism, as an ideology of social transformation, contains "magical" elements, *i.e.*, elements that treat a desired condition as if it were already an accomplished fact.[30] Soviet slogans such as "The People and the Party are One" or "All Socialist States Coexist Peacefully Together" are patently false if taken as statements of empirical fact. Yet, their function is not to describe accurately the present, but rather to change the factual into the desirable (which in Marxist ideology happily coincides with the historically inevitable). In Soviet domestic politics, exhortative declarations are used constantly in an attempt to mobilize people toward fulfillment, say, of the latest five-year plan. Thus, Soviets are conditioned always to act within a larger context, within a declared ethical framework that promises a fundamental resolution of human conflict in the future.[31] Although in the contemporary Soviet Union these declarations are accompanied by a high degree of cynicism, they do significantly reflect the ways Soviets approach problem-solving and social-international change.

Several facts suggest that domestic political culture influences the Soviet approach to relations with other countries. In the 1977 "Brezhnev" Constitution, the Soviets incorporated the ten basic principles from the Helsinki Final Act. During the 1970s, the Soviets sought to institutionalize their relations with other countries through a system of mutually agreed statements of principles to govern relations. Every (published) Soviet international affairs analyst begins his article by referring to those principles and the latest Party statement, always emphasizing the "peace-loving" intentions of the Soviet state. Although to Westerners these statements of benign intent presented as fact seem pretentious and hypocritical, to the Soviets they function somewhat like the ten commandments: they provide an ethical framework intended to serve as a standard to evaluate proper behavior. These declarations can be accompanied by a deep realism that they may in fact not be borne out in reality, but such mutual affirmation of basic principles can, at times, assist in creating an atmosphere conducive to concrete problem-solving.

Hence, the Soviets now have placed renewed stress on the need for restoring confidence through declarations such as on the non-use of force. Such declarations, variations of which have been presented by the Soviet side for decades, are said to provide evidence of that elusive yet very popular Soviet notion of "political will."[32] But, Soviets argue, the declaration not to use nuclear weapons first is not just an empty pledge; it has concrete ramifications for crisis stability as well. Aside from the consequences of such a pledge for extended deterrence and

NATO alliance politics, such a commitment would, if honored, have implications for military doctrine and force structure. In addressing the danger of "the risk of the outbreak of war as a result of error, accident, miscalculation or misunderstanding," Soviet CDE delegate General Tatarnikov noted:

> . . . keeping nuclear forces in a first strike readiness requires constant tension. As a result of this dangerous mistakes in the evaluation of the military situation or the acceptance of false signals by notification systems, leading to tragic consequences, are possible . . . of course, the obligation not to be the first to use nuclear weapons would increase stability and lower the probability of such miscalculations or accidents.[33]

Regarding the alleged practical ramifications of no-first-use for Soviet military doctrine, then Defense Minister Ustinov commented that "In their preparation, the Armed Forces will not direct still more attention to the problem of preventing the escalation [*pererastanie*] of military conflict to the nuclear level."[34] As far as what specific measures are envisioned, one Soviet official elaborated the following: a more strict framework in training troops and staffs, in defining the composition of arms, and in the organization of even more strict monitoring to safeguard against the unsanctioned launch of a tactical or strategic weapon[35] (the Soviets appear to have adopted permissive action links, or PALs).[36]

Combining Political Declarations and Military-Technical CBMs

There have recently been indications that the Soviets may be loosening the tight linkage between CBMs and the overall political relationship and disarmament issues. Soviet statements and writings recently appear to be moving closer to the view that crisis stability requires not necessarily first—and certainly not only—broad political declarations like the 1972 Basic Principles agreement, non-use of force declarations, and the March 1984 Chernenko "norms of relations for the nuclear powers."[37] This may improve the prospects for agreement upon the military-technical measures favored by the West.

Currently, there still appears to be two broad schools of Soviet thought on the linkage question. The first adheres to a rather strict chronology of policy recommendations beginning with declarations to improve the political relationship and to reduce arms as a *prerequisite* to consideration of military-technical CBMs. According to a leading Soviet specialist: "The Soviet Union goes along with the provision of necessary information [pursuant to CBMs] to the degree that it is conditioned by the process of limiting arms. Agreements concerning the exchange of data on quantities of strategic arms were achieved within the framework of SALT. . . the scale of such exchange widens to the degree of this positive process [of limiting arms and improving political relations] and in close organic linkage [*uviaska*] with it."[38] The second school, however, appears to place less emphasis on this linkage. For instance, according to R. Timerbaev, Deputy Chief of the International Organizations Department in the Soviet foreign ministry: "It is not subject to doubt that the CBMs in the military field agreed upon by the participants in the [CSCE] facilitate an increase in stability and security in Europe, in spite of the fact that the general political climate began to change for the worse, the fault of the aggressive forces of imperialism in the end of the 70s and the beginning of the 80s."[39] And according to Yu. Rachmaninoff, General Counselor in the foreign ministry: "the preconditions have ripened for the widening of CBMs between states."[40]

With respect to the actual Soviet negotiating position at the CDE, the Soviets opened with statements that political declarations such as non-use of force should be "combined" with concrete military-technical CBMs. As one Soviet delegate stated: "the development of CBMs in the military field should, if not 'crown' the work of the Conference, at least take place side-by-side with the major steps of a military-political nature proposed by us. Without this, other measures would be of no significance."[41] Although the Soviets did not respond positively to President Reagan's June 1984 offer to discuss reaffirmation of the non-use of force principle in exchange for Soviet willingness to discuss militarily significant CSBMs, following the establishment in December 1984 of working groups at the CDE where both "political-legal" and "military-technical" measures would be discussed "on an equal footing and with equal intensity,"[42] the Soviets began to come forward with more detailed presentations of their own "military-technical" measures, *e.g.*, by specifying numerical thresholds for notification measures.

Conclusion

As noted, there are indications that the Soviets may be loosening the heretofore tight linkage between CBMs and the overall political relationship and questions of disarmament. Such a shift could provide a welcome relief to the arms control process, which has continued to bear the entire burden of improving superpower relations. If they are presented not as a substitute for arms reductions, but as potentially attainable complementary steps, CBMs might serve as an important entering wedge to improve the U.S.-Soviet relationship.

Several trends underlie the apparently growing Soviet receptivity to such an approach. Although public Soviet media continue to stress the danger of advertent war (because of U.S. weapons deployments), private discussions among Soviet specialists show growing concern about the problem of inadvertent war. A serious Soviet study of international conflict in the 1970s argued that "In our time [international] crises have become the main (if not the only) path by which the slip to global nuclear conflict could occur," and noted the danger of the "uncontrollable element" (*nekontroliruemyi element*) associated with third area conflicts, where a third party might create a dangerous crisis, drawing in the superpowers.[43] The shared U.S.-Soviet interest regarding such dangers is clear: the 1973 Agreement on the Prevention of Nuclear War had its origin, for example, according to Kissinger's memoirs, in a Soviet proposal to "prevent" actions taken by third countries that might lead to nuclear war,[44] and in 1985 the U.S.-Soviet Standing Consultative Commission (SCC) agreed on an understanding whereby both sides would consult via the Hotline in the event of a third-party nuclear incident. This shared interest, however, confronts political and institutional questions regarding the development of more ambitious mechanisms.

Among the most promising areas for progress in the CBM and crisis settlement areas, attention might be directed to further operationalizing the "urgent consultations" proposals advanced repeatedly by the Soviets in the CDE and elsewhere. Such a clause currently exists in the 1973 Agreement on the Prevention of Nuclear War, yet there has apparently been little discussion with the Soviets on how to operationalize this clause. Consideration should be given to proposals by several analysts to use the SCC as a model for U.S.-Soviet "risk reduction" efforts, or for a multilateral East-West crisis management body.[45] Looking toward the immediate future, the Soviet proposals for "urgent consultations" could serve as an important initial focal point for concrete development of such a mechanism.

Notes

1. See Douglas M. Hart, "Soviet Approaches to Crisis Management: The Military Dimension," *Survival*, vol. 26, no. 5 (September/October 1984), pp. 214–222.

2. V. K. Sobakin, *Ravnaia bezopasnost'* ("Equal Security") (Moscow: Izd. mezhdunarodnye otnosheniia, 1984), p. 222.

3. O. N. Bykov, *Mery doveria* ("Measures of Confidence") (Moscow: Izd. Nauka Publishing House, 1983), p. 57.

4. *Ibid.*, p. 63.

5. For a recent statement of the Soviet position, see R. Timerbaev, *Problemy kontrolia* ("The Problem of Verification") (Moscow: Izd. Nauka Publishing House, 1984), p. 65.

6. These included advance notification of all ballistic missile test launches exceeding 1800 km range, mutual exchange of data on strategic and intermediate-range nuclear forces, and advance notification of all major military exercises worldwide, including strategic exercises. See appendix A.

7. *Pravda*, November 25, 1982. The Soviets also expressed indignation over the U.S. CBM proposals on the grounds that the USSR had proposed at START "a more extensive" set of CBMs, including operational constraints, which they claimed the U.S. ignored. See also *Pravda* editorial, January 2, 1983, p. 4. There was, however, a U.S. press report claiming that Ambassador Dobrynin had responded privately in a positive manner to President Reagan's proposals. See Hedrick Smith, "Moscow Welcomes Reagan Proposals on Reducing Risks," *New York Times*, December 3, 1982, p. A1.

8. The *Pravda* article cited above rhetorically asks: "It would be useful to have more information on test launches of missiles, which is one thing the U.S. President proposes. However, the main thing is that no missiles be launched in combat. If 100 MX missiles are complemented by 10 telephones—red or blue—directly linking Moscow and Washington, will that make those missiles any less dangerous? This is a specific illustration of how an idea that is not bad in itself can be made meaningless." Likewise, commenting on President Reagan's May 8, 1985, proposal for a joint U.S.-Soviet military communications link (originally proposed on May 24, 1983), Georgi Arbatov stated: "We might welcome some of the steps the president mentioned in the context of a certain policy. But that is not the case. Even if you have 10 hot lines in a dangerous situation, it still would not be productive. It is the policy that is the problem." Jim Hoagland, "After Probing American-Soviet Relations Appear to Be Poor," *International Herald Tribune*, June 15–16, 1985, p. 2.

9. See for example Major General M. I. Cherendnichenko, "Military Strategy and Military Technology," *Voennaia mysl*, no. 4 (April 1972), p. 42, cited by Raymond Garthoff, "Soviet Views on the Interrelation of Diplomacy and Military Strategy," *Political Science Quarterly*, vol. 94, no. 3 (Fall 1979), p. 394.

10. See appendix A.

11. For example, the U.S. has objected to the idea of safe havens for fleet ballistic missile submarines on the grounds that it would be hard to monitor such zones to be sure that surface naval vessels or aircraft were not circumventing the ban on ASW activity, nor would there be controls on the navies of other countries. Moreover, such sanctuaries would probably be the last place SSBNs would be deployed in an alert, thus proving to be of little utility in crisis while interfering with international legal rights of overflight and navigation in peacetime.

12. A. A. Gromyko, "Report on the International Situation, *Pravda*, June 17, 1984, pp. 2–3.

13. *Krasnaya Zvezda*, September 23, 1984, p. 3 (commenting on *Autumn Forge-84*).

14. Hart, "Soviet Approaches to Crisis Management," pp. 220–221.

15. Tatarnikov, CDE plenary statement, March 8, 1984.

16. Bykov, *Mery doveria*, p. 62.

17. Igor Andropov, CDE plenary statement, February 7, 1984.

18. Henry Tromifenko, "America, Russia and the Third World," *Foreign Affairs*, vol. 59, no. 5 (Summer 1981), p. 1039.

19. See appendix A.

20. The primary reason given was the "new correlation of forces" which "objectively requires" international stability and normalization of relations between the two countries. The Soviets lauded the "realistic" tendencies of U.S. policy in the early 1970s, claiming that detente was a policy "forced" upon the U.S. because of its own internal destabilization and loss of its former position in world affairs. See Bruce Allyn, "The Soviet Approach to Crisis Prevention in Third Areas," working paper, Nuclear Negotiation Project, Harvard Law School, January 1984.

21. *Pravda*, July 22, 1983, cited by Coit Blacker in Alexander George, ed., *Managing U.S.-Soviet Rivalry* (Boulder, CO: Westview Press, 1983), p. 127.

22. *Pravda*, December 22, 1982.

23. "Strategic and International-Political Consequences of Creating a Space-Based Anti-missile System Using Directed Energy Weapons," (Moscow: Institute of Space Research, USSR Academy of Sciences, 1984), p. 30.

24. *New York Times*, October 14, 1983.

25. See for example V. Zhurkin and V. Kremeniuk, "Podkhod SShA k mezhdunarodnym krizisnym situatsiiam," *Sovremennaia vneshniaia politiki SShA*, vol. 1 (Moscow: Izd. Nauka, 1984), p. 371; and V. Kremeniuk, *SShA i konflikty v stranakh Azii v 70-akh g.* (Moscow: Izd. Nauka Publishing House, 1979).

26. Some Soviet commentators on the proposed crisis control center were quick to suggest that the idea, in its initial contemporary association with Senator Jackson, was primarily a way to divert attention from the "freeze" movement and to "tranquilize" the U.S. public in a time of rapid military build-up.

27. V. Gantman, ed., *Mezhdunarodnye konflikty sovremennosti* (Moscow: Izd. Nauka Publishing House, 1983), p. 62.

28. V. Zhurkin cited in David Holloway, *The Soviet Union and the Arms Race* (New Haven and London: Yale University Press, 1983), p. 50.

29. A great deal of Soviet literature stresses the key role of the two superpowers in crisis prevention and settlement. "The foreign policy of the great powers," many Soviet writings maintain, "objectively possesses the greatest potential in the area of influencing the process of de-escalation and peaceful settlement of international conflict." V. Gantman, ed., *Mezhdunarodnye konflikty sovremennosti*, p. 79. This is reminiscent of Gromyko's query at the 22nd Party Congress in 1962: if the two "giants" were "to unite in their efforts in the cause of peace, who would dare and who would be in a position to threaten that peace?" Despite the dubious ideological basis for joint superpower efforts, the Non-Proliferation Treaty (NPT) and the 1977 case of the Soviet Union informing the U.S. about an imminent nuclear test explosion in the Kalahari desert allegedly planned by South Africa stand as successful precedents. The Soviet interest in joint "imposition of peace" during the 1973 Middle East crisis was evidenced

by Brezhnev's letter to Nixon, albeit prompting U.S. escalation to DEFCON III. The Soviet interest in collaborating with the United States against third-party threats was evidenced concretely by its back-channel efforts in the early 1960s to enlist U.S. support in preventing China from acquiring nuclear weapons. Once China went nuclear, the Soviets began to be concerned about the role that China might play in provoking a nuclear crisis. This Soviet concern was a key motive in Soviet efforts in the early 1970s in the SALT talks to enlist U.S. support against third-country "provocations." See for example Gerard C. Smith, *Doubletalk: The Story of the First Strategic Arms Limitation Talks* (Garden City, N.Y.: Doubleday, 1980), pp. 93–138.

30. H. Marcuse, *Soviet Marxism* (New York: Columbia University Press, 1958), p. 87.

31. Historically, the Russians as a culture have always had a penchant for the theoretical; they have excelled in sciences such as mathematics and physics, which require only a blackboard and chalk. In the tradition of Dostoevsky and Tolstoi, the Russian national character is also characterized by a preoccupation with abstract philosophical questions about the meaning of life.

32. Soviets frequently argue, for example, that the "real" problem at the MBFR talks is not the data-base issue, which is a "superficial" factor. The "real" obstacle is the lack of political will to reach an agreement, which could easily be finalized by a meeting of foreign ministers if only the West would accept the Soviet proposal that the data issue simply be put aside.

33. Tatarnikov, CDE plenary statement, March 8, 1984.

34. *Pravda*, July 12, 1982.

35. See V. F. Petrovsky, *Sovetskaia kontspetsiia razoruzheniia* (Moscow: Izd. Nauka Publishing House, 1983), p. 46.

36. Stephen M. Meyer, "Soviets Perspectives on the Paths to Nuclear War," in Graham T. Allison, Albert Carnesale, and Joseph S. Nye, Jr., eds., *Hawks, Doves, and Owls: An Agenda for Avoiding Nuclear War* (New York: W. W. Norton, 1985), p. 191.

37. The six norms are: (1) to consider the prevention of nuclear war to be the principal goal of any power's foreign policy, not to allow situations fraught with the danger of nuclear conflict, and if such danger arises, to hold urgent consultations to prevent a nuclear conflagration; (2) to renounce the propaganda of all forms of nuclear war; (3) no first-use of nuclear weapons; (4) no use of nuclear weapons against nonnuclear states; (5) to prevent nuclear weapons proliferation; and (6) to eliminate all nuclear weapons on a step-by-step basis. *Pravda*, March 3, 1984.

38. Bykov, *Mery doveria*, p. 48. A cruder form is found in Vladimir Bogachev, "Pentagon Communications Proposals Will Not Restore Trust," Moscow TASS in English, April 13, 1984, in FBIS *Soviet Union*, April 14, 1983, p. AA2: "The Soviet Union holds that the main road to trust, to preventing any war, including a war capable of breaking out by accident, is the ending of the arms race and return to calm, correct relations between states, to detente."

39. R. Timerbaev, *Problemy kontrolia*, p. 66.

40. Yu. Bachmaninoff, "Evropa na otvetstvennom rubezhe," *Mirovaia eknomika i mezhdunarodnye otnosheniia*, No. 8 (1982), p. 11.

41. Igor Andropov, CDE plenary statement, February 7, 1984.

42. Oleg Grinevksy, CDE plenary statement, January 29, 1985.

43. V. V. Zhurkin and Ye. M. Primakov, *Mezhdunarodnye konflikty* (Moscow: Izd. mezhdunarodnye otnoshenie, 1972), pp. 19, 20.

44. Henry Kissinger, *Years of Upheaval* (Boston: Little, Brown, 1982), p. 275.

45. For a sketch of a multilateral crisis control body modeled on the SCC, see Theodore H. Winkler, *Arms Control and the Politics of European Security*, Adelphi paper no. 177 (London: International Institute for Strategic Studies, 1982), pp. 39–40.

PART 3

FUTURES

We have invented our way into unprecedental insecurity through technological innovation. We must invent our way out of it through political innovation. In that endeavor confidence-building measures are likely to prove indispensable tools.

Alton Frye, "Building Confidence Between Adversaries: An American's Perspective," Karl E. Birnbaum, ed., *Confidence-Building and East-West Relations* (Laxenburg, Austria: Austrian Institute for International Affairs, 1983), p. 44.

8

Beyond the Hotline: Controlling a Nuclear Crisis

William Langer Ury and Richard Smoke

On June 8, 1967, in the midst of a great Mideast war, Israeli planes and gunboats attacked a U.S. communications ship, the *Liberty*, off the coast of the Sinai Peninsula. Washington soon learned of the attack, but as President Johnson recalled, "For seventy tense minutes we had no idea who was responsible."[1] Both the U.S. and the USSR had sizable and vulnerable navies in the eastern Mediterranean. The Soviets' intentions were unclear. U.S. Secretary of Defense Robert NcNamara "thought the *Liberty* had been attacked by Soviet forces."[2]

Johnson ordered carrier planes to investigate, and sent Moscow a message on the Hotline that the United States was not about to intervene in the war. An hour later, when the Israelis discovered they had made a tragic mistake, their apology to Washington was also passed along on the Hotline. McNamara later remarked: "Thank goodness our carrier commanders did not launch immediately against the Soviet ships who were operating in the Mediterranean."[3]

The *Liberty* incident illustrates the dangers of unintended runaway escalation that may lurk in a superpower crisis. It also demonstrates the wisdom of establishing mechanisms, such as the Hotline, for effective crisis control. This chapter briefly sketches the kinds of events that could trigger unintended escalation as well as some of the decisionmaking factors that make subsequent escalation more likely. It then discusses

This chapter represents a synopsis of a Report to the U.S. Arms Control and Disarmament Agency published as *Beyond the Hotline: Controlling a Nuclear Crisis* (Cambridge, MA: Harvard Law School Nuclear Negotiation Project, 1984). A book authored by William Ury and presenting the Report's ideas to the general public was published as *Beyond the Hotline: How We Can Prevent the Crisis that Might Bring on a Nuclear War* (Boston: Houghton Mifflin, 1985).

measures for improving U.S.-Soviet decisionmaking in crisis, both those that exist and additional ones that might be valuable.

Paths To Unintended Nuclear War

Most experts agree that the most likely path to a nuclear war lies neither in a calculated launching of a general nuclear war independent of any crisis, nor in a deliberate Soviet invasion of Western Europe. Rather, the most likely path appears to lie through a nuclear crisis: an intense Soviet-American confrontation which, despite a desire on both sides to avoid war, would generate such tensions and threats that nuclear war could result.

The Cuban missile crisis of 1962 was one occasion when the superpowers appeared to come perilously close to nuclear war. During several other crises, including the Middle East wars of 1967 and 1973 and the Berlin crises of 1948 and 1961, the perceived possibility of a nuclear war rose noticeably.

Three generic triggers of a crisis that might lead to an unintended nuclear war may be usefully distinguished: regional conflicts, inadvertent encounters between deployed U.S. and Soviet forces, and "bizarre" nuclear detonations.

Regional Conflicts

On almost any day, several wars are being fought in the Third World. Others are on the verge of erupting. In many cases, the forces of the superpowers are not far off, in part because American and Soviet leaders hold the view that their countries' national interests extend over much of the world.

Although the scope of their perceived interests is not diminishing, the superpowers do not have as much influence as they once had in the Third World. Global economic, political, and military power is becoming more decentralized. In many regional conflicts, the superpowers are less able to sway their respective clients than they were a couple of decades ago. As their mastery wanes, their capacity to control escalation may wane also. Despite some quiet communication between the U.S. and USSR about restraining superpower involvement in regional conflicts, there continues to exist a worrisome danger of a severe superpower confrontation erupting out of some future conflict in the Third World.

The potential danger grows as nuclear weapons proliferate. Pakistan, India, Israel, and South Africa now have, or are close to having, nuclear weapons. Additional countries may be added to the list in the future.[4] The possibility of a serious nuclear threat, or event of a nuclear detonation, in a regional conflict will make the superpowers more cautious, but will correspondingly make a confrontation significantly more risky.

Inadvertent Encounters

U.S. and Soviet forces operate in close proximity not just in times and places of crisis such as the 1967 war in the Middle East but at all times, over much of the globe. Both navies patrol the same seas, and their planes constantly pass in the skies.

Dangerous incidents occasionally occur. In November 1969, for instance, the U.S. nuclear submarine *Gato* collided with a Soviet nuclear submarine at the entrance to the White Sea. According to a United Press International account of a secret Congressional report, the *Gato* prepared for action with nuclear torpedoes, but the Soviet crew was so confused about what had been hit that the Americans were able to steal away.[5]

More recently, in March 1984, a Soviet submarine collided with the American aircraft carrier *Kitty Hawk* in the Sea of Japan.[6] So far, no serious crisis has ensued from such an encounter. But suppose such an incident took place in a moment of great U.S.-Soviet tension?

A related kind of risk stems from the proximity, and routine interaction, of U.S. and Soviet strategic nuclear systems. When Soviet submarines approach the shores of the United States, for instance, computerized warning and command systems do not just ring bells; they automatically cause actions to be taken that the equally automatic warning systems on the Soviet side can observe. The Soviet warning system may order similar military actions automatically, which of course are noticed and may be responded to immediately by the U.S. system. In a time of crisis, when forces are on alert, this back-and-forth process could ratchet upward.[7]

Safeguards exist, of course, but some danger remains and in fact tends to grow over time as the systems become more tightly coupled and the flight times of missiles become shorter.[8]

Bizarre Detonations

Proliferation dangers are creating one kind of "bizarre" possibility. Terrorist experts take seriously the risk of nuclear blackmail, in which a terrorist group (perhaps acting for, or with the backing of, a "pro-terrorist" nation such as Colonel Khaddafi's Libya) threatens to blow up a major city unless demands are met for some immediate political outcome and/or a large sum of money. Terrorists might also be interested in a nuclear threat or nuclear use to demonstrate overwhelmingly the importance of their cause, or to carry out terrible vengeance against a nation which they perceive as having flouted or hindered their cause. In such cases, it is far from certain that the event would trigger a superpower confrontation, but also far from certain that it would not.

Deliberately causing such a superpower confrontation would be the object of *agent provocateur* attacks, also called "disguised third-party attack." It is possible that an "irresponsible" nation or terrorist group might wish to try to trigger a U.S.-Soviet war, perhaps by the use of one or more nuclear weapons, from a belief that their own nation or group would be in a relatively better position in a post-World War III world.

Such an attack, which to have any hope of success would need to be executed in the midst of a severe East-West crisis, may seem fantastic. But *agent provocateur* attacks have succeeded before. During World War II, for instance, the German air force bombed the Hungarian city of Kassa with Russian bombs in order to make the Hungarians think they were being attacked by the Soviets. The ruse was successful: the Hungarians examined the bomb fragments, discovered them to be of Russian manufacture, and declared war on the Soviet Union.[9]

Yet another possible source of bizarre detonations are accidental or unauthorized launches. The object of considerable preventive effort by both superpowers, an accidental or unauthorized launch of one or more nuclear weapons nevertheless remains a possibility.[10]

A Deadly Combination

The escalation of regional conflicts, inadvertent encounters between U.S. and Soviet systems, and bizarre detonations are three broad types of potential risks. Within these categories one can devise countless scenarios that could conceivably lead to an intense superpower confrontation, and perhaps to a nuclear war. Any particular path to unintended nuclear war may be extremely unlikely, but if all the potential paths are added up, the cumulative risk is impossible to ignore.

Perhaps the most worrisome danger is the possibility of several events occurring at about the same time, interacting to produce effects none of them could by itself. A coincidence of unexpected events and accidents occurring during a moment of high U.S.-Soviet tension could produce consequences almost impossible to foresee, and perhaps a fast-moving train of U.S. and Soviet escalations.[11]

In his book *The Command and Control of Nuclear Forces*, Paul Bracken describes one such instance that took place in 1956, just at the time that the Hungarians were revolting, the British and French were trying to take the Suez canal back from Egypt, and the Soviets were threatening to destroy London and Paris with nuclear missiles:

The headquarters of the U.S. military command in Europe received a flash message that unidentified jet aircraft were flying over Turkey and that the Turkish air force had gone on alert in response. There were additional reports of 100 Soviet MiG-15s over Syria and further reports that a British Canberra bomber had been shot down also over Syria. (In the mid-1950s only the Soviet MiGs had the ability to shoot down the high-flying Canberras.) Finally, there were reports that a Russian fleet was moving through the Dardanelles. . . . The White House reaction to these events is not fully known, but reportedly General Andrew Goodpaster was afraid that the events "might trigger off all the NATO operations plan." At this time, the NATO operations plan called for all-out nuclear strikes on the Soviet Union.

As it turned out, the "jets" over Turkey were actually a flock of swans picked up on radar and incorrectly identified, and the 100 Soviet MiGs over Syria were really a much smaller routine escort returning the president of Syria from a state visit to Moscow. The British Canberra bomber was downed by mechanical difficulty, and the Soviet fleet was engaging in long-scheduled exercises.[12]

If this coincidence had been suggested as a "scenario," it would have been dismissed by many analysts as too improbable to take seriously. Yet it actually occurred. This is not to suggest that such perilous interactions are likely, but simply that we cannot fully predict future events.

Unless counter-trends that make the world safer develop, these hazards of regional conflicts, inadvertent encounters between U.S. and Soviet forces, and bizarre detonations may create, alone or in combination, a growing danger of nuclear crises occurring and of the actual use of nuclear weapons in the coming decades. Unless improved measures can be created for forestalling and controlling confrontation between the superpowers, this global trend, combined with continuing superpower rivalry, may mean a growing risk of unintended nuclear war.

Decisionmaking in Crises

Decisionmaking in moments of high crisis appears to be qualitatively different from the normal flow of governmental decisionmaking. A number of ways have been offered for conceptualizing the "warp," or diminished rationality, that prevails during crisis decisionmaking.[13] One somewhat simplified scheme emphasizes four main factors at work in the minds of decisionmakers: there is little *time* for making crucial decisions; the *stakes* are high; critical information is often lacking, leading to dangerous *uncertainty*; and few usable *options* are available. Let us consider briefly each of these elements.

Little Time

However grave the issues at stake, an event is usually not thought of as a crisis if plenty of time is available. Little available time is a fundamental aspect of crises. The 1973 Middle East war became an acute superpower crisis, for instance, when the Israelis encircled the Egyptian Third Army and threatened to capture it imminently, which would have been a grave humiliation for Egypt and her Soviet patrons.[14]

In the Cuban missile crisis, President Kennedy sought to move the naval blockade from eight hundred miles to five hundred miles away from Cuba, precisely to give Premier Khrushchev more time to think, to develop a response with his advisors, and to negotiate.[15]

High Stakes

From the Western point of view, the Berlin crises of 1958 and 1961 were critical not so much because half a city might be lost but because it was feared that the German alliance would unravel and, with it, NATO.[16] If the stakes are not high, decisionmakers may see themselves as "putting out fires" but not as dealing with a genuine crisis. An international, and especially a nuclear, crisis is distinguished from the normal flow of decisionmaking (which often includes short deadlines and a feeling of urgency) by expectations of severe losses—in other words, high stakes.

The stakes in a crisis can rise in two ways. Either the magnitude of the potential loss or the probability of that loss (or both) can increase. An example of the former is the ongoing Vietnam crisis of late 1965 and early 1966. After tens of thousands of U.S. troops had been committed, the stakes were much higher for Washington than they had been earlier. Examples of the latter are the Berlin crises of 1958 and 1961, during which what was at stake—the Western presence in Berlin, and possibly the West German membership in NATO—remained essentially the same throughout, but, as the crises intensified, the perceived probability of the threat to those stakes rose.

High Uncertainty

Decisionmakers often report that one major feature of the crisis experience is a sense of great uncertainty. Not enough clear information is available, and they feel that they are groping in a fog.

Three kinds of uncertainty in a crisis can be distinguished. The simplest is a lack of critical information about what is going on. To what degree are the opponent's forces mobilized? Where are they deployed? What exactly is occurring? Factual data generally are incomplete.

Almost always there is great uncertainty about the opponent's intentions. During the 1973 Middle East war, U.S. intelligence discovered that the Soviets were shipping nuclear material through the Bosporus. Did this mean that the USSR was about to introduce nuclear weapons into the war? Or threaten to do so? (There was a lack of simple factual information too: were these weapons, nuclear waste, reactor fuel rods, or what?)[17]

Closely related to uncertainty about the opponent's intentions is great uncertainty about the likely escalation sequences that could result from the current situation. In the Cuban missile crisis the ExCom worried that Khrushchev might suddenly move against Berlin or take other drastic action.[18] The Western responses to such moves were uncertain as were, of course, the Soviet counter-responses, and so on.

Few Usable Options

In a crisis, decisionmakers perceive there to be fewer usable policy options available than in normal times, and the ones available are likely to be more extreme. Generally, the more intense the sense of crisis, the more this will be so. In the first two days of the Cuban missile crisis, the only two options seriously examined were to do nothing beyond a diplomatic response, or to carry out an air strike on Cuba, which carried a distinct possibility of escalation toward war.[19] In a crisis, the options often come, as it were, "sliced thick," compared to normal times when more and more differential or "fine-tuned" options are often available or can be developed.

It should be mentioned that in many crises, a considerable number of options *are* actually available. But decisionmakers *perceive* themselves as having few usable choices. Many things could be done, but very few of them meet the demanding criteria of simultaneously defending and furthering national interests, and limiting the risk of severe escalation to follow.

The Intensification of Crises

The four factors of little time, high stakes, high uncertainty, and few usable options all combine to create among decisionmakers a felt need to act. Decisionmakers may or may not be consciously aware of all four factors during an actual crisis, but they certainly will be consciously aware of a pressure to act. Indeed, this feeling of need to act—"to do something"—may be extremely strong.

As a crisis intensifies, decisionmakers typically sense that all of these factors are becoming more serious. The press of time becomes more noticeable. The stakes may be rising. As actions of ambiguous import are taken, the uncertainties may also rise. As a crisis mounts, decisionmakers often have the sense that they are rapidly approaching the point where they will have only a few and extreme options left. This sense of constricting possibilities is one of the psychologically distinctive features of the crisis experience.[20] In the various Berlin crises, Western decisionmakers sometimes found themselves only a couple of steps away from the point where they would have to order major military action, which might well have provoked a European war. At points in the 1973 Middle East crisis, U.S. officials felt they were only a few steps from an intense East-West confrontation.[21]

Crisis Control as an Approach

Various kinds of policies can affect the risks that nuclear crises may create. Four are especially worth distinguishing. First, *force structure* and *force deployments* can contribute to make crises either more or less risky. Configuring both sides' arms to maximize "crisis stability" is one of the classical objectives of arms control. Second, *military doctrine* and *grand strategy* can affect crisis risk for similar reasons. An obvious example is doctrine for the initial use of nuclear weapons. Third, aspects of *overall foreign policy* also contribute to making crises more or less likely and more or less dangerous. Obviously, greater aggressiveness will make crises more probable and more hazardous. But the superpowers' general perceptions of each other are also important—for example, whether each perceives the other as interested in forestalling and/or quickly resolving severe confrontations, or as more likely to try to exploit them. Finally, a nuclear crisis can become more or less probable and dangerous as a result of the *design of decisionmaking processes*. The adequacy of communications, negotiations, internal decisionmaking processes, and prior consultation with the other side may make a considerable difference should a crisis occur.

This chapter focuses on the fourth approach, which commonly goes under the names of "crisis management" or "crisis control." The challenge of nuclear crisis control is to shape U.S.-Soviet decisionmaking during and immediately preceding crises so as to reduce the risk of nuclear war while at the same time preserving other vital national interests.

Steps Taken Toward Crisis Control

Recognition of the dangers of runaway escalation and of the difficulties of decisionmaking in crises have led Washington and Moscow to undertake some measures already to help control crises. The best known is the Hotline, formally termed the Direct Communications Link, which was created in 1963 in the wake of the Cuban missile crisis. During that crisis, the two sides were compelled to improvise awkward and roundabout ways for President Kennedy and Premier Khrushchev to communicate, such as passing notes through a news reporter. The Hotline was created to allow direct, prompt, and confidential communication at the head of state level.[22] Since then, additional steps, discussed previously in this book, have been taken: the 1971 Hotline satellite link upgrade; the 1971 Accidents Agreement; the 1972 Prevention of Nuclear War Agreement; the 1975 Helsinki Final Act; the 1984 Hotline facsimile upgrade; and the 1985 Accidents Agreement understanding whereby the U.S. and the USSR would consult immediately on the Hotline in case of an unauthorized or third-party nuclear detonation.[23] A number of other CBMs have also been proposed, as discussed elsewhere in this book.

Growth in American Interest

The first half of the 1980s witnessed a considerable growth in interest in ways to build on these existing agreements. In part this interest was inspired by a realization among some U.S. Senators and experts of the potentially increasing dangers of a nuclear crisis. In part it may have been a response to the intense and widespread popular concern at the time with preventing nuclear war, and the dissatisfaction felt by many with traditional arms control.

In 1981, Senator Sam Nunn asked the Strategic Air Command (SAC) to study how the United States could identify accurately a nuclear attack from a third party that was disguised as Soviet in origin, and some related questions. SAC reported that dramatic improvements in nuclear crisis control were needed on the part of both superpowers.[24]

In 1982, Senators Nunn and Jackson, later joined by Senator Warner, proposed that the U.S. and the USSR jointly create a "military crisis control center."[25] Such a center, perhaps located in a neutral country, would be staffed by personnel from both nations and would monitor the nuclear weapons of third parties and terrorist groups. (More recently, opinion has favored twin crisis control centers in Washington and Moscow, linked by teleconferencing.)

In September of that year, the Senate, at the initiative of Senators Jackson and Nunn, added an amendment to the FY1983 DoD Authorization Act, directing the Department of Defense to conduct a study of initiatives for improving controls on the use of nuclear weapons, especially during crises.

Secretary of Defense Weinberger responded with a DoD Report on April 11, 1983.[26] As discussed in the first two chapters, the report made several positive proposals: to the Hotline should be added a high-speed facsimile capability but not voice or video (this was the proposal subsequently accepted by the Soviets and adopted in July 1984); a high-speed data link should be added from each national capital to the embassy in the opposite capital; and a Joint Military Communications Link would connect the two national military command centers with a high-speed facsimile transmission capability. This link, said the report, could be used for crisis communications not requiring the attention of the head of state, for transmitting urgent technical and military information in a crisis, for communicating in a terrorist incident, and for some non-crisis functions.

In the spring of 1984 Senators Nunn, Warner, and Bradley introduced a Senate Resolution commending the Administration for the steps it had taken, and urging that negotiations be opened toward making "risk reduction centers" the next step. On June 15 of that year, Senate Resolution 329 passed 82–0.

Three months later, in a speech at the United Nations, President Reagan proposed institutionalizing regular cabinet-level meetings as well as "periodic consultations at policy level about regional problems. . . to help avoid miscalculation [and] reduce the potential risk of U.S.-Soviet confrontation.[27]

On May 8, 1985, in a speech to the European Parliament in Strasbourg, President Reagan proposed instituting "regular, high-level contacts between Soviet and American military leaders to develop better understanding and to prevent potential tragedies from occurring." He went on to re-propose a "permanent military-to-military communications link . . . to reduce the chances of misunderstanding and misinterpretation." "Over time," the President continued, "it might evolve into a 'risk-reduction' mechanism for rapid communication and exchange of data in time of crisis."[28] Government officials later clarified that this "risk-reduction mechanism" was "along the lines specified by Senators Nunn, Warner, and others."[29] In August 1985, the Reagan administration made the centers, in a limited form, an official policy goal.

Soviet Views

The Soviet Union has shown ambivalence about crisis control. At various times, the Soviets have expressed skepticism about U.S. motives in advancing it as a subject for negotiations. In Soviet eyes, Washington may want to create a distraction from the issue of limiting nuclear weapons, which divides the USSR and the United States so deeply.

Moscow has suspected Washington of wanting a visible success on the crisis control front as a way of diverting world public opinion from the current American weapons build-up, which the Soviets believe world public opinion opposes. A *Pravda* article commenting on President Reagan's Berlin speech of November 1982 on reducing the risk of miscalculations asked rhetorically: "If a hundred MX missiles are complemented by ten telephones—red or blue—directly linking Moscow and Washington, will that make those missiles any less dangerous?"[30]

The Soviets also express some skepticism about the substance of crisis control. They question whether a center, for instance, could be misused to make it easier for one side to escalate a low-level crisis. They suggest that the superpowers already have some crisis control procedures in the form of the Hotline and the 1971 and 1973 agreements; they are not yet convinced that more are needed. And they point out that mere technical improvements cannot make up for a hostile and dangerous overall relationship between the two superpowers.

At the same time, the Soviets acknowledge that the superpowers share a true common interest in controlling crises. The Soviets have long been concerned about accidental war, including the possibility that another nation might deliberately draw the superpowers into a mutually annihilating nuclear war. The Soviets say that further crisis control should be built on the foundation of existing agreements, such as the 1971 Accidents Agreement and the 1973 Prevention of Nuclear War Agreement.[31] On March 2, 1984, then Secretary Chernenko made a speech, little noticed in the West at the time, calling for emphasizing the importance of principles in preventing nuclear crises, and even "making them mandatory." Among the principles he proposed were: "not to allow situations fraught with the danger of nuclear conflict"; and "if such a danger arises, to hold urgent consultations to prevent a nuclear conflagration."[32] Although these principles are not new, the fact that Chernenko chose to repeat them in a major address suggested that awareness of the need for crisis control was growing in Moscow too.

At a conference on international security held in Atlanta, Georgia, in April 1985, Ambassador Anatoli Dobrynin signed a joint statement with former Presidents Ford and Carter that urged the United States and the Soviet Union to "address with the utmost priority the question of establishing mechanisms aimed at crisis prevention and crisis management in order to avoid misunderstanding and/or miscalculations that could lead to conflict. Frequent and regular meetings of senior political and military leaders would be desirable."[33]

A further sign of mutual U.S.-Soviet interest in crisis control in addition to the Hotline upgrade came in March 1985 in response to the shooting of a U.S. major in East Germany. Secretary of State George

Shultz met with Soviet Ambassador Dobrynin and agreed to meetings between the U.S. and the Soviet military commanders in Germany in order to discuss how to prevent future incidents.[34] In addition, during a meeting in September of that year with Senators Nunn and Warner in Moscow, General Secretary Mikhail Gorbachev stated that the idea of nuclear risk reduction centers "demands attention."

Risks of Crisis Control

Crisis control contains a basic paradox. The very information and procedures that leaders should have during a crisis in order to control and end it are often the same things that, if available before the crisis, might lead to overconfidence. Having crisis control machinery could conceivably cause leaders to relax in crisis, or even to take risks they would not take without the machinery.

A more concrete danger of many possible measures lies in the vulnerability to misuse. Unless adequate safeguards are adopted, joint centers, for instance, could be used for gathering intelligence or for sending false information at a critical time. Moreover, unless allies and friends are carefully consulted, U.S.-Soviet crisis control measures could be misinterpreted as collusion by the superpowers to dominate the world.

Beyond the Hotline

In September 1982, the U.S. Arms Control and Disarmament Agency asked the Nuclear Negotiation Project at Harvard Law School to suggest a few measures for strengthening the current crisis control machinery. Below are five measures our report recommended for consideration and further study.[35] They are sketched out here not as a final blueprint but rather as ideas designed to stimulate discussion and to elicit criticism and improvements. Although each one has its own specific merits (and risks), what matters most is the overall approach for systematically preventing and defusing dangerous crises.

Crisis Control Centers in Washington and Moscow

If a nuclear bomb suddenly were to detonate in San Francisco, U.S. suspicions would naturally fasten on the Soviet Union. But the weapon might have been exploded by a third nation, a terrorist group, or through a Soviet accident. In such cases, U.S. leaders would want proof and the Soviets would surely want to cooperate. No one would want to go to war over a mistaken assumption.

The Hotline—even the "enhanced" one—might be inadequate for the delicate tasks of interpreting and authenticating information. It might be valuable to the leaders of both countries in such a situation to have on call a group of highly trained military and diplomatic experts from both sides who already knew each other and had prepared together for just such a crisis. Hence, the usefulness of U.S.-Soviet crisis control centers in Washington and Moscow, connected by instant video communication and staffed with American and Soviet specialists. This is the basic concept advocated by the U.S. Senate (see Senator Nunn's chapter) and referred to in President Reagan's speech on May 8, 1985.

In advance of a crisis, this joint professional working group could anticipate potential crisis triggers and develop technical procedures for handling them. The center's officers, moreover, might serve as a support staff to ongoing Cabinet-level talks with the USSR on crisis prevention and control, thus helping to ensure the center's relevance to policy-makers' concerns and increasing the likelihood of its expertise being tapped in time of crisis.

Unless handled with considerable care, a crisis control center could present certain problems, including disinformation at critical moments, intelligence leaks, added bureaucracy, and foreign perceptions of U.S.-Soviet condominium. The center therefore might best be implemented in increments, perhaps beginning with a bilateral standing commission. The commission at first might have a narrow mandate, derived from the Accidents Agreement to develop measures to prevent and control crises arising inadvertently, such as from accidents, a nuclear war in the Third World, or nuclear terrorism.

II. Crisis Procedures

Agreed-upon crisis procedures such as the Hotline and the Incidents at Sea Agreement make it technically possible both to head off potential crises and to cope more effectively with any that do occur. Such essentially non-political procedures are in both sides' interest and could and should function even in times of tension.

Successful crisis procedures created to date provide a basis for developing additional ones. To prevent crises, the U.S. might consider proposing further "incidents agreements" for accidental ground and air intrusions (like that of Korean Airlines Flight 007); and limited but regular consultations on the possibility of nuclear terrorism. The meetings between the U.S. and Soviet generals held in the wake of the shooting of Major Nicholson in March 1985 might be regularized and expanded to pro-active (rather than reactive) study of potential incidents in central Europe.

To contain crises, the superpowers could adopt such measures as procedures for coping with nuclear detonations whose source and motive are unclear; procedures to signal peaceful intent in time of heightened expectation of war; prearranged procedures to facilitate face-to-face negotiations in times of crisis; and enlargement of the existing crisis codes for instant and accurate Hotline communication. For halting inadvertently triggered hostilities, the U.S. might consider a discussion of contingency procedures for a cease-fire and return to *status quo ante*, as well as an East-West communications channel for the supreme commanders in Europe.

In particular, Washington and Moscow (or any two potential adversaries) might agree in advance on a crisis consultation period in the event certain specified contingencies occur. In the case of the superpowers, an unlikely but exceedingly dangerous possibility is the single nuclear detonation on either's territory, the purpose, and perhaps even the origin, of which is not immediately clear. Agreements currently in force require the superpowers to "notify" each other if such an event is imminent, and to "consult" over any imminent risk of war. A feasible next step is to define a period during which no hostile action will be taken, assuming only one or a small number of detonations occur.[36] Although such a period would be unenforceable, top leaders on both sides would have strong incentives to observe it, and even to seize upon it as a means of preventing otherwise uncontrollable escalation.

The essential value of these agreed-upon crisis procedures lies in making sure that when the leaders of each side want to avoid or defuse a crisis, they will not fail for simple lack of the machinery to do so.

Regular Cabinet-Level Talks on Preventing Nuclear War

None of the agreed-upon procedures and institutions can come into being without negotiation between high-level policymakers on each side. Agreement, if it comes, is likely to be in incremental steps. Moreover, as new potential dangers arise, new measures will be required. All this suggests the need not for one-shot negotiations, but for ongoing regular talks. As noted above, President Reagan proposed similar Cabinet-level discussions in his speech to the United Nations in September 1984.

Some agreements, because of their delicacy and susceptibility to misinterpretation by others, would remain necessarily informal. Indeed, useful discussion would likely revolve not just around possible agreements, but around basic assumptions and the intentions of each side, so as to reduce the chance of miscalculation and misunderstanding.

Because of the informal nature of these exchanges, they might best take place between those who would later be centrally involved in the crisis decisionmaking process, such as the U.S. secretaries of state and defense and their Soviet counterparts. Should a crisis occur, officials already would have a working relationship with their opposite numbers, a wish frequently expressed by U.S. participants in past crises.

Such talks carry, of course, a certain risk of misunderstandings and false confidence. While this calls for considerable caution in the talks, it almost certainly does not outweigh their potential benefits.

Briefing the President

While the president receives some preparation for fighting a war and using nuclear weapons, apparently little preparation is given him for defusing a nuclear crisis safely and successfully. Yet decisions in a nuclear crisis would likely be the most important decisions a president would ever make. Controlling such a crisis, moreover, is like launching a mission to the moon: an extremely complex system must work perfectly the first time.

A given president will likely make real "hands-on" crisis decisions only once, if ever; no practice is possible. But it is possible to transfer to a new president and a new staff the accumulated wisdom and experience of past nuclear crises in the form of an intensive briefing over several days. Participants in those past crises, most of whom are still alive, could discuss the lessons they learned, assisted by experts in military affairs, history, and international relations. The president and staff members might also observe or participate in one or more simulations of an emerging crisis to explore the difficulties of keeping a crisis under control. Such a briefing might usefully take place in the pre-inaugural period.

Enhanced Roles for Third Parties
in Defusing Regional Conflicts

Perhaps the most likely source of superpower confrontation is a regional crisis in the Third World which draws in the superpowers. Regional mediation before the U.S. and USSR become directly involved may be the most effective means of forestalling escalation. While there is a long history of third-party efforts, their effectiveness could be enhanced.

Potential third parties include regional organizations like the OAU or OAS, neutral countries, or the U.N. One of the most successful efforts in recent years was the British mediation of the Zimbabwe-Rhodesia conflict, which threatened to escalate into an East-West crisis.[37]

An international mediation service (or a network of regional mediation services) could be created with senior, globally respected figures who could help mediate conflicts before they become superpower crises. A "rapid deployment peacekeeping force" might also be constituted; made up of soldiers from many countries, it would have the ability to arrive quickly in a trouble spot to separate antagonists before fighting begins or is renewed. Greater use should also be made of regional congresses, which can bring together adversarial and mediating nations and groups in search of a resolution, or at least a containment, of a local crisis.

A Stabilization Strategy

The foregoing measures are intended to help head off, or escape from, crisis situations that have arisen at least partly inadvertently. But what if the other side has deliberately initiated the crisis to make a unilateral gain? How can one defuse a dangerous crisis while protecting vital national interests?

One possible approach, which may be labelled a "stabilization strategy," involves two elements: blocking or freezing offensive military action so as to deny the other side any gains by arms, and simultaneously initiating immediate negotiations to protect both sides' essential security and other interests. Blocking military action can gain time for decisionmaking and reduce the perceived stakes; negotiation can reduce dangerous uncertainty and expand the options available for a peaceful resolution. These steps usually require preparatory measures, which ideally would head off crises even before they start.

Khrushchev's sending missiles to Cuba in October 1962 offers a good example of a crisis that began in a bid for unilateral gain. Kennedy's response offers an illustration of a stabilization strategy. His skillful combination of military blocking action—the naval quarantine around Cuba—and high-level personal communication and negotiation succeeded in defusing the crisis while protecting vital national interests.

In some instances it may be possible to block the other side without counter-escalating in a way that threatens its security. Land mines and tank barriers along borders, the interposition of third forces, and other defensive techniques might reduce the risk to one's own vital national interests without increasing the risk to those on the other side. Developing additional techniques of this kind is a promising area for military research and development.

Towards a Crisis Control System

The centers, crisis procedures, Cabinet-level talks, presidential briefing, and enhanced third party roles, together with the Hotline and other existing crisis control measures, could add up to a "crisis control system."

Crisis control deserves attention in its own right for several reasons. First, it deals with what is perhaps the most likely path to nuclear war. More than any other approach, nuclear crisis control focuses on the flaws in crisis decisionmaking which can create a runaway crisis. Deterrence and traditional arms control presume rational actors on both sides; crisis control deals with the irrational, non-rational, and fallible aspects of people and organizations.

Indeed, effective crisis control can sometimes make the difference between peace and war. If the Cuban missile crisis, for instance, had ended in a war, historians would have had little trouble explaining why.[38]

Moreover, significant improvements in the methods and institutional arrangements of crisis control may be possible. Real progress may be more feasible than on many arms control issues where the superpowers' interests clash in negotiations, or in areas of foreign policy and doctrine where one or both superpowers may be primarily concerned with the danger of aggressive, hostile behavior by the other. Crisis control does not appear to evoke the same fears of military inferiority as traditional arms control often does.

Finally, crisis control offers the advantage of relatively unexplored territory. Among national security specialists interested in arms control, the bulk of the attention to date has gone to limiting and reducing quantities and types of nuclear weapons. Far less attention, by comparison, has gone to the complementary approach of focusing on controlling and halting the kinds of crises that could trigger actual war. If it is true, however, that nuclear war is most likely to occur as the result of escalation from a crisis involving the superpowers, preventing and controlling such crises is central to the effort of avoiding nuclear war.

Notes

1. Lyndon Baines Johnson, *The Vantage Point: Perspectives of the Presidency* (New York: Holt, Rinehart & Winston, 1971), p. 300.

2. "Sect. Rusk and Sect. of Defense McNamara Discuss Vietnam and Korea on 'Meet the Press,' " *Department of State Bulletin*, vol. 83, no. 1496 (February 26, 1968), p. 271.

3. *Ibid.*

4. Steve Weissman, *The Islamic Bomb* (New York: Times Books, 1981), p. 64.

5. United Press International report published in the *Indianapolis Star*, February 16, 1976.

6. "US, Soviet Vessels Collide Off Korea," *Boston Globe*, March 22, 1984, p. 1.

7. Paul Bracken, *The Command and Control of Nuclear Forces* (New Haven and London: Yale University Press, 1983), pp. 59–65.

8. *Ibid.*

9. Leo Szilard, *The Voice of the Dolphins and Other Stories* (New York: Simon & Schuster, 1941), p. 49n.

10. Bracken, *Command and Control*, p. 53.

11. *Ibid.*

12. *Ibid.*, p. 66.

13. Thomas Schelling, *A Strategy of Conflict* (Cambridge, MA: Harvard University Press, 1960), p. 21.

14. Scott Sagan, "Lessons of the Yom Kippur Alert," *Foreign Policy*, no. 36 (Fall 1979), p. 168.

15. Robert F. Kennedy, *Thirteen Days: A Memoir of the Cuban Missile Crisis* (New York: W. W. Norton, 1971), p. 71.

16. Alexander George and Richard Smoke, *Deterrence in American Foreign Policy: Theory and Practice* (New York: Columbia University Press, 1974), p. 400.

17. Barry M. Blechman, "The Political Utility of Nuclear Weapons," *International Security*, vol. 7, no. 1 (Summer 1982), p. 137.

18. The description of escalation presented in this chapter is not intended as a full analysis of how escalation occurs in crisis or war. It is, however, a simplified description sufficient for these purposes. For an in-depth analysis of escalation processes, see Richard Smoke, *War: Controlling Escalation* (Cambridge, MA: Harvard University Press, 1977).

19. Schelling, *A Strategy of Conflict*, p. 21.

20. *Ibid.*

21. Blechman, "The Political Utility of Nuclear Weapons," p. 137.

22. Richard N. Lebow, *Between Peace and War: The Nature of International Crisis* (Baltimore: Johns Hopkins University Press, 1981), p. 3.

23. U.S. Arms Control and Disarmament Agency, *Arms Control and Disarmament Agreements: Texts and Histories of Negotiations* (Washington, D.C.: GPO, 1980), p. 112.

24. *Congressional Record of the 97th Congress*, vol. 128, no. 46 (Monday, April 26, 1982), p. S3963.

25. *Ibid.*

26. *Report to the Congress by Secretary of Defense Caspar W. Weinberger on Direct Communications Links and Other Measures to Enhance Stability*, April 11, 1983 (Washington, D.C.: Department of Defense, 1983).

27. "Transcript of Reagan's Address to the U.N. General Assembly," *New York Times*, September 25, 1984, p. A10.

28. "Excerpts From Reagan's Address to the European Parliament," *New York Times*, May 9, 1985, p. A22.

29. "The President's Address to the European Parliament," *Fact Sheet* (Washington, D.C.: Office of the Press Secretary, The White House, May 8, 1985).

30. *Pravda*, November 25, 1982.

31. These observations are drawn from an active unofficial exchange between Harvard's Kennedy School of Government and the Soviet Academy of Sciences on the subject of crisis prevention and settlement.

32. Chernenko, quoted in the *Current Digest of the Soviet Press*, vol. 36, no. 9 (March 28, 1984).

33. "The 14 Recommendations Coming Out of Carter Center Consultation," *Atlanta Constitution*, April 21, 1985.

34. "U.S.-Soviet Talks Called to Discuss Killing of Major," *New York Times*, March 31, 1985, p. A1.

35. *Beyond the Hotline: Controlling a Nuclear Crisis* (Cambridge, MA: Harvard Law School Negotiation Project, 1984).

36. Robert S. McNamara, "No Second Use—Until," *New York Times*, February 2, 1983, p. A19.

37. Larry C. Napper, "The African Terrain and U.S.-Soviet Conflict," in Alexander George, ed., *Managing U.S.-Soviet Rivalry* (Boulder, CO: Westview Press, 1983), p. 169.

38. Lebow, *Between Peace and War*, p. 3.

9

CBMs for Stabilizing the Strategic Nuclear Competition

Michael H. Mobbs

On the eve of the Strategic Arms Reduction Talks (START),[1] while public attention focused chiefly on various proposals to reduce the number of nuclear arms, President Ronald Reagan also stressed the interest of the United States in undertaking new measures with the Soviet Union to reduce the possibility of nuclear conflict through accident, misunderstanding, or miscalculation. During an address in Berlin on June 11, 1982, and again at the United Nations Special Session on Disarmament on June 17, 1982, the President identified three potential measures to enhance mutual confidence and to improve communication between the United States and the Soviet Union: the advance notification of strategic ballistic missile launches, the advance notification of major military exercises, and an expanded exchange of information on strategic nuclear forces.[2]

On November 22, 1982, President Reagan advanced these proposals in a letter to the Soviet leadership and instructed U.S. negotiators at the START talks to present them to the Soviet delegation.[3] In turn, the Soviet Union published a number of proposals in *Pravda* on January 2, 1983, that it had tabled at the START talks. These were the advance notification of a "mass" take-off of heavy bombers and "forward-based" aircraft, a ban on the operation of heavy bombers and aircraft carriers of one country in agreed zones adjoining the territory of the other, and the establishment of zones in which any antisubmarine warfare activities by one country against missile-carrying submarines of the other would be banned.[4]

The views expressed herein are those of the author, and are not necessarily shared by the Department of Defense or any other department or agency of the U.S. Government.

Thus, as in the past, potential measures to enhance the stability of the strategic relationship by reducing the possibility of error or misjudgment became the focus of some attention in negotiations to constrain strategic arms, even though such measures would not directly affect the size, structure, or capability of strategic forces. The United States and the Soviet Union seemed to agree that in START the parties should address CBMs going beyond the limited provisions of previous agreements. It appeared that, at least with respect to prior notification of certain military activities, the proposals of each country were sufficiently similar to permit a negotiated resolution of differences.

In fact, it did not prove possible at the START talks to achieve significant progress toward agreement on new CBMs. While the United States consistently advocated a prompt separate accord upon as many CBMs as the parties could agree, the Soviet Union just as consistently opposed a separate or rapid accord on CBMs but insisted that any agreed CBMs would have to be a part of whatever broader agreement on the reduction of strategic forces the parties might ultimately reach. The Soviet Union also placed greatest emphasis on those proposals, such as constraints on the operational zones of certain military forces, where the parties' positions diverged most and where the prospect for agreement was least.

Given the political and diplomatic setting of the START talks, it was not surprising that the United States and the Soviet Union took such differing stances on the negotiation of CBMs. For the Soviet Union, the larger objective throughout the period of the START talks (June 29, 1982-December 8, 1983) was to prevent the deployment of U.S. intermediate-range nuclear forces (INF). The NATO alliance had decided in 1979 that those forces must be deployed in response to the deployment of Soviet SS-20 ballistic missiles, unless U.S.-Soviet negotiations could render U.S. deployment unnecessary. For the United States, the central objectives were to achieve such progress toward substantial reductions of strategic nuclear forces as might prove possible, to limit deployments of U.S. and Soviet INF to the lowest possible equal global limit, and to preserve a consensus within NATO both on U.S. negotiating positions respecting offensive nuclear force reductions and on the necessity of U.S. INF deployments should negotiations not succeed.

In START, therefore, the Soviet Union tailored its proposals and negotiating strategies to further its fundamental goal of preventing U.S. INF deployments. The Soviet proposal in START to reduce total strategic nuclear delivery vehicles,[5] for example, was expressly conditioned on U.S. acceptance of the central Soviet demand in the INF talks, that is, no U.S. INF deployments. Thus, even a perception of progress on CBMs, or any other issue in START, would have contradicted the Soviet position that no agreement in START was possible so long as the United States insisted on preserving a right of INF deployments responsive to Soviet INF deployments.

Nonetheless, the exchanges on CBMs in START helped to illuminate U.S. and Soviet views on the potential role of CBMs in the strategic relationship as well as to lay the foundation for additional discussion in later negotiations. While the future course of U.S.-Soviet arms control remains uncertain, it seems likely that CBMs will continue to be on the agenda of strategic arms negotiations. Therefore, the positions of each country at START merit closer scrutiny.

The U.S. Approach

The U.S. CBM proposals in START proceeded from the premise that there is inherent value in agreed measures to enhance each country's confidence in its judgments respecting the strategic military capabilities and activities of the other. Not only may such measures reduce ambiguities at times surrounding certain military activities such as large exercises, but they may also provide insight into each country's military capabilities that assists the other's assessment of the balance of strategic forces. If consistently applied and observed in good faith, such measures over time could conceivably help to avoid unnecessary competition by reducing each country's incentive to undertake new strategic programs out of uncertainty or potential misjudgment about the strategic capabilities of the other. It could also be argued that, at substantially reduced force levels,[6] each country would need an even greater degree of confidence in its assessment of the balance of strategic capabilities than required at higher force levels. An acceptable margin of error for a given military capability might become less and less acceptable as that capability was reduced. U.S. CBM proposals in START reflected such considerations.

Notification of Ballistic Missile Launches

Some experts have observed that the consistently high readiness of modern ICBM forces in itself reduces the potential for misunderstanding ICBM operations, since ICBMs "are unambiguously ready for war."[7] In part for this very reason, however, the testing of ballistic missiles can be a source of concern. No matter how rapid early warning systems may be, they nevertheless require a finite time to determine the trajectory and intended impact point of an ICBM or an SLBM, and to determine whether a single or multiple launch has occurred. Since the total flight time of an ICBM is only about thirty minutes (and potentially much less for an SLBM depending on its launch point), any initial uncertainty is potentially dangerous, particularly during a period of tension. An unannounced launch is more likely than an announced one to raise questions about the intent of the launching country and to serve as a means of threat or intimidation.

At the same time, the utility of prior notification is subject to debate. Notification could be used as a deceptive cover for limited attacks, perhaps adding a few moments of hesitation before the operators of early warning systems issued an alarm. Some observers have argued that notification in general, if it consistently lessened the fear of attack, would even encourage attack by contributing to strategic deception: "the aggressor would simply use notification as a smokescreen to confuse the victim, then attack."[8]

In fact, current early warning systems and operational procedures would almost certainly issue the alarm within a matter of minutes in case of an actual attack, whether or not prior notice of launch had been given. On the other hand, failure to give required notice of a launch undoubtedly would provoke an even higher state of alert as soon as the launch was detected. On balance, it seems that prior notification may complicate the possibility of a surprise attack and reduce the utility of ballistic missile test launches as geopolitical gestures.[9]

These considerations assume additional significance from the U.S. viewpoint in light of the Soviet practices of conducting multiple test launches and test launches from operational silos (the United States does not test from operational silos). It has been reported, for example, that a 1982 test of SS-11s, SS-20s, SLBMs, and anti-ballistic missiles could have been mistaken for an attack.[10]

Previous U.S.-Soviet agreements contain limited requirements for the advance notification of ballistic missile launches. The 1971 Accidents Measures Agreement requires each party to notify the other in advance of any planned missile launches that will extend beyond its national territory in the direction of the other party.[11] This provision is of questionable utility, however, inasmuch as neither country conducts test launches in the direction of the other party. The 1972 Incidents at Sea Agreement requires each party to give advance notification to mariners (NOTAMs) of "actions on the high seas which represent a danger to navigation or to aircraft in flight," and each country issues NOTAMs whenever it deems SLBM test launches to fall within this requirement. NOTAMs, however, merely announce closure areas in specified ocean areas for a stated length of time; they do not identify the nature or time of the event requiring the closure, and there is no requirement under this or any other agreement for the United States and the Soviet Union to give one another advance notice of SLBM launches as such.

Article XVI of the unratified SALT II treaty would have required each country to give advance notification of all ICBM test launches, except single launches not planned to extend beyond its national territory. The great majority of Soviet ICBM test launches, however, are single launches confined to Soviet territory and thus would fall within the exception. On the other hand, all U.S. ICBM test launches extend over international waters and would fall within the SALT II notification requirement.

In order to remedy the deficiencies of these previous provisions, the United States proposed at START that each country give the other notice of all ICBM and SLBM test launches not later than a specified period in advance of the test, regardless of whether such launches were single or multiple, whether the missile flight path was confined to or extended beyond national territory, or whether the missile impact point was on land or at sea. The notification would also include certain additional information designed to enhance confidence. As proposed, the U.S. measure in practice would affect the United States and the Soviet Union equally, in contrast to previously agreed notification measures.

Notification of Major Military Exercises

Prior notification of military exercises has long been regarded as a useful CBM. The Helsinki Final Act adopted by the Conference on Security and Cooperation in Europe in 1975, for example, contains a number of provisions concerning the prior notification of military exercises, such as the obligation of parties to give 21 days notice of exercises involving over 25,000 troops. There is currently no provision, however, specifically designed to require notification of exercises involving strategic or other nuclear forces.

Prior notification of military exercises, or a requirement for it, obviously would not stop an aggressor bent on attack, but it could serve to mitigate the potentially coercive aspects of military movements short of attack. Moreover, while preparations for attack could be disguised as military exercises (whether declared or not), a threatened country that discovered a military movement of which required notice had not been given might attempt to take more effective steps to deter or defend against an attack than it would take if no notice were required.

Such considerations could become highly relevant in the setting of a divided Europe, where the Soviet Union more than once has resorted to the threat and use of military action for geopolitical objectives. Furthermore, in a severe crisis military activities might provide a more accurate insight into Warsaw Pact intentions than diplomatic moves, given the Soviet emphasis on *maskirovka*, or deception.[12]

In order to introduce a notification regime for nuclear force exercises, the United States proposed at START that each country give notice a specified period in advance of its participation in any "major military exercise" involving the nuclear forces of concern, that is, an exercise comprising one or more of the following:

- the take-off, within a specified span of time, of more than a specified number of certain strategic aircraft of each country;
- the dispersal, within a specified span of time, of the ballistic-missile submarines of a naval fleet of either country; or
- an exercise involving but not limited to the launch by either country of one or more ICBMs, SLBMs, or longer-range INF ballistic missiles.

Under the U.S. proposal, the notification would include such information as the designation and general purpose of the exercise, the type and strength of the party's forces involved, and the location and duration of the exercise. Each country would also have the right to raise questions and seek additional information on any exercise that had been notified or that, in its opinion, might require notification.

Exchange of Data on Strategic Forces

The exchange of data on forces limited by an agreement serves a useful and necessary function by establishing an agreed baseline from which force reductions or other obligations under the agreement will be performed. In this respect, such a data exchange is frequently and properly regarded as an important aid to verification of compliance. The SALT II treaty, for example, contained a data base on the numbers of strategic offensive arms within broad categories, such as ICBM launchers, SLBM launchers, and launchers of MIRVed missiles.

In a broader sense, however, the exchange of data can enhance each party's confidence not only in its ability to verify the terms of an agreement once concluded, but also to evaluate the wisdom and acceptability of proposed force constraints even during the course of negotiating an agreement. Moreover, CBMs, just as direct constraints on the size and capability of forces, should be effectively verifiable in order not to create new sources of doubt, uncertainty, or controversy over whether a party is complying with the CBMs in question. To the extent such CBMs implicate the testing, exercise, or operation of forces, an exchange of data on those forces can help to avoid such problems.

At START the United States proposed, as a CBM, an expanded exchange of data on strategic forces. Such an exchange would go well beyond SALT II's limited numerical summaries of forces within broad categories and could include numerous other categories of information such as: the numbers of deployed and nondeployed missiles broken down by specific types of systems (*e.g.*, Minuteman IIIs and SS-18s); the number of stages and number of warheads on each type of missile; the launch-weight and throw-weight of each type of missile, etc. Such an exchange of data, during the course of a negotiation on force reductions, could facilitate the negotiation by helping the parties to evaluate the effect that proposed constraints would have on actual force capabilities of each party. If the information a party received at times differed from its own assessment of the facts, that party could seek clarification from the other party or at least internally reexamine its own assessments in light of the other's representations. Such a process in itself could produce useful insights into the merits or demerits of proposed force constraints.

In advancing these various proposals, the United States took the view that an accord on new CBMs need not await final resolution of all issues under discussion at START. Rather, the parties should seek to come to terms on as many CBMs as possible, as early as possible, and implement them in a separate accord. Toward that end, the United States in the fall of 1982 proposed to create a special joint working group on CBMs under the auspices of the overall U.S. and Soviet delegations to START. The United States also proposed that the parties give first priority to those proposals of each country that appeared to converge to some extent with the proposals of the other, in order to facilitate progress where agreement seemed most likely.

The Soviet Approach

As discussed more fully in Chapter 7, the Soviets have historically resisted the Western emphasis on concrete, well defined, at times technical CBMs that could be adopted independently of progress on arms controls. Instead, the Soviets have emphasized general declaratory principles as well as operational constraints on military activities, while typically subordinating CBMs to arms limitations. The Soviets seem to ascribe to CBMs a political, even symbolic utility that overshadows practical or technical considerations, as the Soviet attitude toward the verification of CBMs reveals:

> One of the theories advanced in the West in connection with the development of measures of confidence is the position on the necessity of verifying them. Such a presentation of the question contradicts the logic of the measures adopted. Confidence should beget confidence. Instead it is proposed to subject to verification the very measures of confidence, in other words, to call into question the sincerity of the sides' intentions to strengthen mutual confidence.[13]

Soviet positions at START were consistent with such attitudes. For example, the Soviets claimed that U.S. concerns over the verifiability of certain Soviet CBM proposals were unfounded and reflected a U.S. intent to block progress. They dismissed U.S. proposals to exchange data on strategic forces as premature and of no value in building confidence.

Similarly, the Soviets refused for almost a year to establish a CBM working group, even though the Soviet Union had already tabled its own CBM proposals when the United States first proposed such a group. The Soviets' stated rationale for this position was that to set up a working group would create "an illusion of progress" where, they argued, none existed. The Soviet motive most likely was to prevent any development that would give Western publics, particularly in Europe, any ground for hope that progress was possible in START while INF remained unresolved.

Even after the CBM working group was established in the fall of 1983, the Soviet Union continued to insist that any agreed CBMs must be a part of whatever ultimate agreement on the limitation and reduction of strategic arms might be reached and consistently placed greatest emphasis on "active" measures that, they argued, would impose "real" limits on military activities. These, of course, were the Soviet proposals to create exclusionary zones for certain aircraft and aircraft carriers operating in international airspace and waters, and to establish ocean areas where activities to detect and track submarines would be banned— proposals where U.S. and Soviet positions had the least in common.

Notification of Ballistic Missile Launches and "Mass" Take-Offs of Aircraft. Although the Soviet Union proposed to require advance notification of ballistic missile launches, its proposal exempted single ICBM test launches not planned to extend beyond national territory—*i.e.*, the great majority of Soviet ICBM test launches. Nor did the Soviet proposal require any notification of SLBM test launches. In short, the Soviet proposal would have carried forward the notification provision of SALT II (Article XVI) unchanged and would not have addressed the deficiencies of earlier provisions that the analogous U.S. proposal was designed to remedy. The Soviet proposal for advance notification of the "mass" take-off of heavy bombers and "forward-based" aircraft remained somewhat vague throughout START, although the underlying concept seemed similar to the U.S. proposal to give prior notice of the take-off of a specified number of certain aircraft within a certain time span. Unlike the United States, however, the Soviet Union did not during START specify precisely under what conditions its proposed notification requirement would be triggered. Since the term "mass take-off" was not defined, it is difficult to judge to what extent the two countries were addressing similar concerns.

Ban on the Operations of Heavy Bombers and Aircraft Carriers in Agreed Zones Adjoining the Territory of Either Country. Demilitarized areas and buffer zones have long been employed in international relations as attempted measures to limit military activities, with mixed results. For example, under the Rush-Bagot Treaty the Great Lakes have remained demilitarized since 1817. On the other hand, the Montreux Convention of 1936 prohibits transit of aircraft carriers through the Turkish Straits, yet Soviet Kiev-class warships, which are aircraft carriers in all but name, have transitted since 1976.[14]

The rationale of the exclusionary zones that the Soviets proposed in START appeared to be that the operations of heavy bombers and aircraft carriers are a source of such serious concern and tension that such operations by either country anywhere in the world within weapons range of the other country should be banned. In fact, such exclusionary zones would severely impair freedom of navigation on and over the high seas—a freedom recognized by international law—and in practice would burden the United States more than the Soviet Union, given the global nature of U.S. interests and responsibilities.

The United States has alliance responsibilities that are carried out by air, land, and naval forces with multiple missions not limited to strategic nuclear roles. U.S. aircraft carriers and their aircraft, for instance, are first and foremost conventional forces designed to fulfill tactical and regional functions, including U.S. commitments to the defense of its allies. Exclusionary zones such as the Soviets proposed would prohibit U.S. heavy bombers (B-52s and B-1Bs) and aircraft carriers from the Eurasian land mass and water contiguous to it, while allowing the presence of similar Soviet forces. Thus, the United States in effect would be cut off from many of its allies and from regions vital to its security, while the Soviet Union would not be similarly constrained. The confidence-building value of such a result is difficult to discern.

Antisubmarine Warfare-Free Zones. Under this concept, the United States and the Soviet Union would delineate certain large areas of the oceans in which missile-carrying submarines would be free from antisubmarine (ASW) activities, *i.e.*, exercises or operations aimed at detecting and tracking submarines. Some of these zones would be assigned to one country, and some to the other. Each country would be barred from conducting ASW activities inside the zones of the other. Neither country's military forces capable of conducting ASW activities, as distinguished from the activities themselves, would be excluded from the zones of the other. The ostensible purpose of creating such zones would be to guarantee the survivability of a retaliatory capability at sea, thus eliminating any possibility of a first strike with impunity.

As a practical matter, however, strategic ballistic missile submarines are already virtually invulnerable, since neither country today can, through ASW, threaten the submarine force of the other with a disarming strike. The weight of informed opinion suggests that the development of such a capability in the future is highly remote at best.[15] The more both countries learn about the phenomenology of the oceans, the more insurmountable seem the difficulties of simultaneously locating and successfully attacking a large portion, much less all, of an adversary's submarine force.[16] The increased ranges of modern SLBMs also enhance the capability of submarines to operate safely and effectively throughout the oceans, including home waters.

Moreover, the creation of ASW-free zones as the Soviets proposed could entail serious practical difficulties, the effect of which would be to undermine confidence rather than improve it. For instance, all naval combatants have some type of submarine detection capability for self-defense. Prohibitions on the use of such equipment would seriously impair their ability to conduct routine, wholly legitimate defensive tactics.

In addition, the difficulty of verifying an ASW ban would be enormous and probably intractable. It would be necessary to monitor every combatant of one country within the zones of the other to determine whether or not it was conducting ASW. Indeed, to monitor whether submarines were conducting ASW within the zones would to some extent require the very conduct of ASW that was to be prohibited.[17]

Many noncombatants also have the capability to conduct submarine detection activities. Monitoring the vast array of combatants and noncombatants operating in or through these huge zones, which would perhaps total several million square miles, would seem a practical impossibility. Since countries not party to the agreement could freely conduct ASW within the zones, a party would also need to be able to distinguish the ASW activities of the other party from those of third countries. Uncertainties about whether both parties were strictly observing the agreement would be inevitable.

Prospects and Conclusions

The experience at START again demonstrated that the negotiation of CBMs at times can be as difficult as the negotiation of direct constraints on military forces. While both the United States and the Soviet Union obviously share an interest in reducing the possibility of war by accident or miscalculation, such a possibility is not merely the product of misunderstanding or poor communications between the countries. The possibility of conflict through accident or miscalculation may also spring from more fundamental causes such as the disparate political systems, force structures and capabilities, military doctrines, and geopolitical behavior and objectives of the two countries. CBMs that could effectively reduce the risk of miscalculation flowing from such basic differences would need somehow to narrow the differences themselves and would almost certainly be regarded by one country or the other as an infringement on its fundamental interests. Moreover, a country is likely to grant genuine additional security to a potential adversary only at a high cost that the adversary may be unwilling to pay. These are some of the reasons why mutually acceptable measures to reduce the risk of conflict between the United States and the Soviet Union have been few and often insignificant. Where fundamental interests of nations are perceived to be at stake, CBMs are unlikely to be effective.[18]

Indeed, some would question the soundness of the belief that there exists a significant risk of unintended conflict, in the sense of conflict accidentally arising through a misunderstanding of the other party's actions. Generally, nations have gone to war only as a last resort when they perceived no other means of achieving vital objectives or protecting fundamental interests. In such cases, the initiation of war was not unintentional, even though the outcome of it may have been:

> The idea of "unintentional war" and "accidental war" seems misleading. The sudden vogue for these concepts in the nuclear age reflects not only a justifiable nervousness about war but also the backward state of knowledge about the causes of war. One may suggest that what was so often unintentional about war was not the decision to fight but the outcome of the fighting. A war was often longer and more costly than each warring nation had intended. Above all, most wars were likely to end in the defeat of at least one nation which had expected victory. On the eve of each war at least one of the nations miscalculated its bargaining power. In that sense, every war comes from a misunderstanding. And in that sense every war is an accident.[19]

Even when governments advocate the easing of tension in the abstract, such is not always their most immediate objective. On occasion the competing interests of countries may lead each of them to conflicting assessments on the value of relaxed tension. For example, throughout 1982 and 1983 the Soviet Union sought to convince Western European governments and publics that a deployment of U.S. INF systems in response to Soviet SS-20s would torpedo any hope for arms control negotiations and would produce a severe East-West crisis. During this period, as noted above, any significant relaxation of tension, through perceived progress in arms control or otherwise, would have undercut the immediate Soviet objective of preventing U.S. deployments.

Nevertheless, CBMs will probably continue to play a significant and perhaps enhanced role in the U.S.-Soviet relationship as the negotiation of verifiable and militarily significant arms control measures inevitably becomes more complex and protracted. Measures that substantially reduce the size and military capabilities of strategic forces, such as the United States proposed at START, are by definition more contentious than previous measures that, in general, did not constrain then existing force capabilities but only their potential for growth. In addition, technological advances facilitating the deployment of smaller, mobile nuclear weapon systems are a stabilizing factor insofar as they reduce the vulnerability of nuclear forces to a potential first strike, but on the other hand such developments enormously complicate the elaboration of verifiable arms controls. The increased level of Soviet telemetry encryption in recent years also calls into serious question whether it will be possible to verify constraints on the capabilities of nuclear weapon systems in the future.[20]

At the same time, nuclear arms control and related issues will probably continue to be widely regarded as the touchstone of U.S.-Soviet relations. In such an environment, the United States and the Soviet Union may find it increasingly in their interest to address CBMs that mitigate mutual concerns, such as those raised in START, and that therefore bear some prospect for agreement. In this context, CBMs need not be merely a surrogate for constraints on nuclear forces but may, as suggested above, actually facilitate the negotiation of such constraints as well as help to avoid unnecessary competition in the strategic relationship.

Notes

1. The Strategic Arms Reduction Talks between the United States and the Soviet Union began in Geneva on June 29, 1982, and continued until December 8, 1983, when the Soviet Union refused to set a date for a further round of talks. The Soviets' stated reason for this refusal was that the commencement in November 1983 of U.S. intermediate-range nuclear force deployments in Western Europe required the Soviets to reassess their positions at START. The Soviets had also broken off the Negotiations on Intermediate-range Nuclear Forces (INF) with the beginning of U.S. deployments. For approximately the next 15 months, the Soviet Union declined to resume any negotiation with the United States on either strategic forces or INF. At a meeting between U.S. Secretary of State George Shultz and Soviet Foreign Minister Andrei Gromyko in January 1985, the two countries agreed to commence new negotiations on strategic offensive nuclear arms, INF, and defense and space weapons. Accordingly, the Negotiations on Nuclear and Space Arms began in Geneva on March 12, 1985.

2. "Remarks to the People of Berlin," June 11, 1982, and "Remarks in New York City Before the United Nations General Assembly Special Session Devoted to Disarmament," June 17, 1982, *Public Papers of the Presidents of the United States: Ronald Reagan*, vol. 1, 1982 (Washington, D.C.: U.S. GPO, 1983), pp. 765–768, 784–789. Hereinafter cited as *Reagan Presidential Papers*.

3. "Address to the Nation on Strategic Arms Reduction and Nuclear Deterrence," November 22, 1982, *Reagan Presidential Papers*, vol. 2, 1982, pp. 1505–1510. In the INF negotiations the United States also tabled similar proposals for the exchange of data on INF forces and prenotification of INF ballistic missile launches.

4. "The U.S.S.R. and the U.S.A.: Two Approaches to the Strategic Arms Limitation and Reduction Talks," *Pravda*, January 2, 1983, p. 4; see also "U.S. and Soviets Seek to Prevent Surprise Attack," *New York Times*, December 8, 1983, p. A6.

5. In START the Soviet Union proposed to reduce strategic nuclear delivery vehicles (ICBMs, SLBMs, and heavy bombers) to an aggregate number of 1,800 for each country. This number was twenty percent less than the aggregate number of strategic nuclear delivery vehicles (2,250) that the unratified SALT II treaty would have permitted. The Soviet START proposal stipulated that such a reduction would be made only if the United States agreed not to proceed with deployments of Pershing II and ground-launched cruise missiles in Europe. The Soviet Union also proposed in START to reduce the total number of each country's "nuclear charges" (*yadernye zaryady*), a term by which the Soviets meant all nuclear weapons of whatever description on all strategic delivery vehicles. The Soviets consistently declined, however, to specify the level of nuclear charges to be allowed under their proposal.

6. The United States proposed in START to reduce ballistic missile warheads, including ICBM and SLBM warheads, to 5,000 for each country—a reduction of about one-third from each side's current level. In addition, the United States initially proposed to reduce the total number of ICBMs and SLBMs to 850 for each country—a reduction of about one-half from the current U.S. level. The United States later offered to raise the proposed 850 limit, taking into account Soviet opposition to it as well as the Scowcroft Commission's (see note 15 below) recommendations favoring an evolution to small, single-warhead ICBMs. The United States also proposed a substantial reduction in ballistic missile throw-weight and a limit on heavy bombers of 400 for each country.

7. Alan J. Vick and James A. Thomson, *The Military Significance of Restrictions on Strategic Nuclear Force Operations* (Santa Monica, CA: RAND, 1984), p. 10.

8. *Ibid.*, p. 29.

9. Ronald F. Lehman, unpublished manuscript of a chapter on cooperative measures, scheduled to appear in a forthcoming law school case book on law and national security being published under the auspices of the Center for Law and National Security at the University of Virginia School of Law, Charlottesville, Virginia. Ambassador Lehman is the Deputy Negotiator on Strategic Nuclear Arms in the U.S. Delegation to the Negotiations on Nuclear and Space Arms. His manuscript cited here is an excellent historical and theoretical analysis of

confidence-building and other cooperative measures. The author gratefully acknowledges the valuable assistance of that analysis in the preparation of this chapter.

10. "Soviets' Integrated Test of Weapons," *Aviation Week and Space Technology* (June 28, 1982), pp. 20–21, cited in Vick and Thomson, *Military Significance of Restrictions*, p. 10.

11. See note 9.

12. Douglas M. Hart, "Soviet Approaches to Crisis Management: The Military Dimension," *Survival*, vol. 26, no. 5 (September/October 1984), p. 215.

13. O. N. Bykov, *Mery Doveria* (Measures of Confidence) (Moscow: Nauka Publishing House, 1983), p. 62 (translation by author).

14. See note 9.

15. See, *e.g.*, Cdr. James J. Tritten, "The Concept of Strategic ASW," *NAVY International*, vol. 89 (June 1984), pp. 348–350; Joel S. Wit, "Advances in Antisubmarine Warfare," *Scientific American*, vol. 244 (February 1981), pp. 31–41; Norman Polmar, "Thinking About Soviet ASW," *United States Naval Institute Proceedings*, vol. 102 (May 1976); Richard L. Garwin, "Antisubmarine Warfare and National Security," *Scientific American*, vol. 227 (July 1972), pp. 14–25. See also *Report of the President's Commission on Strategic Forces* (the Scowcroft Commission), April 1983, stating at page 9 that the "problem of conducting open-ocean search for submarines is likely to continue to be sufficiently difficult that ballistic missile submarine forces will have a high degree of survivability for a long time."

16. See, *e.g.*, "Navy Says U.S. Subs Are Safe," *New York Times*, June 25, 1985, p. 9; Richard L. Garwin, "Will Strategic Submarines be Vulnerable?" *International Security*, vol. 8, no. 2 (Fall 1983), pp. 52–67.

17. See note 9.

18. Kevin N. Lewis and Mark A. Lorell, "Confidence-Building Measures and Crisis Resolution: Historical Perspectives," *Orbis*, vol. 28, no. 2 (Summer 1984), p. 286.

19. Geoffrey Blainey, *The Causes of War* (London: Macmillan, 1973), pp. 144–145. See also note 9.

20. The United States has concluded that Soviet telemetry encryption practices are in violation of SALT II. See "Message to the Congress Transmitting the President's Report on Soviet Noncompliance with Arms Control Agreements," January 23, 1984, *Weekly Compilation of Presidential Documents*, vol. 20, January 30, 1984, pp. 73–77.

10

Risk Reduction and Crisis Prevention

Sam Nunn

Over the past several years, the Senate has been in the forefront of efforts to devise practical measures to strengthen controls over nuclear weapons and to reduce the risk that these weapons might ever be used due to accident or miscalculation.

The history of this risk reduction initiative began back in the early 1980s, when I asked General Ellis, then Commander in Chief of the Strategic Air Command (SAC), to undertake a study of the dangers of an accidental war between the United States and the Soviet Union triggered by a third party. The SAC study concluded that under several possible scenarios, neither superpower may have the capability to determine the country of origin of a third party attack, and neither had adequate warning and detection systems to deal with unconventional-type attacks.

In 1982, Senator Warner, our late colleague Senator Jackson, and I introduced an amendment to the fiscal year 1983 defense authorization bill requiring the Department of Defense to evaluate several proposals aimed at reducing the risk of nuclear confrontation.[1] That legislation resulted in an April 1983 report by Secretary Weinberger to the Congress outlining four specific risk reduction measures which were eventually proposed to the Soviet Union. The four measures were: (1) adding a high-speed facsimile capability to the Hotline; (2) creating a joint military communications link (JMCL) between the Pentagon and the Soviet military command; (3) installing high-rate data links between the United States and the Soviet Union with their embassies in the capital of the other; and (4) proposing a multilateral agreement for nations to consult in the event of a nuclear incident involving terrorists.

Of these four measures, the Soviets have showed no interest in the JMCL or the embassy data links. There have, however, been discussions between the U.S. and USSR in the Standing Consultative Commission (SCC) on the nuclear armed terrorist problem, resulting in the signing, on June 14, 1985, of a new Common Understanding to the 1971 Accidents Measures agreement that outlines each side's responsibilities for notifying each other in the event of such incidents.

In July 1984, the two nations signed an accord concerning upgrading the Hotline. Under this agreement, a facsimile capability will be added to the Hotline, enabling each country for the first time to transmit and receive graphic materials. In addition, the planned improvements will allow the U.S. and Soviet heads of government to exchange messages more rapidly than they can with the existing teletype. The increase in the speed of communication and the ability to send pictures and maps could be especially critical in future crises.

The Direct Communications Link will now consist of: three circuits (two satellite circuits plus one wire telegraph circuit); one earth station in each country for each satellite circuit; and terminals in each country linked to the three circuits and equipped with teletype and facsimile equipment.

The agreement specifies that the U.S. Government will sell the Soviet Union at cost the equipment necessary to install and maintain the improved Hotline. This transaction will include facsimile equipment, personal computer (PC) equipment, modem equipment, and microprocessor systems to ensure the privacy of these very sensitive communications. Most of this transaction will be completed in the initial sale of the specified equipment to the Soviet Union. However, sales of services and additional equipment, including consumable items, will recur periodically throughout the life of the Hotline.

On April 4, 1985, Senator Warner and I, joined by Senators Bradley, Byrd, Cohen, and other co-sponsors, introduced Senate Joint Resolution 108, authorizing the Secretary of Defense to provide to the Soviet Union, on a reimbursable basis, equipment and services necessary to implement this agreement. The resolution was passed by the Senate on May 16, 1985, and sent to the President for signature by the House on July 29 of that year.

One important risk reduction measure which was cited in our 1982 legislation, but not acted on by the Administration, was the establishment of risk reduction centers. Basically, the Administration took the position at that time that while these centers might represent a useful long-term goal, it preferred to pursue its own package of proposals before taking on what it regarded as the more ambitious step of establishing the centers.

In November 1983, the Nunn/Warner Working Group on Nuclear Risk Reduction, which we had formed a year earlier, released its report and recommendations. Members of our group included General Brent Scowcroft, General Richard Ellis, Dr. James Schlesinger, William Hyland,

Dr. Barry Blechman, Admiral Bobby Inman, Dr. William Perry, and Dr. Donald Rice. In its report, the working group commended the Administration for proposing the four CBMs. However, it disagreed with the Administration's decision not to adopt the risk reduction center proposal. In its report, the group stated that there are "crucial political aspects" to controlling crises which can only be addressed through "more comprehensive language involving designation of particular representatives and facilities in both nations that would be assigned specific responsibilities for preventing a nuclear crisis."

On February 1, 1984, Senator Warner and I introduced Senate Resolution 329, which incorporated the recommendations of the working group and urged the President to propose to the Soviets the establishment of these centers.[2] On June 15, 1984, the Senate voted 82:0 to approve an amendment which we introduced to the fiscal year 1985 defense authorization bill incorporating the language of Senate Resolution 329. This provision was subsequently approved by the conference committee on this bill and enacted into law.

Despite the overwhelming congressional support for this proposal, the idea has yet to be formally embraced by this Administration. I was, however, encouraged by Secretary Weinberger's testimony of January 31, 1985, before the Foreign Relations Committee, in which he stated that it was very important to negotiate the creation of these centers. I remain hopeful that the Administration will add the risk reduction center proposal to its negotiating agenda in future discussions with the Soviet Union.[3]

One year ago, when Senator Warner and I testified before the Foreign Relations Committee on our resolution, I noted that although the United States and the Soviet Union had in large measure been able to avoid confrontations entailing the risk of nuclear war over the past three decades, there were compelling reasons to be concerned about their ability to continue this into the future. Indeed, there are an increasing number of circumstances that could precipitate the outbreak of nuclear war that neither side anticipated or intended, possibly involving terrorist groups or the growing number of nuclear-armed states that will likely exist by the end of the century.

If anything, I am more convinced today than I was then that the establishment of nuclear risk reduction centers is a crucial, indeed imperative, step. Over the past year, we have witnessed three different Soviet military accidents that could easily have been misinterpreted by one side or the other: the errant Soviet cruise missile incident in January 1985 and two major explosions in the Soviet Union in 1984—one at the naval munitions depot in Severomorsk, the other at a munitions factory in western Siberia.

Even more compelling, though, is the shift that both sides are now undertaking in their strategic posture toward a much prompter launch of land-based systems. As increasingly accurate, MIRVed ICBMs like the MX, the SS-18, and the SS-19 make each side more vulnerable to a first strike, and as warning time decreases, both sides are moving inexorably toward a hair trigger retaliatory posture. In these conditions, there is an extraordinary premium placed on avoiding any misinterpretation of nuclear incidents or military activities, and this is precisely the role that nuclear risk reduction centers could perform.

What we have in mind is separate facilities in Moscow and Washington, linked by the most modern communications equipment. The U.S. center should probably be directed by an ambassador-level official who would report directly to the National Security Council through the President's National Security Adviser. The permanent staff should include such other diplomatic, military, and intelligence personnel needed to maintain a 24-hour watch and support the various other functions performed by the centers. We do not believe that it would be prudent to start out with joint U.S./Soviet manning of the centers, though this step might be feasible at some stage further down the road. For the time being, each embassy could designate liaison officers to coordinate with the center in the respective capitals.

Senator Warner and I believe that there is presently a number of functions that these centers could usefully perform. We recommend that the centers be assigned rather modest tasks in their initial phase of operations, recognizing that a more ambitious set of responsibilities would have to evolve over time as the centers demonstrated their worth.

The first recommended function is one which is most commonly associated with the risk reduction center concept: that of serving as the primary point of contact for the exchange of all military information required under U.S.-Soviet agreements and, if accepted by the Soviets, the types of notifications that were proposed by the United States in the START working group on CBMS (see Chapter 9). This tasking corresponds to a function that was specifically cited in our amendment, the exchange of information about military activities that might be misunderstood during periods of mounting tension.

This communications link would be under political control, as opposed to the military-to-military communications system which President Reagan has proposed. Given the Soviets' longstanding practice of keeping their military under strict political control, we think that they might be more disposed to establishing this kind of communications link if it were not proposed to be under independent military control.

The centers could also serve as facilities for the exchange of information concerning events that might lead to the acquisition of nuclear weapons by subnational groups or terrorists. This function is also specifically cited in the legislation which the Senate passed in 1984.

Another function draws on a proposal by President Reagan in his September 1984 U.N. speech. The President suggested that the United States and the Soviet Union hold regular, institutionalized meetings at the ministerial or Cabinet-level, and that the agenda for these meetings could involve, for example, the exchange of 5-year military plans for weapons development and procurement. Another activity that might be appropriate for these meetings is one that was also outlined in the legislation: discussing procedures to be followed in the event of possible incidents involving the use of nuclear weapons by third parties. We believe the risk reduction centers would be an ideal location for conducting these kinds of discussions.

Another promising option relates to a proposal that President Reagan renewed in his May 7, 1985, speech to the European Parliament in Strasbourg. This is to institute regular, high-level meetings between U.S. and Soviet military leaders. I made a similar suggestion in 1979 after my first trip to the Soviet Union, where I had a most productive dialogue with a senior Soviet general. These meetings could promote a dialogue on nuclear doctrines, forces, and activities, as recommended in the Nunn/Warner amendment. We believe the risk reduction centers would also be a perfect facility for conducting these meetings.

Of these functions, the first is probably the one most directly related to the concept of these centers as it has evolved over time. Obviously, the most important function is the around-the-clock maintenance of communications, facilities, and personnel for *preventing* a nuclear crisis. I would emphasize that the role of these centers would be in the area of crisis prevention, and not crisis management. The centers are not intended to take the place of existing top-level councils in the U.S. Government assigned responsibility for handling crises.

To the extent that the other functions involve activities that could stand on their own absent the existence of risk reduction centers, bringing them under the umbrella of these centers is a symbolic act. But when we are dealing with the profound question of preventing nuclear war, I would argue that symbols matter.

The American people want reassurance. They want to know that the Government which they are entrusting with command authority over tens of thousands of nuclear devices is giving the highest priority to reducing the risks of nuclear war. The establishment of nuclear risk reduction centers can provide such a symbol and also serve crucial substantive functions.

Notes

1. Editor's note: Section 1123(2) of Public Law 97–252, dated September 8, 1982, amending Department of Defense Authorization Act FY 1983, directed the Secretary of Defense to conduct a study of possible initiatives for improving the containment and control of nuclear weapons use, particularly during crisis. It specified that the report should address: (1) establishing a multinational crisis control center to monitor and contain third-party use or potential use of nuclear weapons; (2) developing a forum for U.S.-Soviet information exchange pertaining to third-party nuclear activity; and (3) developing other measures to further confidence-building, such as an improved Hotline, improved verification procedures, reducing the vulnerability of command, control, and communications systems, and lengthening warning time of a potential nuclear attack.

2. Editor's note: See appendix A.

3. Editor's note: At a meeting between Senators Nunn and Warner and National Security Advisor Robert McFarlane on August 26, 1985, the Administration formally accepted the specific concept of nuclear risk reduction centers, albeit in a limited form. The Administration agreed that the centers would be established in Washington and Moscow, linked by communications equipment equivalent to the 1984 Hotline upgrade, manned on a 24-hour basis by military and diplomatic personnel, and serving as communications links for all required military and arms control notifications, as a meeting place for ministerial-level visits and other diplomatic discussions relating to risk reduction and CBMs, and as a meeting place for Incidents at Sea sessions, high-level military exchanges, National War College exchanges, and other discussions that would promote a dialogue on nuclear doctrines, forces, and activities. Designated liaison officers from the Soviet Embassy would be given access to the U.S. Center under controlled escort on a periodic basis, and vice versa. This outline was presented to General Secretary Mikhail Gorbachev by Senators Nunn and Warner at a meeting in the Kremlin on September 3, 1985, along with a list of "Roles That Might Be Added in the Future" representing the Senators' own views of how the Centers might evolve over time—a list to which the August 26 agreement between the Senators and the Administration does not extend. These future roles are: (1) discussion of procedures to be followed in the event of incidents involving the use or threatened use of nuclear weapons by unauthorized parties; (2) maintaining close contact during nuclear incidents or threats precipitated by unauthorized parties; (3) exchange of information concerning events that might lead to the acquisition of nuclear weapons, materials, or equipment by unauthorized parties; (4) joint U.S.-Soviet manning of each Center; and (5) upgraded communications capabilities to include voice and teleconferencing systems. Information provided by the Office of Senator Sam Nunn. See also Don Oberdorfer, "Reduction of Nuclear Risk Eyed," *Washington Post*, September 16, 1985. As of this writing, it was still unclear as to whether the risk reduction center issue would be taken up at the summit meeting in Geneva between President Reagan and General Secretary Gorbachev to be held over November

19–20, 1985, although reportedly the idea was being considered by the Administration, and whereas Gorbachev reportedly stated during his meeting with the Senators that the idea "deserves attention."

Postscript: on November 21, 1985, at the Geneva summit, President Reagan and General Secretary Gorbachev jointly endorsed exploration of the concept of nuclear-risk reduction centers.

11

An East-West Center
for Military Cooperation

David T. Twining

This chapter proposes that European security be stabilized and military relations institutionalized through the creation of an "East-West Center for Military Cooperation." The Center would be an appropriate confidence- and security-building measure (CSBM) within the aegis of the Conference on Confidence- and Security-Building Measures and Disarmament in Europe, or CDE. It would also be the means by which other CSBMs, as may be agreed upon, may be effectuated. The Center would give administrative form to enhanced military-to-military relations, and would serve to institutionalize military interaction, reduce mutual suspicion, and add stability and confidence to the European security environment.

Background

The CDE convened in Stockholm on January 17, 1984. Its charter was adopted at the 1980–1983 Madrid review meeting of the Conference on Security and Cooperation in Europe (CSCE) two months prior to its adjournment in September 1983. Specifically, the CDE is based on a 1978 French proposal that the CSCE Final Act CBM Document be strengthened. Because compliance with the Final Act's provisions for prior notification of military maneuvers and movements, observation of military exercises, and exchange of goodwill military delegations is largely voluntary, further specificity and incentives for compliance were desired.

The CDE represents a realistic opportunity for reducing the possibilities of surprise attack and the dangers of accidental and inadvertent war in Europe. By concentrating on those military activities which may deliberately or unintentionally lead to war, the CDE is seeking practical measures to make a surprise attack by conventional forces less likely by calling for foreknowledge of a potential adversary's military activities. The increased visibility and predictability concerning conventional force activity should, in turn, reduce the danger of conventional war—and, hence, the possibilities for escalation to nuclear war—arising by accident, miscalculation, or failure of communication. Enhancing the practicality and potential of the CDE is its mandate that CSBMs will be verifiable, that compliance shall be politically binding on all 35 CSCE participating states, that the area will include the whole of Europe as far east as the Ural mountains, and that these measures will be militarily significant.

The Atlantic Alliance moved early on in the Stockholm Conference to table six interrelated CSBM proposals to reduce the uncertainties associated with military activity. The measures call for the exchange of military information regarding the disposition and composition of ground and land-based air forces and regulations regarding accredited military personnel; exchange of annual forecasts of notifiable military activities; 45 days advance notification of out-of-garrison land activities, mobilization and amphibious activities; observation of these military activities; noninterference with national technical means (NTM) of verification and on-site inspection; and development of better means of communication between governments (see Appendix A). While it is not possible to predict the final outcome of the NATO CSBMs, it is clear that the six measures would go a long way toward enhancing stability and reducing the misunderstandings inherent in the vicissitudes of East-West military activities.

A Center for East-West Military Cooperation, or CMC, could be a seventh such CSBM. Its formation would be a political act of military significance, it would be politically binding upon signatory states, it would apply to the whole of Europe, and it would be a verifiable symbol of enhanced stability in European military affairs. It would also be a key CSBM through which the CSBMs that may be agreed upon would be implemented.

The Center

The principal *raison d'etre* of the CMC would be to institutionalize the intent of reducing the risks of confrontation in Europe. The CMC would provide a forum where CSBMs agreed upon in the CDE may be initiated and where attendant CSBM data (notifications, observer invitations, inspection requests and the like) would be exchanged among the parties for transmission to their respective governments. It would be the multinational body which would explore other cooperative ventures within the CDE ambit, and it could be an additional circuit-breaker to replace past patterns of independent military activity with more predictable ones.

Indeed, it may be asserted that unless CSBMs are given definitive administrative form their results will never be as successful as first envisioned. This vital consideration is easily overlooked in the commotion surrounding such major international endeavors, yet it is by their practical results that such initiatives will be judged. Policy decisions nearly always overshadow administrative procedures for their implementation. On matters involving CSBMs, where precision and accuracy are central to a broad spectrum of European security issues, the administrative mechanism for advance notification, the provision of observers, and other CSBM procedures must be agreed upon as well. Failure to do so will delay their implementation, create the basis for future misunderstandings, and raise unnecessary obstacles to the reduction of military risk for which they were intended.

To carry out its responsibilities as a functional rather than a policy entity, the CMC would be supported by a professional secretariat. The secretariat would provide the permanent staff necessary to maintain and operate the facility. It would work under the direction of an executive director, who would be appointed by and be accountable to the CDE as a whole, or to a standing consultative mechanism in its stead. It is recommended that the secretariat staff be composed of nationals of neutral and non-aligned nations, such as Austria, Finland, Sweden, Switzerland, and Yugoslavia, who are familiar with the unique requirements for maintaining an environment conducive to sustained East-West dialogue. It is within this neutral institutional setting that CSBM functional tasks will be carried out.

Each participating state would assign to the CMC one colonel-level military officer as its principal military representative and up to three deputies. This grade and personnel limitation are consistent with the CMC mission as a coordinating body for the head of respective national military forces and as a facilitator of other CSBMs. This officer, assisted by a small staff, will be the primary mechanism through which other CSBMs are implemented: the furnishing of data required by CSBMs on information exchange, forecasting, notification of military activities, observation of pre-notified military activities, compliance inquiries and inspections, and monitoring the overall security situation in Europe. Matters which cannot be resolved at this level and by this means will be elevated to the CDE, should it remain in existence in some form, a standing consultative mechanism it may create, or to member states themselves. The CMC, as envisaged, will be functional, neutral, and multinational; however, its significance will be far greater than its modest size may suggest.

As an effort to improve the form and substance of European military-to-military ties, the CMC's sole purpose will be CSBMs and other cooperative military projects. It will not replace or supplant other existing organizations or points of contact, such as military attaches, military liaison missions, or diplomatic posts. It is not an intelligence operation or a mere political gesture. Nor would it replace bilateral crisis action procedures and centers as may be established independently of the CDE process.

The CMC would be patterned on other examples of successful cooperative military ventures, such as the U.N. Truce Supervisory Organization and the 1977 U.S.-Soviet Incidents at Sea Agreement. In both cases, narrowly constrained military-to-military mechanisms have survived larger conflicts and tensions by serving specific, well-defined functions in a quiet, practical, and non-polemical way.

Another specialized U.S.-Soviet bilateral consultative body, the Standing Consultative Commission (SCC), was established in 1972 under the provisions of the ABM Treaty and reaffirmed in 1979 under SALT II to resolve compliance issues involving the strategic arms agreements. While not strictly a military-to-military entity, the SCC has served as an important symbol and useful means for pursuing quiet diplomacy regarding strategic arms issues. As a bilateral structure, of course, the SCC is an incomplete model for a multilateral activity. But a permanent multilateral center such as the CMC, having a charter much like the SCC, would be helpful for coordinating the implementation of a multilateral arms control agreement or for providing a standing forum for rapid consultations on security issues.[1]

Having sketched the general contours of the CMC, the following sections detail how the CMC might evolve in terms of its organization and functions.

Formation of the Center

Stage One

The first and most essential step is for the CMC to be adopted as a CSBM by the CDE. The CMC's charter would explicitly acknowledge its pivotal role as the forum in which the implementation of CSBMs would take place. Agreement by 35 nations to provide military representatives to a single entity dedicated to improving European security would be epochal in itself. As both a CSBM and an integral component of other CSBMs, the CMC's ultimate utility is limited only by that which its participants may agree to do to enhance European security.

To depict the contributions a CMC may make to European security, the six NATO CSBMs tabled in Stockholm on January 24, 1984, are reviewed below as they would operate in the context of a functioning Center. While each NATO CSBM already includes implementation procedures, this discussion illustrates the CMC's role as an integrative and coordinating body.

Exchange of Military Information. Each participating state will exchange air and ground order of battle information, to include unit locations, descriptions, and compositions. This information would provide the data base from which routine and non-routine unit movements and activity are measured. On a predetermined date each year, this data would be exchanged among senior military representatives at the CMC for transmission to their home governments. A record copy of each contribution would be given to the CMC secretariat for archival retention and collation in the Center's annual report to the CDE, or to a successor assembly.

Exchange of Forecasts of Activities Notifiable in Advance. Military activities designated as notifiable will be listed in an annual forecast specifying, *inter alia*, the participating states, size and type of forces, and date, place, and purpose of the activity. On a predetermined date each year, senior military representatives would exchange national forecasts with their counterparts at the Center, with a copy submitted to the Center secretariat.

Notification of Military Activities. Notification in compliance with this CSBM regarding out-of-garrison land activities and mobilization, amphibious, and alert activities would be accomplished by the notifying state's senior military representative at the CMC providing written notice of such activity to his or her counterparts. A second copy would be deposited with the secretariat. Because the activity notified 45 days in advance or, in the case of alerts, upon commencement, may or may not have been included in the annual forecast, further inquiry would be allowed to clarify the nature of the activity in question.

Observation of Notifiable Activities. Participating states would be required to invite observers from other signatory states to pre-notified military activities and to alert activities exceeding 48 hours in duration. Each senior military representative at the CMC would coordinate accommodations, travel, and other arrangements for his or her state's observer team with the senior military representative of the host state. Senior military representatives or deputies would be permitted to escort their state's observer team and conduct liaison with host nation personnel, as may be appropriate.

Compliance and Verification. This CSBM specifies that signatories will not interfere with NTM for monitoring compliance. Concerns regarding suspected cases of NTM interference would first be raised among appropriate senior military representatives at the CMC. Participating states may also request that their inspectors be permitted to view suspect military activities which may involve non-compliance. Such requests would first be made at the CMC, with the official record of requests and responses maintained by the secretariat. The CMC would be the primary venue for questions of possible NTM interference or arrangements for inspection on demand of suspect activities. In general, if good faith were demonstrated by both suspect and challenging parties, the matter would be resolved at the CMC without recourse to more senior consultations among the participating states.

Development of Means of Communication. Because of the co-location of senior military representatives and their immediate military staffs at the CMC, communication links to and from all signatory states could terminate there. These circuits would be appropriate for communicating information concerning military activity or administrative matters from one party to another, crisis or emergency messages, or any other data of a military-to-military nature. Bilateral links could connect one signatory state's military command to another, with the CMC acting as the switch point. Multilateral links could relay communications from one signatory state's military command to more than one counterpart via the CMC.

Communications links at the Center would likely include message and text transmission facilities. They would be of such speed and reliability that crisis action communications could be accommodated. Within this context, communications operations would be supervised by the Secretariat, which would maintain record copies of messages for inspection by all national representatives. Access to these communications by all signatory states would serve as further evidence of the openness and visibility given European military activities by the CMC. Matters of such sensitivity that should not be shared with all signatory states, of course, would be passed by other means, and each state's delegation would be expected to have separate privacy communications as well.

The six NATO CSBMs have been depicted as representative of what could be the CMC's fundamental role in maintaining European stability. These six measures, or elements thereof, would represent incremental steps of the first stage of the CMC's evolution. The second stage would comprise those steps which may be later agreed upon as contributions to enhanced European security. At this next stage, the Center's role would be substantial, as illustrated by the following steps which could be implemented if agreed upon.

Stage Two

Monitoring an Agreed Indicator List. The Center could monitor norms of ground, naval, and air activity of signatory states within the defined geographic area. These norms could consist of known levels of military activity during previous periods, and they would be the standard against which on-going military activity is judged. Such norms could include, for example, air activity during 12, 24, and 48-hour periods, based on one, three, and five-year averages as reported by national air traffic control authorities, and out-of-garrison troop activity, based on similar data from national military authorities.

Based upon these levels of "normal" activity as determined by historical records, activity exceeding a normative threshold would trigger automatic inspection or consultation provisions, at either the military-to-military or political level. Unusual levels of military movements, air activity, logistical preparations, or suspected mobilization activity would initiate a process whereby the suspected state's senior military representative would be asked for an explanation and/or the acceptance of inspectors to monitor the activity. Failure to explain satisfactorily a military buildup or other unusual activities through CMC procedures would lead to multilateral political consultations. The CMC secretariat would monitor the official status of normative indicators for each participating state, and, as with other CMC activities, the current status of each indicator would be available to any signatory at any time.

Neutral Nation Military Inspectors. Military personnel from neutral and nonaligned states, selected and agreed upon in advance by the participating states, could be summoned by the CMC whenever on-site inspections were required. Such inspections could include the routine observation of prenotified military activity, or they could involve on-demand inspections to ascertain CSBM compliance. The CMC would coordinate the deployment of neutral nation military inspectors in conjunction with the host state they are to visit. In some cases, neutral nation military personnel may be the only persons permitted to view a site considered particularly sensitive by the host state. A cadre of neutral nation military inspectors could be on-call for such contingencies. This measure would be particularly useful where a signatory state has already used its quota of two inspections per year under the provisions of NATO CSBM 5 or to provide alternative inspection arrangements should CSBM 5 not be adopted.

Crisis Action SOPs. The CMC could maintain a number of crisis action standard operating procedures (SOPs) which, by prior agreement, would become operational in given contingency situations. Crisis action SOPs could be developed to deal with terrorist incidents, air, ground, or naval intrusions, or nuclear weapons thefts, accidents, detonations or other critical developments concerning nuclear weapons, nuclear materials, nuclear storage facilities, or nuclear power plants. These SOPs could be rehearsed or simulated by the participating states, and would be of particular value in exercising the Center's crisis action communications procedures and equipment. The availability of such SOPs will enable national leaders to quickly defuse a crisis or potential crisis if it were their intent to do so.[2]

Pre-planned and Pre-positioned Mediation Program. Mediators who have been agreed upon in advance by the participating states could be on-call by the CMC to defuse disagreements over CSBM matters. Such efforts would not only provide a means of controlling a developing crisis, but they would also serve to prevent, say, superpower involvement in a regional problem. Mediation efforts, operating independently or in conjunction with other Center programs and procedures, could prevent misunderstandings from escalating to dangerous proportions. Mediators so engaged could be drawn from a regional or international organization, or could be a member of an international mediation service composed of distinguished and respected individuals.[3]

Exchange of Information. The Center could develop and facilitate the voluntary exchange of information concerning national military activities not included within the NATO CSBM package which may be considered aggressive or threatening by other participating states. Such data could include new weapons developments or technology which may be perceived as destabilizing, changes in national conscription or other personnel programs, unusual activity near national borders, and the like. Other information which could be exchanged may be that which would provide greater security for special weapons or enhance the security and survivability of missiles, communications, aircraft, or early warning systems.

Stage Three

A third stage in the CMC's evolution would be its role in effectuating confidence-building and arms control verification measures agreed upon in other arms control fora. This could include the verification of troop withdrawals and the continuous monitoring of compliance with residual troop levels involving both on-demand inspections and permanent observation posts at critical entry and exit points through Central Europe in accordance with a future MBFR treaty. It could also include on-site and on-demand inspections to monitor compliance with a Comprehensive Nuclear Test Ban treaty and its predecessor agreements, and administer whatever verification provisions may be required by an INF treaty. Additionally, the CMC could be an appropriate vehicle for assisting other arms control and disarmament bodies, including the United Nations and its component organizations.

Stage Four

The fourth stage of the CMC's development could encompass the type of low-level CSBMs which may be agreed upon without recourse to senior multilateral political bodies. This stage will largely be the result of and benefit from the effectiveness and utility of the CMC as a successful CSBM. The confidence each senior military representative would gain in counterparts, the ease by which face-to-face communication can reduce minor misunderstandings, and the interpersonal chemistry of what is possible by 35 or more military professionals operating in the neutral environment of the CMC may produce noteworthy results, if permitted to do so.

This fourth stage may yield measures which could serve to improve communications, eliminate misunderstanding, and increase the overall level of trust of one party in another. They could encompass a spectrum of common interests concerned with reducing tensions and improving substantive cooperation, to include arranging exchanges of Commanders in Chief, War College faculty and students, and exchange visits to units and headquarters. Other functions could include organizing events such as sports competitions, visits to cultural affairs and historical sites, and professional exchanges of historians, topographers, training and other military specialists.

Location of the Center

Because of its European orientation, the Center should, quite obviously, be based on the European continent. Possible sites would include Helsinki, location of the conclusion of the CSCE Final Act; Geneva, location of the Standing Consultative Commission and many disarmament fora over the years; Stockholm, the venue of the CDE; or Vienna, another city familiar to arms control specialists.

Another venue worthy of consideration is West Berlin's Spandau Prison, which would provide both a precedent and a facility for continuing the tradition of Allied wartime military collaboration, though now with a new direction and purpose. Following the conclusion of World War II, those Nazi leaders given prison terms were transported to Spandau, located in the British sector of what is now West Berlin. In time, Spandau became one of three sites of permanent Allied interaction in West Berlin, with the Allied Air Control Center and the Soviet War Memorial being the other two. While military liaison missions and military representatives of the four powers continue to exercise their rights of access to both East and West Berlin, these three sites have emerged as significant, long-term points of contact.

At Spandau, four military officers representing each occupying power continue to administer the prison on behalf of their senior military commanders, with the responsibility for perimeter security and logistics rotating monthly. Since 1966, when Albert Speer and Baldur von Schirach were released, Spandau has been inhabited by one individual, Rudolf Hess, Hitler's former deputy. Now over 90, Hess may pass away at any time, and along with his death will come the end of more than 38 years of successful four power cooperation.

The use of Spandau Prison as an East-West facility for monitoring and improving European security would perpetuate the special relationship which has evolved there, and West Berlin itself is central in location and to the issues of security in Europe. Because this proposal has been termed a "circuit-breaker"—a departure from past patterns of arms control and disarmament efforts—the adoption of such a unique site may provide the impetus for unique solutions to European security problems.

Conclusion

The concept of a Center for East-West Military Cooperation would of itself be a major step toward greater European understanding and cooperation. Of even more import are the supportive roles the Center can provide to regional and international bodies, other arms control and disarmament measures, and the host of potential initiatives the CMC makes possible. The Center is both a symbol of progress toward a more peaceful Europe and an effective means by which practical steps for achieving military stability may be accomplished. In a real sense, the East-West Center does not represent the end we wish to attain ultimately; however, it is very likely a point at which we must begin if we are to achieve peaceful change and to reduce military tensions in Europe.

Notes

1. See Richard E. Darilek, "Separate Processes, Converging Interests: MBFR and CBMs," in Hans Guenter Brauch and Duncan L. Clarke, eds., *Decisionmaking for Arms Limitation: Assessments and Prospects* (Cambridge, MA: Ballinger, 1983), p. 254; and Jozef Goldblat, *Agreements for Arms Control: A Critical Survey* (Cambridge, MA: Oelgeschlager, Gunn, and Hain; London: Taylor and Francis, 1982), p. 110. See also "Managing East-West Conflict," Report of the Aspen Institute International Group on East-West Relations, in "Excerpts from Report on Making Nuclear War Less Likely," *New York Times*, November 27, 1984, p. A14. The report called for the establishment of a network of crisis control

centers connecting the capitals of nuclear states and "perhaps other key locations as well," presumably the capitals of major non-nuclear allies and primary and alternative national command centers. The CMC could perform this function in concert with its other European security responsibilities.

2. William Langer Ury and Richard Smoke, *Beyond the Hotline: Controlling a Nuclear Crisis* (Cambridge, MA: Harvard Law School Nuclear Negotiation Project, 1984), p. v.

3. *Ibid.*, p. vii.

12
The Limits of Confidence

Jim E. Hinds

Many historical arrangements between former or potential belligerents serve as examples of confidence-building measures. Modern history most often cites the 1963 "Hotline" agreement as the earliest CBM affecting U.S.-Soviet relations. That will puzzle some readers who may recall that long before 1963 every American soldier serving in the Federal Republic of Germany carried a card showing how to identify and treat members of the Soviet Military Liaison Mission (force prohibited). The 1947 Huebner-Malinin agreement provided for the exchange of military liaison officers between the U.S. and Soviet commanders in Germany. That agreement not only precedes the "Hotline" agreement, but is also more directly related to the usual CBMs currently under discussion.[1]

American soldiers still carry such cards.[2] We can assume that Soviet soldiers do not; or if they do, their cards are radically different, as demonstrated by U.S. Army Major Arthur Nicholson's murder by a Soviet sentry in the spring of 1985. Major Nicholson was performing his duties within the provisions of the 1947 CBM agreement. His job was to give us more confidence in our judgments about Soviet leaders' intended use of the massive Group of Soviet Forces in Germany.

But in what is confidence built when a legitimate military observer is murdered? Since the murder, Soviet officials at the highest levels have offered no apologies. As Soviet soldiers are not known for their initiative or for their lack of discipline, we must conclude that the killing was a matter of policy, not an accident or the action of a trigger-happy guard. After U.S. authorities reported an apparently positive statement by the Soviet Commander in Chief regarding future restraint, Moscow was compelled to refute the notion that liaison officers might not be shot in the future.[3]

The views expressed herein are those of the author and do not necessarily reflect U.S. Government policy.

Regardless of the circumstances surrounding the murder, the question of whether the Soviet sentry killed Major Nicholson on instructions is no longer important because of subsequent Soviet actions. Beginning with Soviet officers' failure to provide or permit medical treatment as Nicholson bled to death (an unacceptable act even between armies at war) up to Moscow's refusal to acknowledge responsibility, every Soviet action has shown that the killing has been accepted by the Soviet leadership as policy. The same conclusion could be reached based on Soviet actions after they had destroyed a Korean airliner. In that case, 269 innocent passengers were killed. The International Civil Aviation Organization's rules, also venerable CBM agreements, had no effect on action by Soviet authorities.[4]

The Nicholson shooting was not an isolated incident. Over the years there have been numerous confrontations within the Soviet sector involving the liaison missions, many instances of harrassment, dangerous interference, and other shootings. Indeed, since the Nicholson shooting a Soviet truck rammed a U.S. vehicle, injuring the U.S. Mission Commander. Whether the ramming was intentional, as many such incidents in the past have been, or harassment that got out of hand, the message of Soviet intimidation is clear.[5]

The liaison agreement has been useful in many ways. From time to time it may even have served as the CBM agreement it is supposed to be, perhaps helping to restore stability, or keeping "nerves and armies steady on both sides. . . ."[6] It has, however, frequently been a source of confrontation and frustration whereby distrust has increased, not decreased.

There are other confidence-building agreements in effect that produce similar if less violent results. Military Attaches accredited to the Soviet Ministry of Defense for the purpose of legitimate military observation are prevented in dozens of ways from observing what they have the right and responsibility to observe. Despite agreements providing for normal diplomatic exchanges, large areas of the Soviet Union are closed to foreign travel. Means of transportation to and through open areas are limited in ways that constitute *de facto* denial of access even to those "open" areas. Vast regions that appear open to travellers can only be reached by flights that terminate in closed cities within the "open" area, and only designated *inturist* highways can be used for automobile travel.

Before any attache trip begins, it must be approved by the Ministry of Defense; that institution accepts no obligation to explain last minute denials. All travel arrangements are made through a diplomatic service directorate. Any number of reasons "not in the Government's control" can be used unofficially to deny travel during this operation, *e.g.*, no vacancies, authorized highways under repair, other transportation booked-up, bad weather conditions in the area, and the like. With tickets in hand, the diplomatic traveller still must cope with unannounced cancellations or unexplained changes in air and rail schedules anywhere along his route.

Assuming the Ministry of Defense does not deny permission to travel, and the traveller has reached his destination, he has then to face various obstacles: heavy surveillance by the KGB, the *militsia* (police), "volunteers" and armed military patrols; intimidation by portable signs; staged "public disturbances," drugs in food or drink, illegal detention, physical abuse, or attempted entrapments (the unexpected passing of "documents," unsolicited attention from people exhibiting "antisocial" behavior—black marketeers, money-changers, or "ladies of questionable virtue"); vandalism, such as slashed tires, crossed or stolen ignition wires, stolen car keys, and so on. This former attache became proficient at arts more suitable to the car thief than to the diplomat by twice rewiring Soviet-made *Zhigulis'* ignition switches, once bypassing the steering lock mechanism after breaking into the car, and once sorting out a badly-mangled distributor.

There is no doubt that attaches (and liaison officers in the German Democratic Republic as well) may become frustrated and cynical, "confident" only that they are being deceived. Western military observers, therefore, try harder; no doubt Soviet security services under strict instructions become more suspicious and use cruder forms of interference as attache activities become more aggressive. No tensions are relieved through bad-faith implementation of these CBMs. And no Western military observer worries much about his Government's "miscalculating" or "misunderstanding" an innocent activity as a threatening act, but about deception and interference with the performance of his legitimate functions and the inadequacy of the information he is able to provide about military activities.

The 1975 Helsinki Final Act included provisions formally designated as CBMs. Western signatories have been no more satisified by the implementation of these measures than by implementation of earlier bilateral arrangements. Though the United States has only had one opportunity to attend a Soviet maneuver under the ten-year-old CBM provisions of the Helsinki Final Act, the experience was no more informative or "confidence-building" than routine attache experiences. Observers were only permitted to witness demonstrations, not maneuvers. They were not permitted to provide their own equipment, but were given faulty binoculars, not permitted freedom of movement, but were transported by Soviet hosts, and were given no opportunities freely to interview Soviet officers or soldiers. Confidence is not increased by the fact that the United States has only been invited to two of the many Soviet or Warsaw Pact exercises requiring notification. Nor is confidence inspired by the fact that the Soviets have violated Helsinki's simple notification and observation provisions.

In short, practical experience with U.S.-Soviet CBMs in these cases has not been encouraging. The Nicholson atrocity has confirmed and reinforced our discouragement. Moreover, the framework for considering future CBMs must take into account the Soviet Union's general record of non-compliance with arms control treaties and other international obligations, including violations of the Helsinki CBMs, not to mention arrogant violations of the Helsinki Final Act's human rights provisions. Such a record will not and should not generate great expectations even if great pieces of paper are produced in the future. The point is: what is written is not reality; CBMs produce nothing positive when implemented negatively. Without positive implementation, CBMs can produce negative results, and perhaps themselves provide the spark to set off serious confrontations.

Theoretical Framework

What then do we hope to accomplish with CBMs? For a time, part of the European academic community seemed to be starting on the right track in setting straight the relationship between political conflict and arms control. In the West, the two concepts have on the one hand come to be treated as discrete problems or, on the other, as if armaments were the source of political conflict. Arms reduction agreements are thought of as the means to reduce tensions in the world, especially U.S.-Soviet tensions. Arms, however, are not sources of political conflict. That is the province of competing historical national interests, aggressive ideology and ambition. Indeed, it is argued that nuclear arms have effectively prevented political conflict from leading to major military clashes over the past 40 years by making conventional war potentially apocalyptic. Some of the early advocates of negotiated CBMs recognized the contradiction that inheres in the idea of reducing political tensions through arms control and hoped to address the sources of conflict.

The majority of those who thought about CBMs, however, made a more direct link between CBMs and arms control. For this larger group CBMs were a simplification of and catalyst for disarmament. CBM arrangements would become the instruments of arms control, mechanisms establishing the conditions of trust necessary to further genuine disarmament.

By making CBMs a part of the disarmament process, however, CBM proponents quickly lost sight of their greater objective: the removal of the sources of conflict. This lofty goal was overly ambitious in any case, unless one believed that CBMs would prove that there were few offensive intentions, goals, or ideologies, but mostly misapprehensions and unwarranted suspicions resulting in increasingly dangerous defensive buildups. The danger within this framework would be the temptation to adopt empty political declarations instead of genuine measures. But the statement of the goal made a better framework for CBM negotiations.

As CBM negotiations become the servant of arms control, however, emotional expectations are skewed, and progress toward agreement becomes the measure of success when the measure should be the effect and content of the agreement. Under these circumstances, CBM negotiations take on the character of other arms control negotiations in which pressures mount for demonstrations of "progress" when pressures should be exerted, instead, in the direction of useful arrangements that actually do what they are supposed to do.

Political Theater

In the context of current CBM negotiations, some Westerners still suggest that CBMs should be seen principally as political measures designed to achieve political understanding. We are struck, however, by how often the "political understanding" these CBM advocates have in mind is simply their publics' understanding that we are approaching solutions to the problems of conflict, improving East-West relations, providing for a dialogue on security issues—in other words, "building confidence" that East and West are working together to lower tensions and lessen the risks of confrontation.

When probed, such CBM defenders may admit that the "confidence" they seek is domestic public confidence in their governments' success in reducing the risks of war. To achieve that goal, it is not necessary to be concerned about the content of proposals; it is necessary only to show "progress." Indeed, this cynical admission is frequently justified on the even more cynical grounds that such East-West dialogues are only political theater out of which no harm can come to real security interests.

On the contrary, however, serious analysis demonstrates that serious harm can be done to security interests, especially if empty progress gives rise to unjustified public expectations. Indeed, one suspects that the erroneous belief in reducing risks through disarmament "progress" (presumably more serious business than political theater) is not always a belief mistakenly held, but a false measure intentionally provided to allay public anxiety.

Such discussions obviously relate to publics that influence governments, that is, Western publics. It is not surprising, therefore, that the Soviet Union and its allies encourage this "political" approach. But the achievement of a public sense of "confidence," if confidence is not in fact warranted, is the least desirable objective or effect of any CBM agreement or process.

The centerpiece of Soviet diplomacy with regard to confidence-building at the Stockholm Conference and elsewhere is just such a "political" approach. At Stockholm, the Soviets propose that the Europeans and North Americans enter into a non-use-of-force agreement. All participants in the Stockholm Conference are already legally bound by the U.N. Charter to refrain from the use or threatened use of force in their relations with other states. And as signatories to the Helsinki Final Act, they have all reconfirmed that commitment. About the Soviet proposal, President Reagan, speaking before the Irish parliament on June 4, 1984, said: "If discussions on reaffirming the principle not to use force, a principle in which we believe so deeply, will bring the Soviet Union to negotiate agreements which will give concrete new meaning to that principle, we will gladly enter into such discussions."[7]

No one can object to a reaffirmation of Article 2(4) of the U.N. Charter. But attempts to redefine and narrow the scope of the article can only weaken its force. A European non-use-of-force agreement cannot be used to excuse, for example, Soviet occupation of Afghanistan or to cause states that abide by such commitments to modify their means of self-defense through the prohibition of specific ways of defending against attack. The simplest example of the latter would be a commitment not to be the first to use nuclear weapons. Such a commitment would, of course, strip NATO of its nuclear deterrent, making Soviet use of its superior conventional forces a safe option.

The U.N. Charter's no-force principle remains the most authoritative statement on the subject by any community of nations. The Helsinki Final Act acknowledges that fact, and all participants pledged themselves anew to the principle. Yet neither the U.N. Charter nor its reaffirmation at Helsinki has restrained the Soviet Union in its use or threatened use of force in pursuit of its goals. There is no need here to rehearse the long list of examples. We know that intimidation and military threats (not to mention use) are common components of the Soviet Union's relations with its allies and not uncommon in its relations with others. Moreover, a regime that uses force against its own people, against a civilian airliner gone astray, and force to the extent of killing an officer of the United States in the performance of his legal duties does not inspire confidence by proposing to address the issue with new declarations on the subject.

The publicly stated political objective of CBM agreements, therefore, is not attainable simply by signing agreements. A political change through improved "understanding," if possible, is only possible after a relatively lengthy period of compliance with concrete agreements without deception or circumvention and, indeed, after demonstration of general intent to abide by the laws and norms of the international community.

Military Measures

Agreements cannot produce "confidence" simply because they exist; sound agreements, however, may be useful. But how is a sound agreement designed? There may be a number of "rules of the road" that are clearly in all parties' interest. It is in the U.S. interest, for example, that the Soviet Union should not misinterpret a U.S. missile test launch or a strategic exercise as an attack. Giving Soviet authorities data and notice in advance can help prevent such misinterpretation. It is also clear that the Soviets have an interest in the United States understanding that Soviet activities are only exercises. Sober, businesslike arrangements governing the conduct of warships operating in peacetime in close quarters can help to avoid accidents by establishing rules of safe operations.

This suggests that while political objectives cannot be *achieved* through empty political declarations, movement toward those objectives might be *assisted* by concrete agreements about military activities. But can we reach a generalization on that basis about what is a "good" measure and what is not? The answer is not easy.

Direct Military Utility

Some attribute a potentially important function to military CBMs. The concept is that CBMs may fail to prevent confrontation or to maintain or restore stability, but they could at least deny an adversary the element of surprise or otherwise complicate his aggressive activities. The confidence-building in this case relates to increased confidence that an enemy might find it more difficult to achieve the element of surprise.

This touches on the idea of CBMs serving a direct military purpose. The concept supposes that warning time can be increased through the monitoring or verification functions of some CBMs, or that CBM procedures can interfere with offensive preparations. Some form of observation or inspection must be agreed upon for the concept to work. According to this theory, even if observers are denied access to suspect Soviet activities, effective warning time would be increased by giving

NATO decisionmakers an earlier signal of offensive intent and, therefore, more preparation time.

Much of the theoretical debate surrounding the issue of the military utility of CBMs began in military circles in connection with the Mutual and Balanced Force Reduction (MBFR) talks and the general proposition of decreasing the levels of conventional forces in Central Europe. Recognizing that MBFR's focus on military manpower as a unit of account largely missed the true measure of combat power and vastly complicated verification, and further recognizing that MBFR already provided the possibility of negotiating CBMs ("Associated Measures" in MBFR), some saw an opportunity to impose controls on military use that would be more militarily significant than force reductions.

Most who supported the idea of militarily significant CBMs in this earlier debate were less interested in control through so-called "constraint" measures than in control through carefully used "transparency" measures. There was always a healthy skepticism about the capabilities of paper constraints under which we knew that only NATO would be constrained. These arguments were based instead on the expectation that tightly designed and coordinated observation and inspection measures could increase the risks involved in the use of a surprise attack option. These measures might increase warning time, enhance warning judgments, and/or actually disrupt attack preparations.[8]

Warning time might be increased, and clear warning indicators might be provided in several ways, it was argued. Proof through observation that an agreed measure had been violated would in itself be a clear indication that a significant political decision had been made to use or threaten to use military force. Moreover, observers provided for by an agreement might be able to detect abnormal military behavior in a timely and conclusive fashion, in some cases better than existing intelligence resources. Furthermore, information obtained overtly by multinational observers or inspection teams could be used freely and understood in the Alliance and by the publics without risk of compromising sensitive national means of intelligence. In fact, just for this purpose, an inspection might be called to confirm information initially detected by national resources. The overt multinational character of a CBM regime, in addition to serving as a mechanism for sound public challenge of violations, might improve the NATO consultative process for reaching more timely political decisions to initiate defensive preparations. Finally, it was argued, active and coordinated use of a CBMs package could permit a more concentrated allocation of other collection means, thus improving the entire system.

As pointed out earlier in this chapter, however, things rarely work in practice as in theory or as written into agreements. The obvious and widely recognized problem with the military effectiveness of CBMs is the general practice of deception. As discussed above, we are concerned with early warning or disruption of surprise attack. It goes without saying that a surprise attack will be accompanied by a deception plan. The military planner may be annoyed by the necessity to avoid responses triggered by CBMs. On the other hand, a good planner will be delighted by the opportunity to manipulate standardized procedures. He might cover some preparation steps by providing notice of out-of-garrison or alert activities. He could attempt to calm the opposing Alliance by inviting observers in accordance with the agreement, if necessary permitting observation of specially staged exercises designed to give a normal peacetime appearance. Reinforcements might be moved surreptitiously under the cover of such maneuvers.

Even without deception tactics, however, the effectiveness of observation will be limited. The usefulness of an inspection or observation measure depends on the details agreed to: the degree of access, freedom of movement, size of area covered, number and frequency of inspections permitted, amount of advance notification required, sensitive areas that might be excluded, and the degree to which the inspected party is obliged to accept the inspecting team. It seems unlikely that we will reach agreement on measures that do not set some kind of quotas and other restrictions on inspections.

Even with an unrestricted agreement, however, observation would still prove intrinsically limited. The administrative and material burdens and requirements for trained observers would necessarily limit the numbers of teams and the size of areas covered. Moreover, concerted and widespread use of the inspection measure (presumably extraordinary behavior) would probably require a multinational decision (at least among NATO participants). If indications of attack preparations were not already relatively clear, and if abnormal activities were covered by seemingly proper notification, inspections above the norm might be thought overly provocative. The decision to undertake inspections aggressively could be difficult to make, even if the resources were available and the right to do so were established.

Different interpretations of the CBM's operation would also complicate the measure's implementation. We might negotiate degrees of observation and access to areas in a way that appeared satisfactory, only to find that each step in operation would be a minor confrontation. While we would have devoted great effort to make the agreement watertight, we can be sure that some elements of misunderstanding will arise in implementing any agreement, and some will never be resolved to our satisfaction. We have only to mention again the Soviet Union's implementation of various agreements already providing for military observation.

It is quite certain, furthermore, that groups of multinational observers, trained to varying degrees and armed with national information perhaps not fully shared, will arrive at differing conclusions. Some of the conclusions are bound to be misleading, and findings are likely to be ambiguous unless there is a very clear violation. This will be especially true if the CBMs are not carefully crafted in detail or are not implemented in good faith (which we assume they would not be if intentions were not benign). In the case of ambiguous findings, the CBMs might easily work to our disadvantage. One can imagine a situation in which response to warning would be *delayed* because of disagreement within the Alliance as to whether a CBM had been violated. The debate would be particularly difficult if a proper response to warning would itself require violation or abrogation of an agreement.

It is also argued that increased warning would be gained simply because the secretive Soviets would never accept inspection that would discover violation of an agreement. Refusal to permit a mandatory inspection would set off the alarm bells. That should certainly be the case. But the case can also be made that such refusal would only set off extended discussions. These discussions would center on the military significance of the violation, on questions of whether this "technical" violation represented a substantive violation or merely a manifestation of Soviet paranoia.

All the inbred limitations discussed above would also complicate the idea of disrupting attack preparations. The need to execute a deception plan covering preparations for a short-warning attack, however, suggests a requirement to expend time and resources in ways not directly related to offensive preparations. Assuming that the West had the right to inspect, and that a timely decision could be reached based on other warning indicators to exercise the right, would well-planned inspections of critical areas disrupt the attack? If the East still felt the need to deceive, an inspection would probably disrupt things in the immediate inspection area (otherwise the inspection team would simply become the first casualties of the war—not an unbelievable outcome). There are different requirements for exercises and the real thing; inspections would presumably target those critical differences (for example, establishment of ammunition resupply dumps and combat command and control communication links). Delay of attack, of course, would be of no value if the deception succeeded, and NATO took no actions of its own during the delay. The use of an inspection for disruptive purposes, therefore, would require fairly certain knowledge that attack preparations were underway.

This specialized use of inspections, while interesting, would seem to be limited in its usefulness. The potential shortcomings of such measures as implemented indicate some of the factors that would negatively affect the concept. Furthermore, the short time envelope for useful application requires accurate intelligence and clear warning in advance. The probable requirement to give notice of intent to inspect some specified time prior to arrival at the location to be inspected and logistics involved in moving inspection teams present complex obstacles in the way of sensitive timing demands. Moreover, localized, temporary delays could be overcome in the whole attack scenario by slack in movement planning, redundancy, and other factors routinely incorporated in major troop movements.

Attributing to CBMs a direct contribution to increased warning and disruption of attack preparations seems to require an imaginative stretch. In addition to questions about the effectiveness of CBMs in general, attaching to them a direct military utility raises the danger of doing harm through excessively developed expectations of their worth. It is possible that warning *could* be increased by a fortuitous discovery, but it is not a possibility upon which to depend. Once the decision has been taken to launch an attack, no CBM will have restraining power. Support for CBMs as military-technical restraints seems based on slim reasoning, and experience with existing measures does not point toward military use in any such direct sense.

Openness or "Transparency"

If CBMs designed directly to improve military security are undependable and perhaps harmful, and political declarations are empty, what is left? It is important to remember that CBMs are supposed to clarify intent. If military activities are undertaken with no hostile intent, then measures can be taken to demonstrate the absence of hostility. It is infinitely more difficult to design measures that will prove the aggressive nature of a military activity or even to prove that the activity is underway. Unfortunately, measures demonstrating benign intent may also be manipulated to give off benign signals under hostile conditions.

The difficulty of designing useful CBMs is also a function of defining the situation about which we wish to be "confident." Indeed, while we are engaged in negotiations addressing CBMs, we find ourselves to some extent deep into talks while still in search of objectives. Nonetheless, we attempt to state the rationale for particular CBMs; for example, ". . . to reduce the possibility of conflict through accident, miscalculation, or failure of communications, and to inhibit opportunities for surprise attack or political intimidation. . . ."[9]

We have addressed the difficulties in connection with inhibiting surprise attack, but it is a worthy goal to reduce the possibility of conflict through accident or miscalculation. Ambassador James Goodby, former Head of the U.S. Delegation to the Stockholm CDE Conference has described the terms: "The Stockholm Conference is different . . . in that it addresses not the capabilities for war, the number of weapons and troops, but rather the most likely causes of war: flawed judgments or miscalculations stemming from fears of sudden attack and uncertainty about the military intention of an adversary."[10]

Avoiding accidental war is a narrow goal, however, and one that itself is open to abuse. It is a worthy goal because it is always worthwhile to limit any risk of military conflict, even if not the major risk. It is subject to abuse if we believe it contributes to the prevention of war in any wider sense. The risk of war beginning as a result of an accident or miscalculation is a minor danger when compared to the risk of war beginning as the result of a deliberate decision in pursuit of a policy goal. The decision to pursue goals by military means in the East-West or U.S.-Soviet environment would most likely call for the initial use of military power to extort desired concessions by threat, not by direct attack. At the same time, care would be taken to justify such extortion as defensive in nature, as a necessary countermeasure to aggressive action. Even in these circumstances, it is, nonetheless, quite possible to achieve strategic and tactical surprise.

In such a situation, the cause of war would not be accident, mis-understanding, or miscalculation, but a deliberate decision based on the conflict of foreign and military policies. There is no doubt that wars are not caused by the numbers of weapons and troops, nor are the weapons the source of instability. Though war might begin in a particular way because of miscalculation, the roots of war are located at depths greater than simple accident or miscalculation.

By tying the problem of miscalculation to fears of surprise attack, we tend to set up a one-sided confidence-building regime. No European government believes that NATO will ever launch a "sudden attack" on anyone. Only NATO, therefore, is subject to flawed judgments or miscalculations stemming from genuine fears of attack. The CBMs we discuss, therefore, often seem designed only to prove ourselves wrong whenever we suspect aggressive Soviet intentions.

No one believes that the most likely cause of war in Europe is that NATO, mistaking peaceful Warsaw Pact activities for aggression, will react too quickly and violently. The West's fear is not that NATO's hammer is cocked behind a hair-trigger. The West's worry is quite the opposite: that NATO will not be able to make timely political decisions to respond to threats for fear of being wrong or appearing provocative.

If there is a crucial calculation about which we should worry, it is the calculation that the Warsaw Pact must make about NATO's will to defend its interests and ultimately the existence of the member nations. We are convinced that NATO will defend, but to do so successfully NATO must make credible military preparations based on timely political decisions. The most dangerous calculation or miscalculation would be, therefore, the Soviet Union's and its allies' determination that they could achieve their military objectives before NATO could react properly. Such a judgment could be the most likely immediate cause of war (though the root causes are still more profound). That suggests that the most effective CBM is a sound NATO military structure and a responsive NATO political process.

Confidence-building must be a lengthy process, unrelated to Western public confidence that things have somehow been improved by a signed agreement. Caution with regard to expectations based on CBM agreements is required: the proof is in the pudding, not in the recipe. And skepticism about a CBM agreement's ability to encourage political stability is essential. Measures designed to prevent war by accident or miscalculation, especially with reference to the European situation, have at best a marginal utility in principle. And this limited utility is, of course, directly related to the danger of overblown expectations. Unwarranted public confidence may damage stability by threatening to weaken NATO's deterrent capabilities.

Though it is clearly in our interest to have our peaceful military activities understood correctly, it is also clear that we should not become confident that the act, for example, of giving notice of military activities means that those activities are not aggressive. To serve a useful purpose, such notification measures must be verifiable in a useful period of time, and the information provided must be reliably designed to aid in verification. Unverifiable measures, even if apparently designed to address significant military issues, are not helpful and may be harmful. This points to a type of CBM that, to be useful, is self-verifying, an action that is either done or not done. Such a measure will likely be a modest arrangement made to avoid conflict only where conflict is not intended.

The concept of "transparency" has become a cliche among confidence-building "professionals." The concept is, however, at the heart of confidence. In effect, we must ask the Soviet Union to join the Western democracies in openness by moving away from its tradition of excessive secrecy. In open societies, through the press and other organs, publics and parliaments guarantee transparency to a degree that is not possible in closed societies. We cannot expect the Soviet Union to become such an open society the day a confidence-building arrangement is signed, but it is unrealistic to expect a state of mutual "trust" before some degree of openness is achieved. Thus, the concrete measures that may give greater effect to non-use-of-force commitments are those that will begin to achieve openness about military activities. Without this kind of openness, more ambitious CBMs can be dangerously misleading.

Conclusion

At this stage in Russian and Soviet history and at the current level of Soviet military strength, the issue involved in negotiating CBMs is not trust; we do not trust each other. The issue is knowledge. Knowledge in this sense is not gained through espionage or other forms of intelligence, but from freely given information and reliable procedures to confirm its accuracy. The issue is surprise attack. The Stockholm Conference is about surprise attack—not because CBMs can prevent it, but because we recognize the potential, and the negotiation and implementation of realistic measures acknowledges and focuses on the danger.

Our task has been to outline some of the pitfalls in the confidence-building business. If this essay seems to have gone about its work with too much enthusiasm, the job may have been overdone. The point is not to abandon the confidence-building process, but to avoid shabby construction or straw skyscrapers. As is often the case when small undertakings that work in specialized areas are discovered, institutionalized and given broader application, the grander version loses the workmanlike quality of the original. Such is the danger in designing CBMs to address broad, political goals or unrealistic military objectives. Most arrangements designed to accomplish specific tasks can and have been usefully made. In current CBM approaches, the designers of new measures must understand the limitations of CBMs, set goals for themselves that can be reached and not be deceived by grander views.

Notes

1. A copy of the Huebner-Malinin agreement can be found in Paul G. Skowronek, *U.S.-Soviet Military Liaison Missions in Germany Since 1947* (University of Colorado Ph.D. thesis, 1976), p. 231.

2. Benjamin F. Schemmer, "US Orders Are Clear About Detaining Soviets: 'No Force Should Be Used Or Lives Endangered,'" *Armed Forces Journal International* (July 1985), p. 15.

3. Bernard Gwertzman, "Soviet Qualifies Report by U.S. on G.I. Patrols," *New York Times*, April 23, 1985, p. 1.

4. Editor's note: Following the Soviet downing of the Korean airliner, the Montreal-based Assembly of the International Civil Aviation Organization (ICAO) approved an amendment in May 1984 embodying a specific ban on the use of

weapons against civil aircraft in flight, urging expeditious ratification by all 152 ICAO contracting states.

5. William Beecher, "Soviet Ramming Reportedly Followed Pact," *Boston Globe*, July 23, 1985, p. 7.

6. "Kill First, Questions Later," *Washington Post*, March 27, 1985, p. A22.

7. President's statement quoted from *New York Times*, June 5, 1984.

8. For discussion of these concepts see James Blaker, "On-Site Inspections: The Military Significance of an Arms-Control Proposal," *Survival*, vol. 26, no. 3 (May/June 1984), pp. 98–106. Editor's note: Blaker argues *contra* Hinds, stating that "inspections could have a direct military utility to the West" in terms of disrupting, by more than two days in certain cases, Warsaw Pact attack preparations. *Ibid.*, p. 104.

9. "Arms Control: Confidence-Building Measures," *Gist* (Washington, D.C.: Bureau of Public Affairs, U.S. Department of State, January 1985), p. 1.

10. James E. Goodby, "Security for Europe," *NATO Review*, vol. 32, no. 3 (June 1984), p. 9.

PART 4

CONCLUSION

In a world that fails to make substantial progress in the field of nuclear disarmament and arms control, confidence-building measures . . . represent our most important insurance policy. If nuclear arms cannot be controlled, at least an effort must be made to control the situations that could lead to their use and to introduce as much rationality as possible in dealing with the conflicts that might lead to the use of military force.

Karl Kaiser, ed., preface, *Confidence-Building Measures* (Bonn: Europa Union Verlag, 1983), p. 2.

John Borawski

This book has attempted to present concisely some of the principal issues involved in past, present, and future efforts to design, negotiate, adopt, and implement effective CBMs in a variety of contexts. In closing, it might be appropriate to highlight a few of the themes that provide common points of departure in the preceding chapters.

First, there exists an extraordinary, and refreshing, degree of congruity of international interest in pursuing the objectives of CBMs. It is not, to be sure, a perfect world of shared interests, as attested to by the diverse points of view exhibited by the various proposals and negotiations. Some differences concern details that can be expected to attain resolution in the normal course of negotiation, *e.g.*, "out-of-garrison" military activities vs. "maneuvers and movements" at the CDE, or defining the thresholds and other parameters for notifying aircraft "take-offs" in the Nuclear and Space Arms Negotiations. Others, however, involve less tractable matters of basic principles, to wit, "legalized espionage" vs. "transparency," that can perhaps be "managed" but not overcome except, if at all, in the very long term. Expectations about how far and how fast progress can be achieved in the several CBM fora, hence, must remain neither overly modest nor overly exaggerated. Nevertheless, when viewed against the backdrop of the apparent road to nowhere that the posterity of SALT and other arms limitation talks seem to be taking in Geneva and elsewhere, coupled with the somewhat energized charges and countercharges reported almost daily as to which side is more "serious" and "flexible" about seeking verifiable and substantial reductions to equal force levels, discontinuing nuclear testing, banning chemical weapons, and so forth, it is encouraging to observe that not only do CBMs offer real opportunities for conducting businesslike and productive negotiations and reinvigorating the process of arms control, they offer genuine prospects for creating a more predictable, cooperative, and secure military environment wherein operational barriers are constructed against the threat or use of force, whether by design or inadvertence, so as "to reduce the pressures from arms on the process of politics during peacetime and on decisionmaking in crisis and war."[1] Although CBMs, like any form of arms control, cannot eliminate the threat of war now or in the future, they can serve to reduce that risk by constructing rules of conduct to reduce the possibilities of confrontation in peacetime and the dangers of accident or miscalculation and the opportunities for surprise attack in times of crisis.

Second, CBMs, unlike many other forms of arms control, are likely to appeal to many sides of the nuclear debate. In part, this is so because many CBMs are multidimensional in effect. For example, proposals for the withdrawal of battlefield nuclear weapons from forward areas in Central Europe are advanced not only with a view to alleviate command and control problems associated with the release of nuclear warheads to local commanders, but to support efforts to improve NATO conventional force posture and to reduce reliance on the early first use of nuclear weapons. Proposals to limit ballistic missile tests to low annual limits could be argued to serve confidence-building in some abstract way by promoting "arms race stability," but such measures will most likely appeal to those who believe that restricting the pace of force modernization serves stability. For those who believe that deterrence requires selective nuclear response options and modernized forces designed to execute those options, CBMs to avoid inadvertent escalation may prove appealing, even though such measures, ranging from communications to operational constraints, do not necessarily favor proponents of mutual assured destruction or selective counterforce. But regardless of one's position on these issues, whereas the crossfire of topical controversy over issues such as the strategic defense initiative, Soviet treaty violations, and nuclear force modernization seems more often than not to limit public opinion choices to either building up or burning down the house of arms control as it has been practiced, CBMs offer a third and more useful option: renovation and renewal.

Third, CBMs are a dynamic process. Although extant CBM foundations, however modest, have served important purposes, no one has argued that more ambitious measures need not be studied and pursued. For analysts interested in delving into this field, Ambassador Goodby has given us our marching orders: "What is needed most of all in this rather neglected area is a concerted effort over a long period of time, using all the ingenuity we can muster to design and build a realistic, workable structure of stabilizing arrangements."

In executing this ambitious tasking, one starting point might involve recognizing that the question is not so much one of contriving completely new ideas. As indicated in this volume, a very large amount of conceptual groundwork has already been accomplished by way of identifying general approaches in the areas of information exchange, observation and inspection, and operational constraints. Indeed, what Alton Frye has observed regarding the European CBM environment may very well hold universally: "The menu from which one may choose future CBM is full; the question is whether the parties have an appetite for a healthy meal."[2]

This is not to suggest that theoreticians should not stay hungry, for invariably any treatment of CBMs, such as suggested in Chapter 1, may raise more questions than it can possibly answer. As indicated in this volume, disagreements will persist as to how likely, say, is the "unintentional" path to nuclear war and, hence, on which CBMs deserve the greatest attention. However, what must be intensified is the translation of general principles into specific policy options. For instance, much work has been done, although it is far from complete, in the area of nuclear risk reduction centers. Similar innovative analysis needs to be applied to other functional and geographic CBM areas in detail sufficient to allow for informed judgments. Outer space constitutes an exciting topical arena for investigation, but the literature could well benefit from more practical appraisals moving out in all directions. This is so especially at the classified level, for a thorough grasp of the operations of military forces does not lend itself to the public domain, but there is plenty to be accomplished in unclassified areas as well.

Some of the more interesting questions that ought to be pursued might include the following: How can the new technologies associated with, say, NATO's new sub-concept of operations termed "Follow-On Forces Attack" for all-weather, real-time surveillance be employed for CBM purposes in terms of warning measures and verification of other CBMs? What are the prospects and requirements for an international or regional satellite monitoring agency that would afford to some extent to other countries monitoring capabilities heretofore possessed by only a very few states? Are there nuclear and conventional operational constraints—the measures most clearly linked to inhibiting surprise attack—that can accommodate different NATO and Warsaw Pact requirements in Europe, and U.S. and Soviet interests in the bilateral nuclear sphere? Are there CBM regimes that can be structured to contribute to deescalating crises or even armed conflict in addition to measures that seem best suited for crisis prevention? What can be done to combat the threat of third party nuclear incidents apart from the mere exchange of information? Can negotiable CBMs be identified for areas outside of the immediate East-West context? What realistic arrangements can be designed to enforce CBM regimes? How can the potential dangers of CBMs elaborated in Chapter 12 be guarded against, and are such dangers near certainties or mere possiblities? Would CBMs have made a difference in 1914, in 1939?

Finally, it should be stressed again that CBMs are only one component of security policy. They are not a substitute for arms reductions and unilateral defense efforts, but nor are the pursuit of force reductions and arms procurement replacements for measures that focus on the operations of military forces and on the intentions underlying those activities. It is vital, therefore, that carefully conceived CBMs be permitted to play a far greater role in endeavors to reduce the risks of war, complementing other tools of national security policy in designing a more coherent approach to assuring stability in the years ahead.

Although arms control has experienced a disappointing past, CBMs may very well represent a promising new wave of its future.

Notes

1. Johan Holst quoted in James E. Goodby, address before *L'Institut Francais des Relations Internationales* (IFRI), Paris, December 3, 1984, reprinted as "The Stockholm Conference: A Report on the First Year," *Current Policy*, no. 639 (Washington, D.C.: Bureau of Public Affairs, Department of State, 1984), p. 3.

2. Alton Frye, "Building Confidence Between Adversaries: An American's Perspective," in Karl E. Birnbaum, ed., *Confidence-Building and East-West Relations* (Laxenburg, Austria: Austrian Institute for International Affairs, 1982), p. 40.

Appendix:
A CBM Handbook

MEMORANDUM OF UNDERSTANDING BETWEEN THE UNITED STATES OF AMERICA AND THE UNION OF SOVIET SOCIALIST REPUBLICS REGARDING THE ESTABLISHMENT OF A DIRECT COMMUNICATIONS LINK (Excerpts)

Signed at Geneva, June 20, 1963

For use in time of emergency the Government of the United States of America and the Government of the Union of Soviet Socialist Republics have agreed to establish as soon as technically feasible a direct communications link between the two Governments.

Each Government shall be responsible for the arrangements for the link on its own territory. Each government shall take the necessary steps to ensure continuous functioning of the link and prompt delivery to its head of government of any communications received by means of the link from the head of government of the other party.

AGREEMENT ON MEASURES TO REDUCE THE RISK OF OUTBREAK OF NUCLEAR WAR BETWEEN THE UNITED STATES OF AMERICA AND THE UNION OF SOVIET SOCIALIST REPUBLICS (Excerpts)

Signed at Washington, September 30, 1971

ARTICLE I

Each Party undertakes to maintain and to improve, as it deems necessary, its existing organizational and technical arrangements to guard against the accidental or unauthorized use of nuclear weapons under its control.

ARTICLE 2

The Parties undertake to notify each other immediately in the event of an accidental, unauthorized or any other unexplained incident involving a possible detonation of a nuclear weapon which could create a risk of

---

Updated from land and undersea wire circuits to satellite circuits by agreement signed September 30, 1971, and by facsimile capability by agreement signed July 17, 1984.

outbreak of nuclear war. In the event of such an incident, the Party whose nuclear weapon is involved will immediately make every effort to take necessary measures to render harmless or destroy such weapon without its causing damage.

ARTICLE 3

The Parties undertake to notify each other immediately in the event of detection by missile warning systems of unidentified objects, or in the event of signs of interference with these systems or with related communications facilities, if such occurrences could create a risk of outbreak of nuclear war between the two countries.

ARTICLE 4

Each Party undertakes to notify the other Party in advance of any planned missile launches if such launches will extend beyond its national territory in the direction of the other Party.

ARTICLE 5

Each Party, in other situations involving unexplained nuclear incidents, undertakes to act in such a manner as to reduce the possibility of its actions being misinterpreted by the other Party. In any such situation, each Party may inform the other Party or request information when, in its view, this is warranted by the interests of averting the risk of outbreak of nuclear war.

ARTICLE 6

For transmission of urgent information, notifications and requests for information in situations requiring prompt clarification, the Parties shall make primary use of the Direct Communications Link between the Governments of the United States of America and the Union of Soviet Socialist Republics.

For transmission of other information, notifications and requests for information, the Parties, at their own discretion, may use any communications facilities, including diplomatic channels, depending on the degree of urgency.

ARTICLE 7

The Parties undertake to hold consultations, as mutually agreed, to consider questions relating to implementation of the provisions of this Agreement, as well as to discuss possible amendments thereto aimed at further implementation of the purposes of this Agreement.

AGREEMENT BETWEEN THE GOVERNMENT OF THE UNITED STATES OF AMERICA AND THE GOVERNMENT OF THE UNION OF SOVIET SOCIALIST REPUBLICS ON THE PREVENTION OF INCIDENTS ON AND OVER THE HIGH SEAS (Excerpts)

Signed at Moscow, May 25, 1972

ARTICLE II

The Parties shall take measures to instruct the commanding officers of their respective ships to observe strictly the letter and spirit of the International Regulations for Preventing Collisions at Sea, hereinafter referred to as the Rules of the Road. The Parties recognize that their freedom to conduct operations on the high seas is based on the principles established under recognized international law and codified in the 1958 Geneva Convention on the High Seas.

ARTICLE III

1. In all cases ships operating in proximity to each other, except when required to maintain course and speed under the Rules of the Road, shall remain well clear to avoid risk of collision.

2. Ships meeting or operating in the vicinity of a formation of the other Party shall, while conforming to the Rules of the Road, avoid maneuvering in a manner which would hinder the evolutions of the formation.

3. Formations shall not conduct maneuvers through areas of heavy traffic where internationally recognized traffic separation schemes are in effect.

4. Ships engaged in surveillance of other ships shall stay at a distance which avoids the risk of collision and also shall avoid executing maneuvers embarrassing or endangering the ships under surveillance. Except when required to maintain course and speed under the Rules of the Road, a surveillant shall take positive early action so as, in the exercise of good seamanship, not to embarrass or endanger ships under surveillance.

5. When ships of both Parties maneuver in sight of one another, such signals (flag, sound, and light) as are prescribed by the Rules of the Road, the International Code of Signals, or other mutually agreed signals, shall be adhered to for signalling operations and intentions.

6. Ships of the Parties shall not simulate attacks by aiming guns, missile launchers, torpedo tubes, and other weapons in the direction of a passing ship of the other Party, not launch any object in the direction of passing ships of the other Party, and not use searchlights or other powerful illumination devices to illuminate the navigation bridges of passing ships of the other Party.

7. When conducting exercises with submerged submarines, exercising ships shall show the appropriate signals prescribed by the International Code of Signals to warn ships of the presence of submarines in the area.

8. Ships of one Party when approaching ships of the other Party conducting operations as set forth in Rule 4(c) of the Rules of the Road, and particularly ships engaged in launching or landing aircraft as well as ships engaged in replenishment underway, shall take appropriate measures not to hinder maneuvers of such ships and shall remain well clear.

ARTICLE IV

Commanders of aircraft of the Parties shall use the greatest caution and prudence in approaching aircraft and ships of the other Party operating on and over the high seas, in particular, ships engaged in launching or landing aircraft, and in the interest of mutual safety shall not permit: simulated attacks by the simulated use of weapons against aircraft and ships, or performance of various aerobatics over ships, or dropping various objectives near them in such a manner as to be hazardous to ships or to constitute a hazard to navigation.

ARTICLE V

1. Ships of the Parties operating in sight of one another shall raise proper signals concerning their intent to begin launching or landing aircraft.

2. Aircraft of the Parties flying over the high seas in darkness or under instrument conditions shall, whenever feasible, display navigation lights.

ARTICLE VI

Both Parties shall:

1. Provide through the established system of radio broadcasts of information and warning to mariners, not less than 3 to 5 days in advance as a rule, notification of actions on the high seas which represent a danger to navigation or to aircraft in flight.

2. Make increased use of the informative signals contained in the International Code of Signals to signify the intentions of their respective ships when maneuvering in proximity to one another. At night, or in conditions of reduced visibility, or under conditions of lighting and such distances when signal flags are not distinct, flashing light should be used to inform ships of maneuvers which may hinder the movements of others or involve a risk of collision.

3. Utilize on a trial basis signals additional to those in the International Code of Signals, submitting such signals to the Intergovernmental Maritime Consultative Organization for its consideration and for the information of other States.

ARTICLE VII

The Parties shall exchange appropriate information concerning instances of collision, incidents which result in damage, or other incidents at sea between ships and aircraft of the Parties. The United States Navy shall provide such information through the Soviet Naval Attache in Washington and the Soviet Navy shall provide such information through the United States Naval Attache in Moscow.

ARTICLE IX

The Parties shall meet within one year after the date of the signing of this Agreement to review the implementation of its terms. Similar consultations shall be held thereafter annually, or more frequently as the Parties may decide.

ARTICLE X

The Parties shall designate members to form a Committee which will consider specific measures in conformity with this Agreement. The Committee will, as a particular part of its work, consider the practical workability of concrete fixed distances to be observed in encounters between ships, aircraft, and ships and aircraft. . . .

AGREEMENT BETWEEN THE UNITED STATES OF AMERICA AND THE UNION OF SOVIET SOCIALIST REPUBLICS ON THE PREVENTION OF NUCLEAR WAR (Excerpts)

Signed at Washington, June 22, 1973

ARTICLE I

The United States and the Soviet Union agree that an objective of their policies is to remove the danger of nuclear war and of the use of nuclear weapons.

Accordingly, the Parties agree that they will act in such a manner as to prevent the development of situations capable of causing a dangerous exacerbation of their relations, as to avoid military confrontations, and as to exclude the outbreak of nuclear war between them and between either of the Parties and other countries.

ARTICLE II

The Parties agree, in accordance with Article I and to realize the objective stated in that Article, to proceed from the premise that each Party will refrain from the threat or use of force against the other Party, against the allies of the other Party and against other countries, in circumstances which may endanger international peace and security. The Parties agree that they will be guided by these considerations in the formulation of their foreign policies and in their actions in the field of international relations.

ARTICLE III

The Parties undertake to develop their relations with each other and with other countries in a way consistent with the purposes of this Agreement.

ARTICLE IV

If at any time relations between the Parties or between either Party and other countries appear to involve the risk of a nuclear conflict, or if relations between countries not parties to this Agreement appear to involve the risk of nuclear war between the United States of America and the Union of Soviet Socialist Republics or between either Party and other countries, the United States and the Soviet Union, acting in accordance with the provisions of this Agreement, shall immediately enter into urgent consultations with each other and make every effort to avert this risk.

ARTICLE V

Each Party shall be free to inform the Security Council of the United Nations, the Secretary General of the United Nations and the Governments of allied or other countries of the progress and outcome of consultations initiated in accordance with Article IV of this Agreement.

ARTICLE VI

Nothing in this Agreement shall affect or impair:

(a) the inherent right of individual or collective self-defense as envisaged by Article 51 of the Charter of the United Nations,

(b) the provisions of the Charter of the United Nations, including those relating to the maintenance or restoration of international peace and security, and

(c) the obligations undertaken by either Party towards its allies or other countries in treaties, agreements, and other appropriate documents.

FINAL ACT OF THE CONFERENCE ON SECURITY AND COOPERATION IN EUROPE (Excerpts)

Signed at Helsinki, August 1, 1975

The participating States,

Desirous of eliminating the causes of tension that may exist among them and thus of contributing to the strengthening of peace and security in the world; . . .

Have adopted the following:

Prior Notification of Major Military Manoeuvres

They will notify their major military manoeuvres to all other participating States through usual diplomatic channels in accordance with the following provisions:

Notification will be given of major military manoeuvres exceeding a total of 25,000 troops, independently or combined with any possible air or naval components (in this context the word "troops" includes amphibious and airborne troops). In the case of independent manoeuvres of amphibious or airborne troops, or of combined manoeuvres involving them, these troops will be included in this total. Furthermore, in the case of combined manoeuvres which do not reach the above total but which involve land forces together with significant numbers of either amphibious or airborne troops, or both, notification can also be given.

Notification will be given of major military manoeuvres which take place on the territory, in Europe, of any participating State as well as, if applicable, in the adjoining sea area and air space.

In the case of a participating State whose territory extends beyond Europe, prior notification need be given only of manoeuvres which take place in an area within 250 kilometres from its frontier facing or shared with any other European participating State, the participating State [the Soviet Union and Turkey] need not, however, give notification in cases in which that area is also contiguous to the participating States's frontier facing or shared with a non-European non-participating State.

Notification will be given 21 days or more in advance of the start of the manoeuvre or in the case of a manoeuvre arranged at shorter notice at the earliest possible opportunity prior to its starting date.

Notification will contain information of the designation, if any, the general purpose of and the States involved in the manoeuvre, the type or types and numerical strength of the forces engaged, the area and estimated time-frame of its conduct. The participating States will also, if possible provide additional relevant information, particularly that related to the components of the forces engaged and the period of involvement of these forces.

Prior Notification of Other Military Manoeuvres

The participating States recognize that they can contribute further to strengthening confidence and increasing security and stability, and to this end may also notify smaller-scale military manoeuvres to other participating States, with special regard for those near the area of such manoeuvres.

To the same end, the participating States also recognize that they may notify other military manoeuvres conducted by them.

Exchange of Observers

The participating States will invite other participating States, voluntarily and on a bilateral basis, in a spirit of reciprocity and goodwill towards all participating States, to send observers to attend military manoeuvres.

The inviting State will determine in each case the number of observers, the procedures and conditions of their participation, and give other information which it may consider useful. It will provide appropriate facilities and hospitality.

The invitation will be given as far ahead as is conveniently possible through usual diplomatic channels.

Prior Notification of Major Military Movements

. . . the participating States recognize that they may, at their own discretion and with a view to contributing to confidence-building, notify their major military movements. . . .

Other Confidence-Building Measures

The participating States recognize that there are other means by which their common objectives can be promoted.

In particular, they will, with due regard to reciprocity and with a view to better mutual understanding, promote exchanges by invitation among their military personnel, including visits by military delegations. . . .

They also recognize that the experience gained by the implementation of the provisions set forth above, together with further efforts, could lead to developing and enlarging measures aimed at strengthening confidence.

CBM PROPOSALS SUBMITTED BY FRANCE IN 1978 FOR A CONFERENCE ON DISARMAMENT IN EUROPE

1. Increase access to military facilities by military attachés.
2. Expanded means of communication among CSCE states, such as by common telex facilities between foreign ministries.
3. Publication of annual schedules of principal military activities.
4. Exchange of information on defense appropriations, command and organization of forces, and location of units and commands.
5. Notification 45 days in advance of air-surface maneuvers involving: (a) over 200 armored vehicles; (b) 100 aircraft; and/or (c) 12,000 troops.
6. Notification 45 days in advance of movements exceeding one division or its equivalent, or one air combat group, for more than 200 kilometers.

7. Notification 45 days in advance of smaller-scale, simultaneous maneuvers involving more than 200 armored vehicles, 100 aircraft, and/ or 12,000 troops.

8. Notification 30 days in advance for all types of air exercises involving more than 100 aircraft.

9. Notification 6 months in advance of mobilization or reserve call-ups of more than 25,000 civilians or reservists.

10. Annual limit on the number and duration of principal military maneuvers and movements.

11. Ceiling on air-surface maneuvers involving more than 1,000 armored vehicles and/or 500 aircraft, or 60,000 troops.

12. Ceiling on simultaneous maneuvers and combined drill exercises.

13. Limit on frequency, scope, and duration of military activities in "identified sensitive zones."

14. Ban on certain notifiable military activities in zones to be agreed.

15. Observation of notified military activities.

16. Verification of limited and banned military activities.

SALT II TREATY (Excerpts)

Signed at Vienna, June 18, 1979

ARTICLE XVI

1. Each Party undertakes, before conducting each planned ICBM launch, to notify the other Party well in advance on a case-by-case basis that such a launch will occur, except for single ICBM launches from test ranges or from ICBM launcher deployment areas, which are not planned to extend beyond its national territory.

First Common Understanding. ICBM launches to which the obligations . . . apply, include, among others, those ICBM launches for which advance notification is required pursuant to the provisions of [the Accidents Measures and Incidents at Sea agreements]. Nothing in Article XVI of the Treaty is intended to inhibit advance notification on a voluntary basis of any ICBM launches not subject to its provisions, the advance notification of which would enhance confidence between the Parties.

Second Common Understanding. A multiple ICBM launch conducted by a Party, as distinct from single ICBM launches referred to in Article XVI of the Treaty is a launch which would result in two or more of its ICBMs being in flight at the same time. . . .

2. The Parties shall agree in the Standing Consultative Commission upon procedures to implement the provisions of this Article.

CONCLUDING DOCUMENT OF THE 1980–83 MADRID REVIEW MEETING OF THE CONFERENCE ON SECURITY AND COOPERATION IN EUROPE (Excerpts)

Issued September 9, 1983

Conference on Confidence- and Security-Building Measures and Disarmament in Europe (Excerpts)

The aim of the Conference is, as a substantial and integral part of the multilateral process initiated by the Conference on Security and Cooperation in Europe, with the participation of all the States signatories of the Final Act, to undertake, in stages, new, effective and concrete actions designed to make progress in strengthening confidence and security and in achieving disarmament, so as to give effect and expression to the duty of States to refrain from the threat or use of force in their mutual relations.

Thus the Conference will begin a process of which the first stage will be devoted to the negotiation and adoption of a set of mutually complementary confidence- and security-building measures designed to reduce the risk of military confrontation in Europe.

The first stage of the Conference will be held in Stockholm commencing on 17 January 1984.

On the basis of equality of rights, balance and reciprocity, equal respect for the security interests of all CSCE participating States, and of their respective obligations concerning confidence- and security-building measures and disarmament in Europe, these confidence- and security-building measures will cover the whole of Europe as well as the adjoining sea area* and air space. They will be of military significance and politically binding and will be provided with adequate forms of verification which correspond to their content.

As far as the adjoining sea area* and air space is concerned, the measures will be applicable to the military activities of all the participating States taking place there whenever these activities affect security in Europe as well as constitute a part of activities taking place within the whole of Europe as referred to above, which they will agree to notify. Necessary specifications will be made through the negotiations on the confidence- and security-building measures at the Conference.

---

*In this context, the notion of adjoining sea area is understood to refer also to ocean areas adjoining Europe.

Taking into account the above-mentioned aim of the Conference, the next follow-up meeting of the participating States of the CSCE to be held in Vienna, commencing on 4 November 1986, will assess the progress achieved during the first stage of the Conference.

Taking into account the relevant provisions of the Final Act, and having reviewed the results achieved by the first stage of the Conference, and also in the light of other relevant negotiations on security and disarmament affecting Europe, a future CSCE follow-up meeting will consider ways and appropriate means for the participating States to continue their efforts for security and disarmament in Europe, including the question of supplementing the present mandate for the next stage of the Conference on Confidence- and Security-building Measures and Disarmament in Europe.

NUCLEAR ARMS REDUCTION NEGOTIATIONS

United States (1982)

START

- Advance notification of all major military exercises involving heavy bomber take-offs, SSBN dispersals, and/or launches of one or more ICBMs, SLBMs, or longer-range INF ballistic missiles.
- Advance notification of all ICBM and SLBM launches.
- Exchange of data on strategic forces.

INF

- Advance notification of all LRINF ballistic missile launches.
- Exchange of data on INF.

Soviet Union (1982)

START

- Ban on heavy bomber flights, aircraft carrier patrols, and ASW activity in SSBN sanctuaries in agreed zones adjoining national territory.
- Advance notification of mass take-offs of heavy bombers and of forward-based aircraft.
- Advance notification of ICBM launches, except of single launches not planned to extent beyond national territory (SALT II Art. XVI).

INF

- Advance notification of medium-range (1000–5500 km range/radius) ballistic missile launches, except of single launches not planned to extend beyond national territory.
- Advance notification of mass take-offs of medium-range aircraft.

MBFR ASSOCIATED MEASURES PROPOSALS

NATO (December 1979)

1. Notification 30 days in advance and by annual calendar of out-of-garrison activities by one or more division-size formations; alert activities to be notified upon commencement.

2. Observation of prenotified out-of-garrison activities.

3. Notification 30 days in advance and by annual calendar of major ground force movements into the guidelines area whose home territory is outside the guidelines area.

4. 18 annual ground and/or air inspections.

5. Permanent exit/entry points to monitor movements into and out of the guidelines area, with permanent observers.

6. Annual exchange of information on forces in guidelines area.

Warsaw Pact (June 1983)

1. Advance notification of movements and maneuvers exceeding 20,000 troops.

2. 40,000 troop ceiling on ground force maneuvers.

3. Observers at reductions of "the most substantial contingents" of troops.

4. Notification of reductions initiation and completion.

5. Periodic exchange of data on force strength.

6. 3–4 permanent exit/entry points to monitor collective ceilings.

7. Voluntary on-site inspection.

STOCKHOLM CDE CONFERENCE CSBM PROPOSALS (Highlights)

NATO (January 24, 1984, as amplified March 8, 1985)

1. Annual exchange of information on military command organization and on regulations for accredited military personnel.

2. Annual forecast of activities notifiable in advance (measure 3).

3. 45 days advance notification of: out-of-garrison land activities at the division level or at 6,000 troops; mobilization activities at 3 divisions or 25,000 troops; and amphibious activities at 3 battalions or 3,000 troops. Alert activities to be notified at the time troops are ordered to carry out the alert activity.

4. Observation of notifiable activities, including alerts with a duration exceeding 48 hours. Each participating state will be permitted to send up to two observers to a military activity.

5. Noninterference with national technical means of verification, and inspection on demand of military activities, include suspect activities not notified. Each participating state may carry out up to two inspections per year. Restricted areas exempt from inspection.

6. Establishment of dedicated communication links (bilateral hotlines) for the expeditious handling of CSBM information and for communications on matters of urgency related to agreed CSBMs.

Romania (January 25, 1984)

1. 30 days advance notification of military maneuvers in which take part: land or combined forces exceeding 18,000–20,000 troops; special forces, such as paratroops and amphibious, in excess of 5,000 troops; more than 10–12 surface battleships having a total displacement of 50,000–60,000 tons; and more than 45–50 aircraft.

2. 30 days advance notification of major military movements involving: two or more divisions or their equivalent; major transportation of heavy armaments and other war materiel with which two or more divisions or their equivalent could be equipped.

3. Prior notification, or as soon as possible in emergency situations, of the placing in a state of alert of national or foreign armed forces.

4. 40,000–50,000 ground troop limit for maneuvers and establishment of ceilings for the number of battleships and aircraft fighters.

5. Renunciation of multinational maneuvers within a zone along each side of the borders between sides.

6. Creation along borders of security zones in which there would be no maneuvers, movements, or concentrations of armed forces and armaments, and no placing in a state of alert of important components of such forces; limitation of the armed forces, armaments, and military activities in such regions as a step toward the establishment of demilitarized zones.

7. Nuclear-weapon-free border zones between NATO and Warsaw Pact states and, in the long term, border zones free of any military forces except for order and border forces.

8. Ban on maneuvers and movements of ships and aircraft with nuclear weapons aboard within land and maritime border areas.

9. Ban on stationing of additional troops and nondeployment of additional military bases on the territory of other states, as well as cessation of the extension and modernization of existing bases.

10. Encouragement of and support for the establishment of zones of "peaceful cooperation and good neighborliness," free of nuclear weapons, in the Balkans, Northern Europe, and in other regions of the continent.

11. Establishment of a system of information, communication, and consultations among states on problems relating to their security, and on the prevention and management of crises, including consultations whenever necessary, a standing consultative body, and a system of telephonic communications for consultations and arranging emergency summit meetings.

12. Adoption of measures to prevent nuclear conflict by error or accident, including: creation of a mechanism of rapid communication between governmental representatives; and adoption of emergency procedures and development of technical means.

13. Conclusion of an all-European Treaty on the nonuse or threat of force, containing concrete provisions and measures designed to give practical effect to the duty of states to refrain from the use or threat of force in their mutual relations, as a corollary of efforts underway at the Stockholm Conference.

14. Freezing of military expenditures at the level of 1984 until agreement can be reached on their gradual reduction.

15. Accompaniment of the above measures with a ban on war propaganda, encouragement of peaceful relations, and availability of public information on progress achieved in the Stockholm Conference.

Neutral and Nonaligned (November 15, 1985)

1. Notification 42 days in advance of major military maneuvers concerning engagement of military formations at the division or equivalent formation in combat-related exercises.

2. Notification of notifiable activities by annual calendar.

3. Invitation of observers to notifiable activities.

4. Notification of short-notice maneuvers and non-maneuver-related military movements if they reach the notifiable level.

5. Constraints: (a) no maneuver can exceed five times the notifiable level, and no maneuver can exceed 17 days in duration; (b) no more than five notifiable maneuvers per year per state less than two times the notifiable level, and no more than one such maneuver can be carried out at the same time (no restrictions if notified by annual calendar); (c)

no more than five maneuvers per year per state which are twice the notifiable level or above, no more than two such maneuvers permitted at the same time, but once a year two such maneuvers may be combined but cannot exceed seven times the notifiable level (roughly 70,000 troops).

6. Observation upon military request of military activities (to be granted absent reasons of supreme national interest).

7. Telecommunication links.

8. Consultative arrangements.

9. Non-use of force recommitment.

(Originally proposed, in general form, on March 9, 1984.)

Soviet Union (May 8, 1984, as developed)

1. No-first-use of nuclear weapons obligation.

2. Urgent consultation, inquiry, and information exchange "to preclude situations fraught with nuclear conflict."

3. Treaty on the non-use of force and maintenance of peaceful relations.

4. Non-endangerment of international air, sea, and space communications.

5. Non-increase and reduction in military spending.

6. Ban on chemical weapons in Europe.

7. Nuclear-weapon-free-zones in Balkans, Northern and Central Europe.

8. 40,000 troop limit on ground force maneuvers.

9. Notification 30 days in advance of major ground, air, and naval maneuvers exceeding 20,000 troops, 200 aircraft in the air simultaneously, and 30 ships + 100 aircraft, respectively.

10. Notification 30 days in advance of troop movements (transfers) exceeding 20,000 troops into, within, and out of Europe, and of aircraft movements into the CSBM zone exceeding 100 aircraft.

11. Development of observer exchange at major maneuvers (but not all CDE states need be invited).

12. "Adequate" verification with primary reliance on national technical means but possibly including "requests for information" and "consultations."

(Note: as of January 1986, the Soviets dropped measures 1, 5, 6, 7, and "deferred" consideration of naval activities.)

Malta (November 8, 1984)

1. Notification by annual calendar of: information on the number and structure of armed personnel stationed in the Mediterranean whose

duties are directly related to naval movements; information on the type and number of amphibious and other troop-carrying seaborne units stationed in the Mediterranean; and information on the type and number of major surface combat units stationed in the Mediterranean.

2. Prior notification of: all instances of the exercise of the right of innocent passage through the territorial waters of the Mediterranean CSCE participating states; naval movements involving the sea transportation at any one time across Mediterranean waters of armed personnel exceeding ( ) troops; amphibious activities involving a combined troop transportation capacity exceeding ( ) troops; and naval maneuvers involving more than ( ) surface combat units having a total displacement of ( ) tonnage.

3. Restrictions on deployments and maneuvers involving naval units and/or equipment of vital importance for sustained offensive operations in the Mediterranean.

4. Reductions in the number of major naval maneuvers involving combined amphibious, airborne, and surface combat units.

5. Ceiling on armed personnel and on surface combat units for any independent or joint naval exercise in the Mediterranean.

6. Observation facilities for prenotified naval maneuvers, and adequate verification measures corresponding to the restraint measures (the three preceding CSBMs).

7. Ban on use of land, sea, and/or air forces in the Mediterranean against riparian states except in self-defense.

8. Ban on utilizing foreign armaments, forces, bases, and military facilities against Mediterranean riparian states.

9. Desisting from deploying naval forces in a manner that constitutes a threat of the use of force against Mediterranean riparian states.

10. Ban on stationing of nuclear weapons in Mediterranean waters.

ADDITIONAL REAGAN ADMINISTRATION CBM PROPOSALS

Establishment of high-speed facsimile capability to upgrade the Hotline (concluded with the USSR on June 17, 1984) (May 24, 1983).

Establishment of a Joint Military Communications Link between U.S. military command and Soviet counterpart (May 24, 1983).

Establishment of high-rate data links between U.S. State Department and U.S. Embassy Moscow, and between Soviet Foreign Ministry and Soviet Embassy Washington (May 24, 1983).

Multilateral agreement providing for consultation in the event of a nuclear incident involving third parties (May 24, 1983).

Institutionalization of regular cabinet-level meetings between the United States and the Soviet Union "on the whole agenda of issues before us, including the problem of needless obstacles to understanding" (September 24, 1984).

Exchange of outlines of five-year military plans for weapons development and schedules of intended procurement (September 24, 1984).

Exchange of observers at military exercises and locations (September 24, 1984).

Regular, high-level military-to-military contacts "to develop better understanding and to prevent potential tragedies from occurring" (May 8, 1985).

SENATE RESOLUTION 329

Introduced February 1, 1984, Passed June 15, 1984.

Expressing the support of the Senate for the expansion of confidence building measures between the United States and the Union of Soviet Socialist Republics, including the establishment of nuclear risk reduction centers, in Washington and in Moscow, with modern communications linking the centers.

Whereas an increasing number of scenarios, including misjudgment, miscalculation, misunderstanding, possession of nuclear arms by a terrorist group or a state sponsored threat, could precipitate a sudden increase in tensions and the risk of a nuclear confrontation between the United States and the Union of Soviet Socialist Republics, situations that neither side anticipated, intended, or desired;,

Whereas there has been a steady proliferation throughout the world of the knowledge, equipment, and materials necessary to fabricate nuclear weapons;

Whereas this proliferation of nuclear capabilities suggests an increasing potential for nuclear terrorism, the cumulative risk of which, considering potential terrorist groups and other threats over a period of years into the future, may be great;

Whereas the current communications links represent equipment of the 1960s and as such are relatively outdated and limited in their capabilities;

Whereas Senators Jackson, Nunn, and Warner sponsored an amendment adopted by the Senate to the 1983 Department of Defense authorization proposing certain confidence building measures,;

Whereas President Reagan, responding to congressional initiatives, proposed the establishment of additional and improved communications links between the United States and the Union of Soviet Socialist Republics and other measures to reduce the risk of nuclear confrontation, and has initiated discussions at a working level with the Soviet Union covering:

(a) The addition of a high-speed facsimile capability to the direct communication link (hotline);

(b) The creation of a joint military communications link between the United States Department of Defense and the Soviet Defense Ministry;

(c) The establishment by the United States and Soviet governments of high rate data communications links between each nation and its embassy in the other nation's capital.

Whereas the establishment of nuclear risk reduction centers in Washington and Moscow could reduce the risk of increased tensions and nuclear confrontations thereby enhancing the security of both the United States and the Soviet Union;

Whereas these centers could serve a variety of functions including: (a) discussing procedures to be followed in the event of possible incidents involving the use of nuclear weapons by third parties; (b) maintaining close contact during nuclear threats or incidents precipitated by third parties; (c) exchanging information on a voluntary basis concerning events that might lead to the acquisition of nuclear weapons, materials, or equipment by subnational groups; (d) exchanging information about United States–Union of Soviet Socialist Republics military activities which might be misunderstood by the other party during periods of mounting tensions; and (e) establishing a dialogue about nuclear doctrines, forces, and activities;

Whereas the continuing and routine implementation of these various activities could be facilitated by the establishment within each Government of facilities, organizations, and bureaucratic relationships designated for these purposes, such as risk reduction centers, and by the appointment of individuals responsible to the respective head of state with responsibilities to manage such centers; Now therefore, be it

Resolved, That the Senate of the United States commends the President for his announced support for the aforementioned confidence building measures, and his initiation of negotiations which have occurred and urges the President to pursue negotiations on these measures with the Government of the Soviet Union, and to add to these negotiations the establishment of nuclear risk reduction centers in both nations.

MISCELLANEOUS WESTERN CBM PROPOSALS
(not proposed by governments)

- Ban on multiple ballistic missile launches within short time periods.
- Restricting ballistic missile tests to low annual limit.
- Constraints on maneuvering reentry vehicles.
- Sensors at ICBM silos.
- Ban on close-in basing of nuclear forces (*e.g.*, SSBNs).
- Nuclear weapon "signatures."
- Withdrawal from forward areas of offensive combat forces and support equipment.
- Ban on "stand-down" of nuclear-capable aircraft.
- Ban on coded radio traffic.
- Ban on nuclear delivery training flights.
- Ban on high-altitude ASAT tests and distance limitations between ASAT vehicles and satellites.
- Monitoring agreed-upon indicator list of military activity "norms."
- Enhanced crisis codes.
- Incidents in the Air and on the Ground agreements.
- Joint teams for data-sharing and examination of nuclear detonations of unknown origin.
- Standard ceasefire procedures.
- Postnuclear detonation "pause."
- Observers at major ammunition storage areas.
- Reduction of restrictions on accredited military personnel.
- Simultaneous maneuvers by opposing states.

MISCELLANEOUS SOVIET CBM PROPOSALS

Nonexpansion of "military and political groupings and alliances" in Europe (Belgrade CSCE meeting, 1977).

Extension of CBMs to "Mediterranean basin" (Belgrade CSCE meeting, 1977).

Nonextension of sphere of activity of military alliances to Asia, Africa, and Latin America (Brezhnev, October 12, 1982).

Extension of CBMs to the Far East (CPSU Congress, February 23, 1981).

Mutual restriction of naval operations, including removal of SSBNs from their present combat patrol areas, and restrictions on their cruises (Brezhnev, March 16, 1982).

Extension of CBMs to the seas and oceans, and especially to areas through which the busiest shipping routes pass, "we stand for the largest possible part of the world ocean becoming a zone of peace in the very nearest future" (Brezhnev, March 16, 1982).

Nuclear-weapon-free-zone in Central Europe extending 250–300 km to the west and to the east of the Warsaw Pact–NATO line of contact (TASS, January 27, 1983).

Nuclear-weapon-free-zone in northern Europe. "We would not only assume the commitment to respect such a zone but also would be ready to study the question of similar measures, and substantial ones at that, concerning our own territory adjoining the zone. . . . The Soviet Union also could discuss with the interested sides the question of giving nuclear-free status to the Baltic Sea" (Andropov, June 6, 1983).

Limitation on naval activities and extension of CBMs to particular regions, such as Indian, Atlantic, and Pacific oceans, and to Mediterranean and Persian Gulf (Gromyko, September 17, 1984).

Endorsement of chemical-weapon-free-zone in Central Europe (Gorbachev, September 11, 1985).

Selected Bibliography

Although CBMs have largely eluded the type and extent of analysis that other forms of arms control have received over the years, among the most useful works in English to date would include the following publications:

Alford, Jonathan, ed. *The Future of Arms Control, Part III: Confidence-Building Measures*. Adelphi Paper No. 149. London: International Institute for Strategic Studies, 1979.

———. "The Usefulness and the Limitations of CBMs." William Epstein and Bernard T. Feld, eds. *New Directions In Disarmament*. New York: Praeger Publishers, 1981: 133–144.

Allison, Graham T.; Carnesale, Albert; and Nye, Joseph S., Jr., eds. *Hawks, Doves & Owls: An Agenda for Avoiding Nuclear War*. New York: W. W. Norton, 1985.

Barton, David. "The Sinai peacekeeping experience: a verification paradigm for Europe." *World Armaments and Disarmament, SIPRI Yearbook 1985*. London and Philadelphia: Taylor & Francis, 1985: 539–562.

Betts, Richard K. *Surprise Attack*. Washington, D.C.: Brookings Institution, 1982: 303–309.

———. "A Joint Nuclear Risk Reduction Center," *Parameters*, vol. 15, no. 1 (Spring 1985): 39–51.

Birnbaum, Karl E., ed. *Confidence-Building and East-West Relations*. Laxenburg, Austria: Austrian Institute for International Affairs, 1983.

Bomsdorf, Falk. "The Confidence-Building Offensive in the United Nations." *Aussenpolitik*, vol. 33, no. 4 (1984): 370–390.

Borawski, John. "The Stockholm Conference on Confidence and Security Building Measures in Europe." *Arms Control—The Journal of Arms Control and Disarmament*, vol. 6, no. 2 (September 1985): 115–149.

———. "Progress in Stockholm talks." *Bulletin of the Atomic Scientists*, vol. 42, no. 2 (February 1986): 40–42.

Brauch, Hans Guenter. "Confidence-Building and Disarmament-Supporting Measures." William Epstein and Bernard T. Feld, eds. *New Directions In Disarmament*. New York: Praeger Publishers, 1981: 145–160.

Brayton, Abbott A. "Confidence-Building Measures in European Security." *The World Today*, vol. 36, no. 10 (October 1980): 386–391.

Burt, Richard. "Building Confidence: Strategy for Enhanced Security," *Harvard International Review*, vol. 6, no. 5 (March 1984): 23–29.

Bykov, Oleg. *Confidence-Building Measures: An Essential Factor in Strengthening Peace*. Moscow: Nauka Publishing House, 1983.

Darilek, Richard E. "Separate Processes, Converging Interests: MBFR and CBMs." Hans Guenter Brauch and Duncan L. Clarke, eds. *Decisionmaking for Arms Limitations: Assessments and Prospects*. Cambridge, MA: Ballinger, 1983: 237–258.

Freedman, Lawrence. *Arms Control in Europe*. Chatham House Paper No. 11. London: Royal Institute of International Affairs, 1981: 29–37.

Garwin, Richard L. "The Interaction of Anti-Submarine Warfare With the Submarine-Based Deterrent." Kosta Tsipis, Anne H. Cahn, and Bernard T. Feld, eds. *The Future of the Sea-Based Deterrent*. Cambridge, MA: MIT Press, 1973: 87–120.

Gnesotto, Nicole. "Conference on Disarmament in Europe Opens in Stockholm." *NATO Review*, vol. 31, no. 6 (1983); 1–5.

Goodby, James E. "Security for Europe." *NATO Review*, vol. 32, no. 3 (June/July 1984); 9–14.

———. "Security for Europe: Stockholm Revisited." *NATO Review*, vol. 33, no. 1 (February 1985): 12–16.

Haass, Richard. "Naval Arms Control: Approaches and Considerations." George H. Quester, ed. *Navies and Arms Control*. New York: Praeger Publishers, 1980: 201–212.

Holst, Johan Jørgen, and Melander, Karen Alette. "European Security and Confidence-Building Measures." *Survival*, vol. 19, no. 4 (July/August 1977): 31–45.

Holst, Johan Jørgen. "Confidence-Building Measures: A Conceptual Framework." *Survival*, vol. 25, no. 1 (January/February 1983): 2–15.

Ikle, Fred C. "Constraints on Usable Military Power." Uwe Nerlich, ed. *The Western Panacea: Constraining Soviet Power Through Negotiation*. Cambridge, MA: Ballinger, 1983: 189–202.

Kaiser, Karl, ed. *Confidence-Building Measures*. Bonn: Europa Union Verlag, 1983.

Landi, Dale M. *et al.* "Improving the Means for Intergovernmental Communication in Crisis." *Survival*, vol. 26, no. 5 (September/October 1984): 200–214.

Larrabee, F. Stephen, and Stobbe, Dietrich, eds. *Confidence-Building Measures in Europe*. New York: Institute for East-West Security Studies, 1983.

Lewis, John W., and Blacker, Coit D., eds. *Next Steps in the Creation of an Accidental Nuclear War Prevention Center*. Stanford, CA: Center for International Security and Arms Control, Stanford University, 1983.

Lewis, Kevin N., and Lorell, Mark A. "Confidence-Building Measures and Crisis Resolution: Historical Perspectives." *Orbis*, vol. 28, no. 2 (Summer 1984): 281–306.

Lynch, Allen C. *Confidence-Building in the 1980s: A Conference Report*. New York: Institute for East-West Security Studies; Toronto: York University Research Program in Strategic Studies, 1985.

Macintosh, James. *Confidence (and Security) Building Measures in the Arms Control Process: A Canadian Perspective*. Ottawa: Department of External Affairs, August 1985.

Nye, Joseph S., Jr. "Arms Control and Prevention of War." *The Washington Quarterly*, vol. 7, no. 4 (Fall 1984): 59–70.

Perry, William J. "Measures To Reduce the Risk of Nuclear War." *Orbis*, vol. 28, no. 3 (Winter 1984): 1027–2035.

Roderick, Hilliard, ed. *Avoiding Inadvertent War: Crisis Management.* Austin: University of Texas, LBJ School of Public Affairs, 1983.

———. "Crisis Management: Preventing Accidental War." *Technology Review*, vol. 88, no. 6 (August/September 1985): 50–59.

Schelling, Thomas C., and Halperin, Morton H. *Strategy and Arms Control.* New York: Twentieth Century Fund, 1961.

Schelling, Thomas C. "Confidence in Crisis." *International Security*, vol. 8, no. 4 (Spring 1984): 55–66.

Sharp, Jane M. O. "Confidence Building Measures and SALT." *Arms Control*, vol. 3, no. I (May 1982): 37–61.

Swedish National Defense Research Institute (FOA). *Symposium on Verification of Disarmament in Europe.* Stockholm: FOA, 1985.

Ury, William Langer, and Smoke, Richard. *Beyond the Hotline: Controlling a Nuclear Crisis.* Cambridge, MA: Harvard Law School Nuclear Negotiation Project, 1984.

Ury, William L. *Beyond the Hotline: How We Can Prevent the Crisis that Might Bring On a Nuclear War.* Boston: Houghton Mifflin, 1985.

In addition, two very useful annual volumes that follow the various CBM negotiations are the *Arms Control Reporter* (Brookline, MA: Institute for Defense and Disarmament Studies) and the SIPRI Yearbook *World Armaments and Disarmament.*

About the Contributors

Bruce Allyn is a Research Associate with the Nuclear Negotiation Project, Harvard Law School, and a Research Fellow with the Project on Avoiding Nuclear War, Kennedy School of Government, Harvard University.

Richard E. Darilek is a Senior Analyst with the Rand Corporation, Santa Monica, California. He previously served as Director of the MBFR Task Force in the Office of the Secretary of Defense.

Charles C. Flowerree served as U.S. Ambassador to the Conference on Disarmament, Geneva, Switzerland, over 1980–1981.

Raymond L. Garthoff is a Senior Fellow at the Brookings Institution, Washington, D.C. He formerly served as a member of the U.S. SALT I delegation and as U.S. Ambassador to Bulgaria.

James E. Goodby is currently Research Professor at the Institute for the Study of Diplomacy, Georgetown University. Over 1983–1985 he served as the U.S. Ambassador to the Conference on Confidence- and Security-Building Measures and Disarmament in Europe, Stockholm, Sweden.

Robert T. Herres, General, U.S. Air Force, is Commander in Chief of the North American Aerospace Defense Command.

Jim E. Hinds, Colonel, U.S. Army, Retired, is Principal Director for Negotiations Policy in the Office of the Assistant Secretary of Defense for International Security Policy.

Sally K. Horn is Director of Verification Policy in the Office of the Assistant Secretary of Defense for International Security Policy.

Sean M. Lynn-Jones is a Research Fellow with the project on Avoiding Nuclear War, Kennedy School of Government, Harvard University.

Michael H. Mobbs is Assistant Director, U.S. Arms Control and Disarmament Agency, for Strategic Programs.

Sam Nunn is the senior U.S. Senator from Georgia and ranking Democrat on the Senate Armed Services Committee.

Richard Smoke is Research Director of the Center for Foreign Policy Development, Brown Univeristy.

David T. Twining, Lt. Colonel, U.S. Army, is Director of Soviet and East European Studies at the U.S. Army War College, Carlisle Barracks, Pennsylvania. Over 1984/1985 he served as a National Security Fellow at the Kennedy School of Government, Harvard University.

William Langer Ury is Director of the Nuclear Negotiation Project, Harvard Law School.